NIGHTMARCH

'A story that could not be more important, told with the perfect balance of clear-eyed realism, thoughtful criticism, and abiding love. Shah brings the Indian forests to life, from the terrors and intimate details of daily existence to the visions of the future that move rebels to risk everything. *Nightmarch* reveals what anthropology can do in the hands of a master willing to take genuine risks in the name of human freedom.'

— David Graeber, author of *Bullshit Jobs and Debt: The First 5,000 Years*

'Compassionate, courageous and uncommonly observant. This is an extraordinary work of rigorous, reflective and deeply engaged scholarship, full of unexpected insights. At the same time, it manages to be haunting, lyrical, occasionally harrowing—more compelling than some of the best fiction writing.'

— Harsh Mander, human rights activist and author of *Fatal Accidents of Birth*, *Looking Away* and *Ash in the Belly*

'One of the most gripping, engaging and accessible books I've encountered on the Naxalites. Shah fearlessly bears witness to the upheavals caused by India's rising inequalities, while also asking many urgent, difficult questions. She addresses head-on the guerrillas' zero-tolerance policy towards informers, their tenuous relationship with mining corporations, their dogmatic political philosophy and their blind faith in the future of the armed struggle.'

— Meena Kandasamy, author of *When I Hit You*

'An eloquent and compassionate account of revolutionaries whose voices are rarely heard. Shah skilfully analyses the individual motivations for the Naxalites' radical commitment, their failures, and the deep history of exploitation and neglect that has provoked their struggle for liberation.'

— David Lan, theatre producer and author of *Guns and Rain*

'Brave, brilliant and beautifully written, *Nightmarch* is an anthropological tour de force. Shah portrays the Naxalites' revolutionary dedication with love, respect and analytical acumen, while laying bare the tragic contradictions of their armed struggle.'

— Philippe Bourgois, author of In Search of *Respect: Selling Crack in El Barrio* and *Righteous Dopefiend*

'*Nightmarch* is an outstanding work, combining ethnographic depth with almost cinematic vividness. From an extraordinary inside perspective, Shah reveals a complex interplay among the Naxalites of political ideals, cultural values, personal attachments, and the lure of money.'

— Sherry B. Ortner, Distinguished Professor of Anthropology, UCLA

'Riveting, finely textured, and acutely perceptive, *Nightmarch* is a model of what ethnography can offer. Shah captures both the Naxalite insurgency's contradictions and its human promise against the background of the crippling indignities and exclusions of Indian society.'

— James C. Scott, author of *Against the Grain*

ALPA SHAH

Nightmarch

*Among India's Revolutionary
Guerrillas*

HURST & COMPANY, LONDON

First published in the United Kingdom in 2018 by
C. Hurst & Co. (Publishers) Ltd.,
41 Great Russell Street, London, WC1B 3PL
© Alpa Shah, 2018
All rights reserved.
Printed in the United Kingdom by Bell & Bain Ltd, Glasgow

A Cataloguing-in-Publication data record for this book
is available from the British Library.

ISBN: 9781849049900

This book is printed using paper from registered sustainable
and managed sources.

www.hurstpublishers.com

For Kundan and Madhu

NOTE ON THE TEXT

This is a work of nonfiction. To protect the identities of the people involved, I have used pseudonyms. I have also pseudonymised the *noms de guerre* used by the guerrillas, as these names are themselves widely known in the local villages and by the police. I have only kept original names of those people who have died whose families will no longer be under threat. Where changing names is not enough to protect someone's identity, I have muddied some of their identifying features, usually by drawing on a similar character, at times having to merge parts of their stories. The point of the central characters is to represent archetypal figures who have come together in this movement. I have also changed the names of most places. I was present at all of the events described in this book.

CONTENTS

ix

CONTENTS

LIST OF ILLUSTRATIONS

1. Marching with the guerrilla platoon from Bihar to Jharkhand, 2010.
2. Maoist State-level conference in a forest in Jharkhand, 2010.
3. Rudimentary drawing of Prime Minister Manmohan Singh, Congress Party President Sonia Gandhi and a helicopter representing government counterinsurgency operations, found pinned to the wall of a tent in the Maoist State-level conference in a forest in Bihar, 2010.
4. Roll call in a Maoist platoon, Jharkhand, 2010.
5. Arriving at a temporary guerrilla forest camp for a 'cooking lesson', Jharkhand, 2008.
6. A Naxalite guerrilla reading a newspaper in an Adivasi house in Jharkhand, 2009.
7. Painting the Maoist flag, Jharkhand, 2009.
8. The collection of *kendu* leaves, used for making the Indian cigarette *bidi*—one of the main sources of Maoist funding, Jharkhand, 2009.
9. The forested hills of the guerrilla stronghold in the Chotanagpur Plateau, Jharkhand, 2009.
10. Burning the effigies of Prime Minister Manmohan Singh, Deputy Chairman of the Planning Commission Montek Singh Ahluwalia and Home Minister P. Chidambaram at a Maoist demonstration in the forests of Jharkhand, 2008.

LIST OF ILLUSTRATIONS

All photos were taken by Alpa Shah.

PREFACE

Deep in the forested hills of Jharkhand, on a freezing December night in 2008, I made my way past three sentry posts to a solitary mud hut set apart from the rest of the village. The soft-spoken, slightly balding, middle-aged man inside went only by a *nom de guerre*, Gyanji. Like the guerrilla platoon outside guarding their leader from assassins dispatched by the Indian state, Gyanji was dressed in olive-green fatigues and carried all his worldly belongings in one small rucksack. But in the dim light spreading from the kerosene lamp, I noticed the tender soles of his light-skinned feet. Over the years that I have lived in those forests, I found out that for twenty-five years Gyanji had been constantly on the move in the rural backwaters of India, often sleeping under the stars in the forest, rarely staying more than a few days in one place. But in contrast to the dark broad feet of the tribal soldiers outside, layered with years' worth of skin which made them as tough, dry and cracked as the red earth they had walked barefoot since they were born, Gyanji's feet were still soft from the childhood care and protection they had received in his parents' upper-caste home.

In the hills, where the local tongue of Nagpuria trilled through the forests like song, and even India's majority language, Hindi, was a rarity, Gyanji's polished English stood out. I discovered that he could recite Shelley and Shaw, that he had a master's degree in mathematics, and that his siblings included a bank employee, an accountant, and a computer scientist who had emigrated to Canada. It was only Gyanji who had gone astray from the upper-middle-class path laid out by his parents. Inspired by the revolutionary spirit in the universities around him and by the peasant rebellions that had been sweeping through India in the three decades before, at the age of twenty-four, Gyanji cut ties with his family and took the oath of becoming a 'professional revolutionary'. He joined a group of men and women who had renounced the comforts of their homes and their university classrooms, 'declassed' and 'decasted' themselves and, in a long tradition of revolutionary Marxism-Leninism, resolved to fight oppression, injustice and inequality to make a more humane world. It was the Indian equivalent of being a '68 Parisian rioter or an American counterculture drop-out—except that while radicalism, for many in the West, proved a temporary home, for Gyanji and his comrades it was a life-altering choice. Today these people call themselves the Communist Party of India (Maoist)—also known as the Naxalites, or Maoists—and are leading what is now the world's longest ongoing armed revolutionary movement.

Although an armed force of less than 10,000, and now mainly confined to the hills and forests of central and eastern India, the Naxalite rebels have haunted and taunted the Indian state for the last fifty years. The foot soldiers of their 'People's Liberation Guerrilla Army' come mainly from India's tribal communities, popularly called Adivasis. The Advisasis make up 8.6 per cent of the total population of India, accounting for more than 100 million people—about the number of inhabitants of Germany or Vietnam. Considered lowly, 'savage' and wild by the dominant castes and classes, for centuries Adivasis were left on the margins of Indian society. They survived in the jungles by cultivating whatever little land they had, living off forest resources by hunting and gathering fruits and flowers, and chopping wood to build their houses, fuel their hearths and make their ploughs and digging sticks. Increasingly squeezed out of their forest homes by the state and corporations, today they migrate for a few months far away from their homes to the construction sites and factories of the towns and the cities, where they are used for the most gruelling, backbreaking and hazardous work, providing the cheap labour fuelling the Indian economic boom.

The Adivasi foot soldiers were often fighting for reasons very different from the abstract ideals of leaders like Gyanji. On a wider level, theirs is a struggle for tribal autonomy, against a state that they see as repressive, brutal, and prejudiced. But for any individual Adivasi, their reasons for joining the Maoists were often more personal. Take, for example, Kohli, a gentle, sensitive sixteen-year-old Adivasi youth with radiant dark skin and a coy smile, whose rifle was nearly as tall as himself, and who insisted on carrying my bags when he was once assigned as my bodyguard. He had run away to live with the guerrillas after a trivial fight with his father about a glass of spilt milk while working in his tea-shop. Rather than breaking with their pasts, as Gyanji did, the Adivasi youth found in the guerrilla armies a home away from home, and often moved in and out of them as though they were visiting an uncle or aunt.

To the government in New Delhi, however, both Gyanji and Kohli are simply terrorists, a dangerous cancer that must be eradicated. Fifty years after the rebels initiated their fight, India's media and government bodies were driven into an anti-Maoist frenzy by an attack on Central Reserve Police Forces patrolling the construction of a road in the central state of Chhattisgarh. On 25 and 26 April 2017, the bodies of twenty-six soldiers were wrapped in the Indian tricolour and garlanded with marigolds, a flower used in most Hindu rituals. They were airlifted from the forests of Sukma District to their far-flung hometown cremation sites, from the foothills of the Himalayas to the banks of the Yamuna more than 700 miles away. Many of them came from backgrounds just as poor as the men who had killed them, joining the security forces being one route out of rural destitution.

That was just one of the many bloody skirmishes between the Naxalites and the Indian state. In recent years, the insurgents have blown up security forces, derailed trains that defy their blockades, killed people they deem are police informers and delivered summary justice in their 'people's courts'. Reporting these incidents, news bands reading 'Latest Terrorist Attack' appear regularly across national TV channels, creating a climate of fear among the Indian middle classes for whom large sections of rural central and eastern India are now 'no-go zones'. In 2016, the Maoists were presented as the third deadliest terrorist group in the world, after the Islamic State of Iraq and Syria (ISIS) and the Taliban, in data collected by the National Consortium for the Study of Terrorism and Responses to Terrorism for the U.S. Department of State's annual 'Country Report on Terrorism'.[1]

The latest Indian government campaigns against the rebels began over a decade ago. In 2006, two years before I began living in their guerrilla strongholds as a social anthropologist, and two years after the three major armed Naxalite groups united as the Communist Party of India (Maoist), the then Prime Minister Manmohan Singh declared the rebels the gravest single internal security threat facing the country and labelled them 'terrorists'. This signalled a new wave of security operations to hunt down the Maoists and to silence their sympathisers and supporters. Painting a 'Red Corridor' from the borders of Nepal in the north down to Andhra Pradesh in the south, the Indian intelligence agencies claimed that 40 per cent of India's land area was affected, encompassing twenty of the twenty-eight states, and 223 of 640 districts. The numbers are hard to verify and were possibly inflated to justify an increase in security and defence budgets. Indeed, more than 100,000 soldiers were dispatched to surround the Maoist guerrilla strongholds in the centre and east of the country. They were accompanied by a squadron of helicopters and special forces teams with exotically implausible names such as 'CoBRA', 'Jharkhand Jaguar', and 'Greyhounds', who were trained in jungle warfare schools to fight the guerrillas with their own tactics.

Many human rights activists argue that behind the state's desire to destroy the Naxalites and 'civilise' the Adivasis is the aim of cleansing the region for the extraction of minerals. Under the Adivasi forests in the states of Jharkhand, Chhattisgarh, Odisha, Andhra Pradesh and Telangana lie some of India's most lucrative reserves of coal, iron ore, bauxite, copper, manganese, mica and more. Business analysts have claimed that Indian mining is a success story in waiting. Powerful corporations have signed deals to exploit the resources and to acquire land for mining operations, steel factories and power plants. Mittal, Essar, Vedanta, Rio Tinto, and Posco are scouting out the landscape. But, the historic laws, which the Adivasis fought for in colonial times, prevent their lands from being easily sold to non-Adivasis, to outsiders. The Adivasis, and the Naxalites who live among them, stand squarely in the way of India's economic boom.

In the villages where I lived among the guerrillas, the security forces' search-and-destroy missions generated terror. Those who could, fled to neighbouring villages as the patrols mounted the hills. Villagers had been used as human shields by the security forces and as informers to find the Maoists in the forests. Others had been caught in the crossfire and brutally beaten by soldiers during raids, accused of harbouring the rebels. Scenes from Vietnam War movies played out regularly in the forests of India. Like Vietnam, generals boast of better 'kill ratios' to the media. In the last decade, according to the South Asia Terrorist Portal, almost 7,000 people have been killed, of which 40% have been civilians, 34% Maoists and 26% security forces.

In the aftermath of the Sukma attacks, the home minister, Rajnath Singh, called a high-level meeting of government ministers, police, security forces and intelligence agencies, to plot the final battle. 'We need to bring aggression into our policy. Aggression in thinking, aggression in strategy, aggression in deployment of forces, aggression in operations, aggression in development and aggression in road construction,' Rajnath Singh said.[2] The government promised a final objective: a coordinated battle on security and development fronts that would be fought to the finish and won.

New Delhi has pledged many times in the past to destroy the Maoists and yet they endure. Every year in November, across the forests that are their strongholds, the Maoists celebrate the deceased in a martyrs' week. These meetings of guerrillas in clearings in the forest, lined with crepe paper bunting and memorials draped in red cloth, are ephemeral as all traces of their presence must be erased to evade the security forces. Nevertheless, they fly their red flags painted with a hammer and a sickle, sing the socialist 'Internationale' and, in remembering the thousands that have been killed, they seek to regenerate life in the revolutionary spirit from the dead.

How and why does this armed rebellion for a communist society, a struggle that seems anachronistic to the rest of the world, persist in the heart of the world's largest democracy, the birthplace of non-violence, a country poised to become one of the most powerful economies in the globe?

I crossed paths with the guerrillas when, towards the end of my doctoral field research in 1999–2002, they started to enter the Adivasi rural area of Jharkhand where I was then living. At the time, I saw them as protection racketeers, not unlike the Sicilian Mafia, extorting money from state development schemes and big business in return for safeguarding against their own violence. But in later years, as I followed their progress from London,

PREFACE

I was intrigued by the fact that so many Adivasis were joining the Maoists, and felt compelled to understand why.

I knew I had to return to Jharkhand to conduct ethnographic research and that hallmark praxis of social anthropology, participant observation: deep immersion over a long period of time—at least a year or more—into the lives of people who are initially strangers, learning their language, seeking to know and experience the world through their perspectives and actions in as holistic a manner as possible. Undertaking such long-term, open-ended, field research seemed crucial in order to move beyond the cursory impressions, based on interviews or a visit of a few days, that had begun to emerge of the Maoists. Staying with the Adivasi communities in a guerrilla stronghold seemed the obvious way to arrive at a more nuanced understanding of their predicament than those that had often emerged in comparable contexts—whether in the Vietnam War or Peru's Shining Path insurrection—which argued that people were stuck between two armies, coerced into revolutionary support, or, turned to the guerrillas because of either some utilitarian benefits or the long-standing grievances they addressed. But it was not until 2008, coincidentally as the latest round of its counterinsurgency campaigns were launched by the Indian government, that I was finally able to return to Jharkhand.

I went with modest ambitions: to spend time among the Adivasis in order to understand how life had changed for them in the face of this revolutionary movement allegedly fighting for a more equal society. I didn't expect to see a guerrilla, let alone meet one. But during my stay, I soon realised that the guerrillas were everywhere—in every house, in every village and in every forest. I had by chance ended up living in what the Naxalites considered their 'Red Capital', one of the two guerrilla strongholds in India. As the state's counterinsurgency operations escalated, outsiders were prohibited from entering the guerrilla areas unless accompanied by the security forces. Those who dared to venture in without informing the authorities rarely stayed more than a few hours, at most a few days.

As the situation became increasingly dangerous, I considered returning to London. But the stories of the people I had met in the Red Capital had already pulled me too far into this little-known world. I was compelled to venture increasingly under-cover. My field research had grown into something far more ambitious than I could have ever imagined.

Nightmarch refers to an unexpected seven-night trek with a Naxalite guerrilla platoon, undertaken in 2010 alongside new intensive counterinsurgency operations, when I found myself dressed as a man in an olive-green guerrilla uniform. The only woman, and the only person not carrying a gun, I set out with a group of fighters, under the cover of darkness, to walk 250 kilo-metres from one part of India to another. Unravelling across this march, the book draws on four and a half years of living as an anthropologist amidst India's Adivasi people, with one long spell outside the guerrilla strongholds and another within. *Nightmarch* is then my journey into this underbelly of the subcontinent, to understand why, behind the mask of a shining 'new India', some of the country's poor shunned the world's largest democracy and united with revolutionary ideologues to take up arms against rising inequality. Revealing one of the world's most intractable and under-reported rebellions, the book reflects on why a seem-ingly failing revolution has endured in India and the ways in which it is undermined. It shows how, amidst proliferating con-tradictions, revolutionary motivations are sustained and sub-verted at the same time.

Focusing on both the perspectives of the revolutionary ideo-logues and the poor rural communities who were joining them, at the heart of *Nightmarch* are the nuances, complexities and iro-nies of the protracted encounter between guerrilla leaders and their foot soldiers. *Nightmarch* reveals the story of young tribal boys, born into mud huts, who seasonally migrate for work—carrying bricks on their shoulders in faraway kilns, building the skyscrapers of a brand-new India—but also march in the guerrilla columns to recite poetry, sing revolutionary songs and bear arms. It tells the story of well-heeled, highly-educated Indians who leave the security of their families when their conscience and sense of justice are assaulted by the inequalities of their country, and move underground for years on end in the service of higher ideals. But *Nightmarch* is also the story of youth who grow up learning to read and write in the guerrilla armies and yet come to have more ordinary dreams—of money to buy a plot of land in the city to build a two-storey brick house and to send their children to English-medium private schools—and who eventually betray the guerrillas. It is the story, too, of women who run to the revolutionary family in the hope of finding more egalitarian homes, and of their struggle with patriarchy within the guerrilla hierarchies. And it is also the story of villagers whose lives get ripped apart by the conflict between the guerrillas and the counterinsurgency security forces who turn for solace to the spiritual sects of extreme Hindu right-wing organisations.

In short, *Nightmarch* not only shows why people from very different backgrounds come together to take up arms to change the world, but also what makes them fall apart and turn against each other and their goals. It is a meditation on the contradictions, limitations and paradoxes of emancipatory ambitions, revolutionary desires and guerrilla action. It highlights the fundamental dilemmas of dreamers and reformers who choose revolutionary pathways to make the world a more just and equitable place and how, despite their sacrifices and commitments, their ideals are undermined by their own human frailties. It is a reflection on economic growth, rising inequality, dispossession and conflict at the heart of contemporary India.

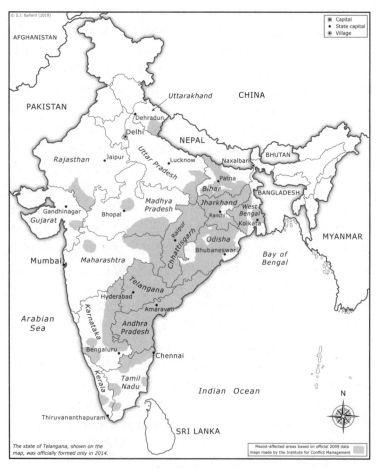

Map of India showing Maoist-affected areas at the time of field research

PART ONE

GOING UNDERGROUND

1

FOLLOWING THE CALL

I began the journey from Ranchi city in the dark, in the bracing bitter cold before sunrise one February morning in 2010. The message had arrived the night before. The phone rang and I recognised the voice at the other end. 'Two p.m. tomorrow,' was all it had said. And then the line went dead.

By dawn the bus was slowly climbing into the hills. Through the cracked panes of the window glass I watched a procession of men pushing bicycles heaped with jute sacks bursting with coal. Like a line of ants carrying food crumbs three times their size, the men were walking alongside the vehicles on the road, their dark naked backs shining with sweat. They would have started work at two in the morning, packing coal scavenged from working mines, from abandoned beds, or dug out of seams found in village common lands. They were transporting the coal to local traders who would sell it to city households, local businesses, small factories and brick kilns.

It was Sebastião Salgado, known for travelling the world documenting the perilous conditions of human existence created by globalisation and economic liberalisation, who first painted a penetrating picture in my imagination of the men and women in the coalfields of what is today the Indian state of Jharkhand, literally meaning 'land of the forests'. The Royal Festival Hall was hosting an exhibition of his photographs and I happened to be walking along the South Bank of the Thames. With their pick-axes on their backs and their faces and clothes covered in coal, the silver lips of the coal miners of eastern India stood out as though they had been painted on with an expensive fluorescent white lipstick. In a curious subversion of signs of exhaustion, the bags under their eyes were similarly a silvery white. It was as though they were signalling their dignified resolution to fight on, saying that this grinding work in these bleak surroundings could never break them. Their intent and determination was hauntingly piercing. Now they were so close, just on the other side of the bus window.

The bicycles disappeared up a mud track at the side of the road. I realised why when we came to an abrupt halt amidst a discord of honking buses, jeeps and cars. It was by now unbearably hot. The forests had given way to dry barren land. Clouds of dust engulfed us and smoke rose out of cracks in the ground. Finding it hard to breathe, I tied a handkerchief covering my nose and mouth.

The road had caved in along a half-kilometre stretch leaving a huge crater with a roaring fire in its pit. This was one of the infamous subterranean coal fires of Jharkhand that turn large tracts of ground into a burning honeycomb. This one had begun in an abandoned coal mine and then spread rapidly along the seam of coal that ran right under the road, making it subside. No one had yet taken responsibility for fixing the damage. Not the private mining companies, the Central Coalfields (a subsidiary of Coal India, which was an undertaking of the government of India), or the district administration. It could take years to repair.

Nearby villagers had ingeniously created a dusty rocky track, going past their mud huts, for the vehicles to manoeuvre through. Groups of young men in their late teens and early twenties, dressed in jeans, their chests bare, with caps or bandanas tied around their heads, blocked three sections of the new dirt road. From the bus, I watched middle-class passengers shrink into the back seats of their cars, instructing their chauffeurs to roll up the windows, apparently afraid of the youths who had surrounded their cars and were knocking at their windows with sticks. The young men were demanding a fee of 10 rupees (10 pence), shouting angrily at those who didn't comply.

The owners of the national and multinational corporations behind these mining developments lived a life of opulence. Indian billionaires were buying some of the most expensive houses in London's Mayfair and Kensington. One mansion was rarely enough. Stately homes in the English countryside were as likely to be among their assets as multi-storey houses in India's metropolitan cities. Yet, at night, the footpaths of Mumbai are crowded with the slumbering bodies of people who have nowhere else to make their home. Indeed, India remained a country of extreme polarities with more poor people than anywhere else in the world, with 800 million people living on less than two dollars a day and eight states having more poor people than twenty-five of Africa's poorest countries put together.[1]

With no access to the privileged worlds of the Indian developers behind the mining, 10 rupees seemed a pittance to demand as some kind of taxation for the suffering of those who lived here, whose homes had either subsided into the crater, or, if left standing, were caked in the dirt, dust and pollution of the traffic.

By noon the pace of the bus had picked up again. I knew we had crossed from Jharkhand into the state of Bihar when we left the winding hill roads behind, and flat rice fields began to whizz past. The sun was now so strong that a mirage hung above the tarmac.

The instruction was to arrive in a town just over 200 kilometres from Ranchi city, in the middle of the great Asian route, the

Grand Trunk Road. Sher Shah Suri, founder of the Sur Empire with its capital in Delhi, built the road in the sixteenth century to stretch from Chittagong in Bangladesh to Kabul in Afghanistan. My destination was a town flanked by the Morhar and Sorhar rivers, a spot where Sher Shah Suri had once hunted down a lion. It was now just another dusty nondescript place with no characteristics to reflect its imposing name: Sherghati, 'Lion Pass'.

Sherghati was also the place where the first known meteorite from Mars landed on Earth in 1865, the Shergottite meteorite. Famous amongst astronomers, I had seen a part of the meteorite in the Sedgwick Museum of Earth Science in Cambridge on my way to lectures in the Geography Department next door. What with the meteorite, the spontaneous combustion of coal, and now the insurgents, the area has been explosive for the last three centuries.

As the bus veered off the tarmac and jolted to a dusty stop, I anxiously peered out through the window at Sherghati's bazaar. I had been told that the guerrillas would send a 'receiver', a person to meet me, and guide me to their forest hideout. But how long would it take to spot the man? Vegetable vendors, watch sellers, chicken and goat dealers and cosmetics merchants, traders of all sorts swarmed between the buses, vans and jeeps. People were buying and selling, drinking chai, or just loitering and passing time. What would happen if the 'receiver' was not there? How long should I wait? When did the last bus back to Ranchi leave?

There were many tales of what could go wrong at this stage. One that would send the guerrillas into great hoots of laughter was about a Naxalite leader from the south of India who was waiting for his 'receiver' outside a busy temple in Jharkhand, holding a bunch of bananas as a signal. As he stood in anticipation under a banyan tree, a monkey crept up on him, snatched the bananas and ran up the tree. Unperturbed by the stones being thrown at it from below, the monkey calmly ate the bananas, watching the angry man beneath him. To the leader's further distress bananas were out of season in Jharkhand and, though he searched high and low, there was no way of buying them in the vicinity. In the end, the allotted time for the meeting came and went and he had no choice but to return to the city where he had begun. It took six months to rearrange his trip to the forests of Jharkhand. From then on, the Naxalites agreed that both parties needed at least two objects to recognise each other, a common greeting, and, in many cases, a second meeting time in case things went wrong at the first.

A short podgy man climbed onto the bus with a carton of small tins. His well-rehearsed chant, almost a song, advertised a coal-black powder that miraculously left teeth sparkling white. No doctor, dentist or toothpaste could match its magic, he claimed, as passengers bought his product. An old woman in a rainbow-striped sari, carrying a basket of small newspaper packages full of peanuts, followed him. Behind her a teenage boy selling a multitude of battery-powered torches squeezed on board. Torches were an essential item, as there were no streetlights in the town and the villages were not electrified.

As the hustle and bustle of the bus stop engulfed us on the vehicle, I became ever more anxious about the 'receiver'. I scanned the horizon and, from the height of the bus, spotted a red cap in the distance. The cap's owner was a tall dark man with a newspaper rolled up under his arm. Everything was as it had been described.

My black hair was neatly oiled into a slick bun and I had wrapped a cheap flowery red and yellow chiffon sari around me to blend in among the local people. But taller and lighter skinned than the local women, I knew I still stood out in this male-dominated environment and thought that the 'receiver' would be able to identify me. Nevertheless, as agreed, I carried a loaf of bread. Object in hand, I approached the 'receiver'.

The man did not look at me. He wore a neatly ironed, plain white collared cotton shirt, beige trousers, and a pair of imitation black leather slip-on shoes which, although gleamingly polished, had worn-out soles, and I could see that he had a squint. 'You must be tired?' he asked. 'Yes,' I replied. A sigh of relief. Passwords uttered. Job done.

I followed the man in silence, not knowing what lay ahead. Nobody was expected to speak except to get from one place to the next. It was essential to protect our anonymity, especially with the counterinsurgency operations now surrounding us.

The man walked to another bus stand. It was for intra-state transport but was busier than the inter-state terminal. The bus we boarded was heaving with people to such an extent that it leaned precariously to one side. Men sat across the roof. The fittest youths hung from the ladder at the back. A line of legs even dangled across the windscreen. The 'receiver' disappeared halfway down the crowds standing in the aisle of the bus. As a woman, I was offered a space to sit perched on top of the piping hot gearbox gurgling with oil, and shared this with five other women. My knees knocked against the woman on the seat opposite me and one of her two young daughters climbed onto my lap. To my right a row of dusty plastic gods lined the cracked windscreen. Ganesh, the elephant god, was surrounded by garishly flashing lights.

With great ceremony, the bus hooted its departure out of Sherghati. The conductor chanted the bus's destination at the top of his voice, in a repetitive machine-gun mantra. As the bus left the stand, there was a last-minute dash of people trying to climb aboard, ramming their bodies into any remaining space. We were soon on the highway and then we turned down a quieter potholed mud road. Despite the bumpy, uncomfortable journey, I was overcome with tiredness and fell asleep.

The thunder of heavy vehicles made me jump up with a start. We were surrounded by tanks and armoured troop carriers, some as large as the bus. It was an Indian security force patrol out on what had become popularly known as 'Operation Green Hunt', the intense counterinsurgency measures that were aimed at eliminating the guerrillas and that had escalated over the last few months. About 100,000 state counterinsurgency forces, called the Central Reserve Police Forces, had been sent to reinforce state police forces and surround the hilly forests of central and eastern India. Border Security Forces and Indo-Tibetan Border Police were also mobilised. Ten CoBRA battalions, elite forces specially trained to fight a guerrilla like a guerrilla, were being raised and dispersed. A fleet of ten armed helicopters from the Indian Air Force were to be at hand to support these troops.

Journalists were increasingly being kept out of the guerrilla areas unless it was to show some dreaded terrorist encounter. Some journalists had reported that they were being paid not to write at all.[2] Anyone found 'supporting' the Maoists could be prosecuted under Section 39 of the Unlawful Activities (Prevention) Act, the Indian Ministry of Home Affairs declared in 2008. Human rights activists had already been arrested and imprisoned. One of the most famous cases was that of Binayak Sen, a paediatrician and human rights activist, who was first arrested in 2007, under the Chhattisgarh Public Security Act of 2005, charged with sedition and with allegedly helping the Maoists set up a network to fight the state. He would later, in 2010, be sentenced to life imprisonment and only granted bail after an international campaign for his release supported by dozens of intellectuals including Noam Chomsky, and the award of several international human rights and peace awards. But most such acts of silencing were going unreported. Scores of activists, lawyers and journalists who tried to enter the guerrilla strongholds to pressure the police into upholding its constitutional responsibilities, keep a civil war at bay, or even simply to find out what was happening in the heart of India, were chased out with violence or its threat. The military might of the Indian state was silently but stealthily being brought to control and clear the regions and extinguish news from within.

I shrank down into my makeshift seat, worrying that even though I was of Indian origin, my 'Western-ness' would stick out. If the security patrol noticed me, too many questions would have to be answered.

We got off the bus at the next village. It was built around a strip of roadside shops with a busy open-air market in front of them. The locals seemed to ignore the convoy of the security forces, but my mouth was dry and my stomach in knots. This was the machinery of war deployed to kill the people I was hoping to meet.

Quickly slipping past the men and women sitting on the roadside with baskets of aubergines, peas and tomatoes to sell, we made our way into a small hardware stall. From there we watched the security forces drive through the village. I counted at least twenty vehicles. This would have meant at least 500 armed men.

I was on my way to conduct a long-awaited interview with one of the Maoist Central Committee leaders. One of India's most wanted men, he had been underground for more than thirty years. This was someone I was yet to meet, even though for the past year and a half I had been living amongst the Adivasis of Lalgaon, a place the Naxalites called their 'Red Capital', deep in the forested hills of Jharkhand. This was only meant to be a short trip. Two days at most, I had been told. But it already promised to be much more than that.

My stomach heaved. Perhaps it was something I had eaten? Or was it from the constant jolting and lurching of the bus and the stench of diesel and exhaust fumes that had engulfed us as we bounced along the bumpy roads? Or maybe it was anxiety about the military convoy I had just seen?

2

HALF A CENTURY OF ARMED RESISTANCE

It is hard to imagine now that Soviet Russia or Maoist China inspired an Indian revolutionary struggle that endures. But the Naxalites did indeed emerge from the world communist movement and from the Communist Party of India this movement had nurtured in the early 1920s. Like other communist organisations, their goal was to fight through all available means, including armed force, for the overthrow of the bourgeoisie, the abolition of the state and for the creation of a communist society. No one knew what this society would look like except that it would be one where there was no private property, no division of mental and manual labour, and above all no social and economic inequality. Although the experiments to achieve those ends failed in China and Russia as the state turned capitalist and grew, rather than withering away, the dream of this classless society of freedom, equality and creativity has continued to inspire revolutionaries.

How to get there has always been the key question that divides the left. Anarchists promoted various means involving direct action to overthrow the authority of the state and organise small autonomous communes. Others, following the Bolsheviks in Russia, argued for a strategy to build broad mass movements involving peasants, soldiers and all oppressed groups, with the organised working class at its heart. In most parts of the world this meant the creation of communist parties, led by those people considered more 'conscious', sometimes called a vanguard. Over the years, parties have differed in opinion on several matters—whether to work within the parliamentary systems of states or whether to turn to arms and go entirely underground; whether the actions should be organised in stages of development or whether they should be spontaneous; whether the movement should be led by the urban working classes or centrally involve the peasantry; whether the struggle should begin in the cities as an insurrection or whether it should seep in from the country-side and slowly take over the urban areas.

After India's independence from British colonial rule, major factions began to develop in the Communist Party in the sub-continent. In the mid-fifties, as the US built a Cold War alliance with Pakistan, the Soviet Union developed a closer relationship with India. The Soviet communist government wanted the Indian communists to be supportive of India's first prime minister, Nehru, and his Congress Party, tone down their criticism of the Indian state and work within the parliamentary system. But Nehru had earlier—in the 1940s—ordered a brutal attack on the communists in Telangana, which divided the Indian left on the direction they were receiving from the Soviet Union. Moreover, relations between the Soviet Union and China were souring. Mao Zedong had begun criticising the Communist Party of the Soviet Union for turning capitalist and repudiating the need for revolutionary underground war, and the Sino-Soviet split which followed left some of the Indian communists sympathising with Mao while others backed Russia's Nikita Khrushchev. The 1962 India-China border disputes that led to the Sino-Indian war accentuated the divide among the Indian communists. Hundreds of Communist Party of India members supporting China were imprisoned for betraying India while their comrades simply looked on. And so, as those incarcerated debated and remobilised in Kolkata's Dum Dum jail—prisons are so often a conduit for further mobilisation—the party finally split into those who were pro-Russian, and those who were pro-Chinese and who argued that it was important to set up a different revolutionary tradition in India.

These Indian radicals—who would later call themselves the Communist Party of India (Marxist-Leninist)—said that despite the separation of India from Britain, colonialism persisted and the economy was still overwhelmingly feudal. They claimed that the country had not gained real independence but had simply been passed over to Indian friends of the colonial empire. Inspired by the protracted war of the Chinese peasantry that Mao Zedong once led, they said that what India needed was the revolutionary strategy that Mao had deployed against the Japanese in the 1930s when conditions in China were similar to those of India, and that Mao had continued to pursue against Chiang Kai-Shek's Chinese Nationalist Party, the Kuomintang. They set the stage for a protracted people's war that would mobilise peasants in the countryside, establish rural bases and organise an army of poor landless labourers and exploited peasants. The hope was that they would eventually encircle the cities in a bid to capture state power in the fight for a global communist society.

These revolutionaries began with a small uprising in May 1967 in the West Bengal village of Naxalbari, from which they get their name. There, led by Charu Majumdar and Kanu Sanyal, peasants and labourers occupied land, reclaimed it as theirs and demanded that the landlords cancel all their debts and end inter-generational bondage. After several months of demonstrations and occupations, protest escalated after one of the largest tea plantations undermined the workers strikes by laying them off. The workers seized the harvest, a landlord was lynched, other landlords ran away. When the police mounted an operation to crush the resistance, an arrow released by the occupiers instantly killed a police inspector. The next day the police retaliated. They opened fire on the protesters, killing eleven people, including eight women and two infants, and ignited rebellion across the countryside.[1]

The uprising in Naxalbari was brutally crushed. But the Chinese Communist Party declared that a 'peal of spring thunder has crashed over India.' They broadcast the Naxalbari events widely on Peking Radio, announcing the establishment of a red area of rural revolutionary armed struggle in the country. There had already been communication between Charu Majumdar and the Chinese Communist Party. A communist farmer had travelled across the Himalayas to give Majumdar's 'Historic Eight Documents' to Mao Zedong. These writings outlined the ideological principles of the militant communist movement that the Naxalite leader was proposing for India and that were a tribute to the path laid by the Chinese leader.[2] Later, in 1967, Kanu Sanyal and three other comrades also travelled through Nepal and across the mountains to China, where they met the People's Liberation Army, received three months of military training and political education and eventually even had an audience with Mao Zedong and Zhou Enlai before returning to India. Sanyal reported that Mao Zedong's parting words to them were, 'Forget everything you have learnt here in China. Once back in Naxalbari, formulate your own revolutionary strategies, keeping in mind the ground realities over there.'[3] But 'China's Chairman is our Chairman; China's Path is Our Path' became one of the main slogans raised by those early Naxalite revolutionaries.

News of the Naxalbari rebellion spread quickly across India and similar struggles erupted far away in the forested and hilly tracts of Srikakulam in Andhra Pradesh, Koraput in Odisha, and the plains of Bhojpur in Bihar and Birbhum in West Bengal. In some of these places the mobilisations drew on an older history of rebellion. For instance, there was the Telangana uprising of 1946–51 against the feudal lords and the Nizam of Hyderabad, who, the local communists said, continued to rule as a monarch even after the proclamation of Indian independence. There, the Indian communists had raised the Maoist slogan and mobilised peasant farmers and labourers against feudal lords to take over 3,000 villages, redistributed the land to the poor, and established village communes reminiscent of Soviet mirs to administer the region. The government had retaliated and sent in the army to erase the resistance and annex the Hyderabad state into the Indian union. That military invasion was brutal and it has only been recently acknowledged that, at a modest estimate, 30,000–40,000 people were killed and at least 10,000 alleged communists arrested.[4] Yet, the idea of guerrilla insurgency and peasant rebellion had also inspired and empowered people in the region. In the late sixties, revolutionary parties all over India sought to rekindle these earlier memories of rebellion, overthrow and sometimes annihilate oppressive landlords, redistribute land to the poorest, remove them from bondage and cancel their debts.

Drawn by the romance of the Naxalbari rebellion, many bright urban youths from upper- and middle-class families felt compelled to leave their homes and their college classrooms to work with the poor in the villages. They saw themselves aligning with a range of anti-colonial Maoist movements emerging across the globe. At the time, Maoism inspired people to engage in revolutionary change in widely different places in the world. The Cultural Revolution had just been launched as a radical movement to get rid of capitalism and traditional elements in Chinese society and the violent purges and killings of the period were not yet known. Maoism became an ideological repertoire of some note not only in many countries of the global South, but also in Europe, notably in France and Italy, and in Denmark and other Scandinavian countries. It influenced many intellectuals, from Simone de Beauvoir and Jean-Paul Sartre, to Michel Foucault and Julia Kristeva.[5]

In Latin America, a whole range of guerrillas led by urban intellectuals adopted Maoist guerrilla warfare, establishing themselves amongst marginalised populations in mountainous and hilly terrains, appropriating various indigenous symbols and beginning protracted people's wars. This is as true of the initial spread of the Sandinistas and the Popular Liberation Army (EPL—Ejército Popular de Liberación) in Colombia (who later turned to electoral politics) as it is of the Zapatistas in Mexico (who then became what is essentially an indigenous people's autonomy movement) and the Shining Path in Peru.

In Zimbabwe, the anti-colonial Zimbabwe African National Union (ZANU) guerrilla movement, led by Robert Mugabe, adopted various Maoist elements in its spread. In Haile Selassie's 'feudal' Ethiopia, the militant Eritrean People's Liberation Front (EPLF), heavily inspired by Maoist ideology, established the Republic of Eritrea. In Congo, Kabila formed a People's Revolutionary Party, supported by the People's Republic of China, which established a secessionist Marxist state to the west of Lake Tanganyika. In Turkey and northern Iran, the Kurdistan Workers' Party (PKK—Partiya Karkerên Kurdistanê) was for decades influenced by the strategy of Maoist people's war (although, like the Zapatistas, today their struggle is most often cast as an eco-feminist autonomy movement). In Southeast Asia, the Communist Party of the Philippines and its New People's Army, also influenced by Maoism, was being formed. In Cambodia, the Khmer Rouge army, with support from the People's Republic of China, was amassing in the jungles to the east of the country. Maoism was flourishing everywhere.

Perhaps one of the main reasons why Maoism as an idea spread widely across much of the global South in comparison to other forms of leftist social movements was Mao's theorisation of the role of the peasantry in revolutionary change. Earlier forms of Marxism saw the proletariat—of which the classic image was the dehumanised urban factory worker—as the truly revolutionary class that would usher in a classless society. They regarded the peasantry as reactionary and a force that would disappear from history because they would be uprooted from their land and would eventually join the urban proletariat. Mao turned this received wisdom on its head and argued for revolutionary history to be made by peasants who would lead a war from the countryside. In a context in which mass industrialisation and the formation of a proletariat was absent from the history of many nations, Maoism therefore enabled a vast swathe of the global South to be the potential harbinger of revolutionary social change.

In addition to this focus on the peasantry, Maoism as an idea was also popular for at least two other reasons. First, Mao saw capitalism as inextricably tied to foreign imperialism and therefore argued that revolutionary change had to be thought of as a worldwide struggle of the forces of socialism against those of imperialism. Mao thus became immediately relevant for many who were fighting colonialism and who either headed anti-colonial movements against the imperial nations or were developing critiques against their own national elites who they argued had allied with colonial forces. Second, Maoism allowed for the translation of a wide range of local conditions and problems through the political, organisational and leadership method which Mao called the 'mass line', central to which was consulting with the masses and interpreting and incorporating their suggestions within the revolutionary framework. 'From the masses to the masses'—as the mass line was referred to—was based on investigating the conditions of people, learning about and participating in their struggles, gathering ideas from them, and creating a plan of action based on their concerns in light of the revolutionary goal. The implication was that Maoism could flourish in discrete ways in different parts of the world, based on local conditions, and with little to do with Maoism elsewhere, or, for that matter, as it existed in China.

In India, the mobilisation of peasants and the landless poor was accompanied by intellectual and cultural activity, as well as attacks on government buildings and the educational system. New journals and periodicals such as *Liberation* and *Dakshin Desh* (Southern Country, referring to India in relation to the Himalayas, with China being the Northern Country) were published to circulate and disseminate the ideology behind the struggles: why India was semi-colonial and semi-feudal; why Indian independence was a 'sham'; why elections must be boycotted. Images and idols of national leaders like Gandhi, who were said to sustain the colonial system in India, were smashed. New radical theatre developed with plays to uphold Naxalbari, such as *The Arrow*, *The Call of Lenin*, and *Vietnam Unvanquished*.

The government continued its unyielding crackdown and many leaders and sympathisers were killed by the police or disappeared after being arrested. Charu Majumdar was imprisoned and died in police custody in 1972. Almost 32,000 suspected Naxals were imprisoned by 1973, many held for years in jail without trial. Splits had already developed between the different revolutionaries on what should be the way forward and critiques of Majumdar had emerged. Nevertheless, a whole generation of city youth had been radicalised and the seeds of rebellion had been sown in the countryside. On the streets of Kolkata and on college campuses, demonstrations had broken out supporting peasant uprisings and protesting police repression. Those not imprisoned carried out slow and patient underground work amongst the peasants and, from the late seventies on, some of those who had come out of jail went to colleges and villages to fight again in various parts of the country. The initial Naxalite uprising continued to inspire new generations of youths in India to take up arms to fight for revolutionary change.

Over the years, the Indian revolutionaries sought to form alliances with and learn lessons from the Shining Path in Peru and the Communist Party of the Philippines. They nurtured the Nepali Maoists who, from 1996, fought a ten-year civil war against the Nepali government, and were later instrumental in the dismantling of Nepal's Hindu monarchy. They formed an emerging set of revolutionary parties working in various parts of the country, all adopting Mao Zedong's strategy of protracted people's war, with their own cultural troops and their own magazines and journals.

They had differing positions on various issues—for instance, the balance in focus between use of arms and mass organising, or the extent to which parliamentary electoral politics should be used. Marxist-Leninist revolutionaries all over the world had taken the position that participation in parliamentary elections could only ever be a means to an end and that the right to vote for a particular candidate or policy must not be mistaken for real power or democracy.[6] Electoral participation was thus seen by many revolutionaries as an invaluable (if limited) tool for the working classes to present their ideas, programmes and counter the forces of the ruling classes. But the eventual revolutionary goal was to take power to establish something much more democratic that would include direct control of the workplaces and the land by the producers. Some parties—like the Communist Party of India (Marxist-Leninist) Liberation—turned to electoral politics. But others took the position that participation in elections in India meant being a part of a system that was corrupt to the core with bribes, extortion and the syphoning off of public funds crucial to its entire operation, and which would corrupt anyone who tried to fight for a seat;

and it was therefore best to boycott electoral participation entirely. There was the Maoist Communist Centre in Bihar, Jharkhand, and parts of West Bengal, the Communist Party of India (Marxist-Leninist) Party Unity in other parts of Bihar, the Communist Party of India (Marxist-Leninist) People's War in Andhra Pradesh in the south, and several other smaller groups, sometimes fighting each other over territories.

Everywhere the high theory of the Indian Maoist analysis of the economy translated on the ground into a fight against inequality and for social justice; the fight against oppression by landlords, against caste discrimination, for labour rights and land rights. Everywhere they sought to mobilise the most margin-alised people and demand their dignity be respected and their rights protected. Urban educated city youths were sent to work amongst the rural poor in 'go-to-the-village' campaigns. They armed themselves with sickles and knives until raids on police stations produced guns. As armed squads spread in the rural areas, so too did cultural troops singing revolutionary songs and staging plays. Everywhere the revolutionaries were criticised for their excessive use of violence, in particular their willingness to kill those they called 'class enemies'—landlords, state officials and police informers. Everywhere they faced state repression.

* * *

In the 1980s some of the agricultural plains of the country became infamous as India's 'flaming fields', due to the fierce caste wars fought between the Naxalites and their supporters, and the dominant-caste landlords. In the state of Bihar, for example, one of the poorest areas of India, the plains were marked by great disparities between the high-caste landlords who controlled large swathes of land, and the smaller farmers and especially the land-less Dalits who worked for the landowners as agricultural labour-ers and were treated like serfs.

Labelled as impure and polluted, the Dalit castes, once popularly known as 'untouchables', had been treated all over India as though they should not be touched. Forced to carry out the most lowly and 'polluting' of tasks, such as removing dead cattle and human excrement, their alleged impurity—which was religiously prescribed—affected every aspect of their life. Their bodily fluids were believed to be contaminating. Dalits were not allowed to touch the food of higher castes, drink water from their wells, walk across the thresholds of their houses or pray in their temples. The 'impurity' of Dalits was even said to affect the air, and therefore defined where they were allowed to live. Their hamlets were restricted to the southern edges of villages, in the belief that wind rarely blew from south to north, limiting the risk of polluted air contaminating higher-caste settlements.

Treated akin to animals, Dalits were expected to remove their shoes when passing through common or upper-caste parts of the village, to hold their heads low in front of a person of higher caste, to never dare look them in the eye. Paid a pittance for their labour, they were often forced to take loans from their higher-caste employers for expenses related to births, marriages, deaths and health, at interest rates that they would never be able to repay, tying them to work for these dominant castes, often across generations, like slaves.

Although some of the makers of the modern independent nation state recognised and tried to address the problems of these extreme hierarchies and inequalities in India, social discrimination based on caste and tribe persists in India. Under the Dalit leader Bhimrao Ambedkar, a new constitution was adopted that not only abolished untouchability but also reserved special places for India's low castes and tribes in higher educational institutions, government services, and in the lower houses of the central and state legislatures. Classsifying the Dalits 'Scheduled Castes' and the Adivasis 'Scheduled Tribes', some Dalits (and Adivasis) have indeed benefitted from these measures of affirmative action and over time the ritual dimensions of caste have declined. But, far from dying out as an anachronism, caste oppression continues to be entrenched in the modern economy.[7]

Across India, it is still overwhelmingly the low castes who do the jobs no one else will, who work for the higher castes as low-paid agricultural labourers usually bonded by advances they have to take to survive, who do the most difficult insecure casual manual labour in factories and in construction where they are hired through labour contractors, on zero-hours contracts, and fired at a moment's notice. Caste violence prevails in many forms—from verbal abuse and discrimination in schools and jobs, to rape and murder. And although, as late as 1989, a Prevention of Atrocities Act was introduced in Parliament to further protect Adivasis and Dalits, when people dare to rise against their oppression and exploitation, they are most often repressed and silenced, the police complicit.

When the Naxalites spread their struggles in the plains of Bihar, inspired by Mao Zedong and replicating the strategies against feudalism taken by Peru's Shining Path and the Communist Party of the Philippines, they tried to infiltrate the Dalit households to free them from their servitude to the dominant castes. They held secret night-time meetings in the Dalit colonies, mobilising them to hold their heads high against their oppression and join the Naxalite armies. They killed several of the most oppressive landlords, chased others away to the cities, seized their land and redistributed it among the landless and small farmers. They organised rallies, protests and labour strikes demanding that landlords raise wages for labourers, eliminate forced and bonded labour and give more equitable terms for redistributing the fruits of sharecropping. They publicly beat men who had sexually harassed working women and they descended *en masse* into government offices to demand clean drinking water, better housing and healthcare.

The high-caste landlords retaliated against the Naxalites and their supporters. They wreaked havoc in the villages that sympathised with the Naxalites by forming private armies or militias which went by names such as Ranvir Sena, Bhumi Sena and Sunlight Sena. The Senas (armies) came with their own war cry: 'There is only one remedy for the Naxalites, cut them down by 6 inches.' Dalits, in particular, were massacred overnight. They were often decapitated, as the slogan promised, to make them 6 inches shorter. Men, women and children were killed. Eight one night, nine another night, twenty-two another, twenty-five and thirty-five—so the growing slaughter continued as the police looked on. The houses of Naxalite supporters were burnt to the ground. The guerrillas could no longer take shelter in the houses, and the rice fields provided safety only when the crop was tall. There was nowhere to hide.[8]

So, in the late eighties, following Mao Zedong and Che Guevara's tactics, hoping to find India's Yan'an, a base area away from the Indian state from which they could progress their fight, the Naxalites went in search of better geographical terrain for guerrilla warfare and began to retreat into the hills and forests of central and eastern India—into what are now the states of Jharkhand and Chhattisgarh, and into southern Odisha, northern Andhra Pradesh and Telangana, southeastern Madhya Pradesh and parts of Maharashtra and West Bengal.

One such ideal guerrilla territory was Lalgaon, where I lived. A thickly forested vast flat-topped plateau of about thirty dispersed villages and 40,000 people, it rose from the plains as a mesa, locally known as a *pat*, composed of Deccan lava. It was bound to the north by the wide Auranga River, to the south by the North Koel River, and dissected by many smaller streams and rivulets so that in the monsoons it was completely cut off from the plains.

These new lands were also ideal territory to develop guerrilla zones as they were virtually devoid of state presence. And so it was that while in most other parts of the world, armed communist struggles began to decline after the fall of the Berlin Wall and China's shift to state capitalism, in India, despite episodes of intense repression and periods in which it seemed all was quiet in the countryside, the Naxalite movement continued to mobilise the most socially discriminated groups: this time its Adivasis.

* * *

Although they had encountered Adivasis before, when they arrived in these remote regions, the Naxalite leaders, who came from the cities and the agricultural plains, knew little about the tribal people that dominated these forested hills, the communities of Hos, Santhals, Gonds, Konds, Murias, Koyas and many other Adivasi groups. In Lalgaon, there were the Oraons, the Mundas, the Kherwars, the Lohras, the Birhors, the Paharias, the Birjias, the Asurs and the Agarias—some of whom still lived off hunting and gathering from the forests and moved their homes seasonally depending on what they were collecting.[9]

For centuries before, these Adivasis had migrated further and further into the shelter of the forests and the hills, seeking to move away from the hierarchies and oppression they faced elsewhere, creating communities that were rather different to those of the caste-divided plains.[10] Although government programmes, activists and scholars in India often consider Adivasis alongside Dalits as India's most oppressed and poorest communities, in the hills where Adivasis had some direct access to land and forests, they were not dependent on other groups for their everyday survival in the way that Dalits were in the agricultural plains. In the plains, different caste groups lived in close proximity in nucleated villages, unequally dependent on each other. Higher and dominant castes marked the top of the social hierarchy, controlling the land and most other important resources. Dalits were right at the bottom with no land of their own to farm in most places and nothing but their labour to sell to make ends meet. But the closer you got to the forests, the less the influence of interdependency and hierarchy between groups that mark caste society in the plains, and the greater the autonomy people had over their own lives.[11] In the remotest of such areas, Adivasi communities lived in dispersed houses, surrounded by the forests in which they hunted and which they cleared to grow grain and crops, some groups still practising shifting cultivation, clearing one patch of forest to cultivate for a few years and then moving on to other areas. This autonomy to sustain themselves on their own terms, though, has come to be persistently undermined.

Like tribal groups all over the world, outsiders who came to these areas thought its forest dwellers to be savage, barbaric and primitive. In India they were called '*jungli*', a derogatory term accusing them of being as wild as the forests they inhabited. The British colonial state and the Mughals before them nevertheless wanted revenue from their land as they did across the country. They introduced outsiders—usually higher castes from the plains—to control, 'tame' and settle the populations. The newcomers tried various strategies, like forcibly moving the people and resettling them in villages that looked more like those of the plains and indebting them through outside moneylenders, turning them into bonded labourers. Although some Adivasi communities succumbed, many either retreated further into the hills or fought the outsiders off. In the end, while some higher castes scattered across the forests and hills,[12] most of these outsiders preferred to stay in the more accessible towns away from the forests and the hills, trying to do their jobs from a distance.

From the late nineteenth century, alongside attempts at land settlement and alienation, commercial logging developed when the forests were found to be a rich resource for railway sleepers, for the building of military ships, and for hardwood furniture. The pattern of extraction was old and global. It was what colonial empires across the world—whether British, Spanish or Dutch—were built on. Timber taken by the Raj can today be traced in the well-preserved stately homes of England. Grand rooms in Buckinghamshire, Bedfordshire and Berkshire can be found bursting with delicately carved chests of drawers, ivory inlaid dressing tables, the occasional Bengal tiger rug, and antique clocks made of the teak and ebony extracted from these forests of central and eastern India and those of the Himalayas.

The forest dwellers suffered in more ways than one. From roaming the landscape, living on different patches of land, hunting and gathering, and cultivation by shifting, as the forests became 'reserved' or 'protected' the forest dwellers were slowly forced into more permanent settlements on the forest fringes. Many small villages, some of fewer than fifty households, developed. The settlement of the forests also introduced a new population of outsiders who came to work the forests and serve the markets opened by forest harvesting and moneylending. In Lalgaon these were middle-caste Hindu (Sahus—termed OBC, or Other Backward Classes, by the Indian government) and Muslim traders who came from the plains of Bihar. They lived together in the most accessible part of the region where the weekly market, called the *haat*, was based. Most of them were businessmen and traders. Not interested in farming, they did not try to accumulate land for tilling and mainly left the Adivasis to cultivate the terrain and to gather the forest fruits. But they introduced new markets of money which heavily indebted the Adivasis while, at the same time, the forest officials tried to deny the Adivasis access to the forest resources they had lived off.

The Adivasis fought back against the persistent attempts at their dispossession. The Mundas, the Kols, the Hos, the Santhals, the Bhumij, the Chero all strung their bows and arrows to attack the outsiders responsible for their plight. Rebellions in various parts of the central and eastern Indian hills arose across the late eighteenth, nineteenth and early twentieth centuries.

One of the most striking of these rebellions (although not the first) was the Santhal Hul. It in fact began two years before the 1857 Sepoy Mutiny against the British East India Company that is otherwise thought of as India's First War of Independence. In 1855–56, tens of thousands of Santhals, led by two brothers, Sidhu and Kanhu, tried to kill the landlords and moneylenders introduced by the British government who had dispossessed the Adivasis of their land and forests and turned them into bonded labourers. But the simple bows and arrows, sickles and knives of the Santhals were no match against the British Government who sent in troops on elephants with cannon and muskets. These colonial forces destroyed and burnt down entire villages, killed 10,000 Santhals, including the two brothers who had led them, and crushed the rebellion.[13]

But the resistance persisted in various parts of the country. The rebellion that is perhaps the most well known is that of Birsa Munda in 1899–1901.[14] Although only said to have lasted a month and killed fewer than thirty people, it lives on today as a symbol of tribal resistance against their alienation from their land and forests, and Birsa's portrait hangs in the Indian parliament as the only Adivasi to have such an honour. The Birsa movement became a historic marker of Adivasi resistance perhaps because in its aftermath some protective measures were finally put into place. Mediated by Christian missionaries, the Chotanagpur Tenancy Act—often considered the Magna Carta of the Adivasis—was an attempt to stop Adivasi land and forests from being sold off to outsiders so that they wouldn't simply be turned into abject wage labour.

Despite the introduction of various such land protection measures—which eventually got enshrined in the Fifth and Sixth Schedules of the Indian Constitution—these laws have been persistently undermined. And, when India separated from British rule, although heavy logging was by then officially prohibited, the Indian state continued the exploitative legacy of the forests in new ways. A black market endured for lucrative forest products and the looting of Adivasi resources continued.

From the seventies, after most of the forests had been depleted, the Indian forestry agenda turned from harvesting the forests to protecting them under a new conservation agenda that was taking over the world. Parts of Lalgaon became a Tiger Sanctuary and National Park, further curtailing the rights of Adivasis from those forests, this time to protect the tiger.

The new conservation agenda also affected the outsiders who had come from the plains of Bihar. While in the heyday of forest harvesting, the outsiders had earned a good living, when forestry turned to conservation, although some continued to run the illicit rackets of logging and smuggling out other forest products (usually moving out of the forests to live in the district head-quarters), many became increasingly impoverished. They sought to earn a living from grocery shops, trading in non-timber forest products such as flowers from the *mahua* tree used to make wine, taking government contracts—for example for Public Distribution Shops which sold subsidised rations provided by the state for the poor—and other small enterprises such as tailoring. Those who failed in enterprise migrated away seasonally as casual wage labour to other parts of the country, although rarely doing the heaviest manual labour jobs which Adivasis and Dalits are used for. Meanwhile, the Adivasis continued to try to farm and live off the forests. As their access to the resources around them was increasingly restricted, they also migrated seasonally as casual wage labour to do the most gruelling of work—like making and carrying heavy loads of bricks in brick factories—that the higher castes would consider demeaning.

Neither the British Raj nor the Indian state made substantive attempts to develop basic infrastructure for the people who lived in these regions. The idea of their savagery and barbarism had stuck and the officials who were given responsibility for these Adivasi forests and hills considered them as beyond the pale of civilisation and made few attempts to integrate them as equal and rightful citizens of the Indian state. They considered their deputations to these areas as 'punishment posts'.

Even at the cusp of the new millennium, as the world marvelled at India's economic growth rates, there was no provision of electricity or running water, healthcare or sanitation, in any of the villages in which I lived in Jharkhand. Efforts to encourage literacy were also negligible and in most of the villages I visited, up to 90 per cent of the Adivasi population was illiterate. Although there were a few schools dotted around the landscape, it was not until the 2000s that schools were being built everywhere. Most people I knew did not have enough education to consider applying for the ambitious constitutional provision for jobs in the state sector that were to be reserved for Adivasis and Dalits in proportion to their representation in the total population.[15]

Although they lived right under the state's extractive regime, historically the Adivasi response to these outsiders was to keep them at arm's length, resisting with a culture that was antithetical to that of the outsiders. 'We are people of the *Jungle Raj* (the Forest Kingdom),' many an Adivasi elder proudly said to me. I came to understand *Jungle Raj* as emblematic of an Adivasi counterculture, a way of life formed in negotiation with but also opposition to the high-caste outsiders.

* * *

In a country whose society is often seen as one of quintessential hierarchy—as exemplified by its caste system—these forest-dwelling communities were exceptional for their relatively egalitarian values, and the dignity and pride with which they held these values, when compared to the caste-divided hierarchical communities of the plains of India. This is not to say that there was no hierarchy amongst Adivasis or to suggest that all Adivasis groups were equally egalitarian, but to mark that in relation to the stark, caste-based inequalities of the agricultural plains, the communities of these hills and forests were notable for their egalitarian spirit that left them relatively free from unequal social divisions. Egalitarian values appeared in many aspects of Adivasi life: in how families were organised in autonomous kin groups; the ways in which communities were led; in their attitudes to production and consumption; and especially in gender relations.

Some scholars have said that India's forest-dwelling communities were marked by social systems of anarchy in that they were ordered societies without the forms of rule that represent enduring structures of domination and exploitation.[16] In some of the Munda and Oraon villages that I came to know intimately, local leaders were selected through an exceptional randomised process. A spirit possessed a blindfolded person, the possessed person moved around all the houses of the village, and the house where the spirit left the person was the house of the new leader. These practices of spiritual sortition were so democratic that it was a lottery as to who would be the next leader. This was an Ancient Athenian form of democracy, once regarded as the principal model of democracy, with a tribal twist. Leaders did not dictate orders but facilitated discussions to resolve disputes by consensus, a process that could take days to reach agreements—what anarchists have called 'democracy by consensus'. They were also responsible for cultivating communal fields whose crops were to be used for feeding the entire village three times a year and given to anyone facing hardship, as a kind of social security net or a welfare state. Not everyone felt that they could hold the responsibility of leading and some passed on the role to others they considered more appropriate. Although not prevalent everywhere, this ideal of leadership was remarkable for being based on the values of society marked by the egalitarianism of sharing responsibility in looking after each other, and not on status, rank, charisma or wealth.[17]

Indeed, internal stratification based on the accumulation of wealth has not typically been encouraged within Adivasi society.[18] Foraging and producing to meet not much more than subsistence needs was common, as many lived mainly just for the moment. Eating, drinking and making merry were a central part of daily Adivasi sociality but this consumption was first and foremost about sharing with others and not about showing your superiority, or marking yourself apart from others. Mutual and collective aid through systems of non-monetised labour exchange between households was crucial for survival. Adivasis proudly continued collective hunting and gathering and shared the fruits of their labour just as they participated in communal labour exchange: you help me build my house, I will help you build yours, or, you help me sow my fields today, I will help you sow yours tomorrow. People were valued as masters of their own production and consumption and when they couldn't survive on what they found around them and had to participate in wage labour for some parts of the year, they often did so in a similar spirit, as 'wage gatherers', seeing wages as just another form of gathering for subsistence.[19]

Perhaps most strikingly, in a country so marked by inequality between men and women, was the relative gender equality and the social, sexual and economic freedom that women had across the forests of central and eastern India in comparison to the higher-caste societies of the plains. Not only did women work outside the household (with some women even going on hunts), but it was common to find men cooking and doing other domestic work, such as washing clothes, collecting water, sweeping and looking after children. And when there was drinking and dancing, Adivasi women participated alongside men with equal fervour. It often struck me that the communities that I lived with had a form of gender equality that surpassed the conditions in the West that decades of feminist movements had fought hard for.

Although these values were constantly being undermined and attacked, Adivasis could maintain their egalitarian countercultures partly because state officials had not taken an interest in co-opting them into their project of citizen-making, but especially because they still had some direct access to the material resources of forests and land, which gave them the autonomy to live on their own terms, and to reproduce their communities and values, without much interference from or being too dependent on others.

It was in the lands of these relatively egalitarian communities that the Naxalite leaders found themselves, seeking to nurture their revolutionary struggle for an egalitarian society. A protracted encounter of different egalitarian ideals and practices—that of the Naxalites and that of the Adivasis—followed, albeit surrounded by the tensions of hierarchy and inequality fraying at the possibilities of their conjuncture. Nevertheless, although so many outsiders had failed to infiltrate these forests, from the 1990s in particular, the people of these areas became the main support base of the Naxalites and it is here, in the heart of the country, that the guerrillas grew in strength, consolidating their armies.

* * *

For many years, the underground leaders of the various revolutionary parties had talked of unity, and in 2004 these talks bore fruit, creating what is now called the Communist Party of India (Maoist) and their People's Liberation Guerrilla Army (PLGA) to escalate their war against the Indian state. Since then, they have been called Maoists in the press and by the police. They themselves use both Naxalite and Maoist and in the villages in their strongholds they take on several names including 'The Party' and '*Jungle Sarkar*' (the Forest State).[20] Although the numbers change all the time, and with such clandestine armies that are constantly on the move it is easy to project a greater force than is in fact the case, by 2010 there were an estimated 10,000 guerrilla soldiers and the numbers were said to be rising.

Working outside of the Indian state boundaries, they created their own parallel state with state-like structures and their own geographical demarcations, which superseded the Indian borders and were based mainly on topographical continuities and the homes of the various oppressed communities. Heading it all, in a pyramidal structure, was the Central Committee with its Politburo overseeing the various State-level Committees that executed the political-organisational work of the movement. Bihar-Jharkhand-Chhattisgarh was the state area in which I lived and Dandakaranya, which straddled southern Chhattisgarh, northern Andhra Pradesh, southern Odisha and Maharashtra, was considered the foremost guerrilla stronghold. Within each of these Maoist states were Regional Committees, followed by Zonal Committees, under which there were Area Committees overseeing the work of party cells and mass organisations (the latter were non-violent and led by and consisted of people who were not underground). Those who were mobilised to contribute to the political work began right at the bottom and were slowly promoted up the ladder. Although each region had its own socio-cultural history and specific tactical needs, the aim was to achieve unity in strategy across the areas. Programmes of mobilisation and also leaders could therefore be found deputed across states; for example, in Jharkhand it was common to find people from Andhra Pradesh working alongside those from West Bengal and Bihar.

These political structures were supported by the military force of the People's Liberation Guerrilla Army. Villagers who wanted to join the armies were first recruited into local area squads. If they lasted, they would be promoted to a platoon (a force of about thirty soldiers), then a company (around eighty to ninety soldiers) and finally a battalion (of several hundred soldiers). People's militias consisted of villagers who could come together to fight with arms—usually swords, sticks, bows and arrows—only when necessary. There were also mass fronts—farmers' movements, anti-displacement and anti-mining fronts, women's movements—organisations that worked openly to mobilise people to fight against issues that affected them daily. But these mass fronts were usually kept separate from the armies to protect them as they were open and not underground and therefore more vulnerable to state repression.

The Indian state's solution to this growing force was development under the barrel of a gun, although there were those in government who had argued against such a security-centred approach.[21] The links between the economic growth model of the government and the war to be waged against the Maoists were explicit. In 2009, Indian Prime Minister Manmohan Singh said in parliament, 'If left-wing extremism continues to flourish in important parts of our country which have tremendous natural resources of minerals and other precious things, that will certainly affect the climate for investment.' The brain behind the offensive which followed, Home Minister P. Chidambaram (also the erstwhile finance minister), was previously a corporate lawyer representing several mining corporations as well as a non-executive director of Vedanta—a British mining company owned by the billionaire Anil Aggarwal—which planned to excavate bauxite in many parts of India. The following year, the home secretary said that the insurgents blocking $80 billion of investments would be subdued within three years. But, in 2014, the Maoists persisted and the new home minister, Rajnath Singh, promised to wipe them out in another three years. In 2017, another end was promised with a renewed aggressive fight to choke the rebels.

There were some attempts at 'peace negotiations', most notably in Andhra Pradesh in 2004. A ceasefire was agreed for a period in order to facilitate talks. Senior leaders came out of the forests, and engaged in talks with the government. The first round discussed many of the Naxalite demands including the withdrawal of cases against people who had been agitating, the release of political prisoners and the removal of awards for the arrest of wanted revolutionary leaders. Also discussed was land distribution to the poor. But no agreements were made and after this round, the government was reluctant to continue the ceasefire for the second round of talks. The talks broke down in January 2005. The government claimed that the Naxalites had used the ceasefire to consolidate their armies while the Naxalites said that the government had used the period of the talks to get information about their top leaders and networks. The government repression that followed was intense, destroying the movement in Andhra Pradesh.[22]

In 2010 peace negotiations were considered again but ceased when the Maoist Central Committee leader responsible for the negotiations, Cherukuri Rajkumar, who went by the *nomme de guerre* Azad (meaning Freedom), was killed. The Maoists claimed that the government was once again using the talks to wipe out their leadership. They said that Azad had been killed in a 'fake encounter'—an extra-judicial killing that was presented as a staged confrontation—marking a long history of such fabrications. Villagers, foot soldiers and leaders have been picked up by the police, brutally tortured in custody and killed, and then had their bodies strewn in faraway forests to be presented to the world as having been killed by the police acting in self-defence during an encounter with the Naxalites, even though there were marks of torture all over their mutilated bodies. Over the time I spent in Lalgaon, the National Human Rights Commission recorded that there were more than 200 reported cases of fake encounters across the country, most of which were in Naxalite areas.[23]

The most brutal form of counterinsurgency measures began after the 2004–5 'peace negotiations'. In the Dandakaranya region of southern Chhattisgarh, to which the Naxalites had retreated after the repression in Andhra Pradesh, from 2006, local youth were armed and mobilised to cleanse the area of people in what was called Salwa Judum, meaning 'purification hunt' in the local Gondi language. Headed and nurtured by a local politician—who called the mobilisation a 'Peace March'—the hunt recruited upwardly mobile educated youth from both the middle castes and the Adivasis, and backed by the police and government funding and weapons, they attacked the Adivasi villages and villagers who were seen as Naxalite supporters. Entire villages were plundered and burned down, children thrown into fires and pregnant women killed; hundreds of women were raped, others mutilated and murdered, and more than 350,000 people were forced to leave their homes, according to human rights activists.[24] It was reminiscent of the brutality of British counterinsurgency tactics used to kill the support of the National Liberation Army of the Malayan Communist Party more than sixty years before. In Chhattisgarh, many people were killed and others forcibly evacuated into resettlement camps that they saw as being like prison compounds. The corporations were waiting to enter the region. But the Naxalites claimed that these counterinsurgency programmes only served to increase their ranks.

As their village support grew, the Naxalite cadres expanded and so did the territories they controlled—at least for a while, before the security forces boxed them in—so that they could walk from one Indian state to the next and rely on support from sympathisers along the way.

3

LIVING IN A MUD HUT

How did I find myself here? It is difficult to say where exactly my journey began. Perhaps it was before I was born in an Indian suburb of Nairobi. In the late 1920s my grandparents sailed the monsoon winds from the poor, dry and dusty villages by the Gulf of Kutch in Gujarat, India, to eke out a living in Africa. They followed a well-trodden path, promoted at the turn of the twentieth century by the British Raj, who, having laid the Indian Railways in the late 1800s, took contract labourers from India to build train tracks from the Kenyan port of Mombasa to Lake Victoria. Upon his arrival in Mombasa, my grandfather, then aged sixteen, headed for Nairobi to make a new life for himself.

My grandmother, Moti, who had not laid eyes on my grandfather before she was married off to him by uncles and aunts, went to join him a year after their marriage. She set sail on a small dhow carrying eighty passengers. A few weeks into their journey the monsoon winds failed. Stuck in the doldrums of the Indian Ocean for three days, they were running out of drinking water. There, in the crowded heat of the hull, is where fifteen-year-old Moti, on her way to an unknown land and an undiscovered husband, thought that they would all die. In the toughest moments of my journeys in eastern India, I would think of my grandmother's fortitude in the face of this uncertainty and my own fear and suffering would pale into insignificance.

Although my grandparents were illiterate, they worked hard and invested everything into the education of future generations, sending my father to medical school at the Makerere University in Uganda. By the time I was born, from sweeping the floors of other people's shops, my grandfather had established his own. Our story was fairly common of a certain generation of migrant East African Gujaratis. Others were more ambitious. Some of my father's friends set up the first sweet factories of Africa, the first textile mills and the first oil refineries in Kenya. Others expanded their industries across the globe to West Africa and South East Asia and now feature high up on the global lists of wealthy Africans and British Asians worth at least two billion dollars. My father taught me, though, to question the inequities that this accumulation of wealth entailed and made me acutely aware of the plight of the local Kikuyu, Akamba and Luo labourers on the backs of whom it was built.

Over the years my father responded to the values being embraced by those around him with a strong anti-materialist outlook. While his friends sat luxuriously in air-conditioned Mercedes Benzes, my father proudly insisted on filling his twelve-seater van with twice the number of people it was meant for and driving them across the country, arguing that a car was for one purpose only: to get as many people as possible from point A to point B. And as his friends poured their newly accumulated wealth into seeking the advice of spiritual gurus, venerating Jain monks and sinking gold into the foundation of new marble temples, my father turned more and more secular. From my father I learnt to question the injustices of the world around me. But I also learnt to question him.

I was fifteen when my family moved to England, and by then it was expected that girls would go to university and find paid work because it was no longer possible to sustain most middle-class Gujarati households on just one salary. Like the choice of a suitable boy for marriage, a suitable job for a woman had strict boundaries. From my father's point of view at that time, the purpose of higher education for me and my three sisters was to find dignified jobs in public service—to become a dentist, optometrist or pharmacist, for instance—that would allow us to have reasonable working hours and fulfil our main duty—to look after our children, husbands and wider family. I had different desires, however. Naïve as I was, I wanted to reach beyond the family and make the world a better place for all.

I read geography at Cambridge and then went on to work with various international development organisations. From teaching displaced children in the slums of Delhi for a small charity, I found myself walking through the sparkling glass atrium of the World Bank in Washington, DC, working as an intern in their Poverty Reduction and Economic Management unit. But I became disillusioned by what seemed to be a widespread approach that turned poverty into an industry, benefitting from poverty-related activities, rarely questioning the underlying inequalities that produced it. I increasingly believed that projects aiming to tackle inequality must begin from the diverse perspectives and experiences of the marginalised, oppressed and excluded people whose lives they wished to change but whose voices were rarely heard, often silenced. I returned to university to embark on a PhD, with these thoughts uppermost.

It was at university that I discovered both the Naxalites and what social anthropologists call 'participant observation', that rather quaint praxis of ethnographic research that few anthropologists have the time to pursue today. Participant observation was proposed in the early twentieth century by the Polish-born

British anthropologist Bronislaw Malinowski, returning from field research in the South Pacific Trobriand Islands, as an antidote to research done from distant armchairs, through data obtained second-hand from missionaries or travel writing, or through a few interviews or short investigative visits. Involving an intense involvement with people in their own cultural environment by living with them over an extended period of time, learning their language, observing and participating in their daily lives, exploring all aspects of their lives in as holistic a way as possible, long-term participant observation had the ability to give us novel insights about the world and unveil hidden processes that we might never be able to see otherwise.[1] It seemed important to be trained as an anthropologist as a route to the answers I needed for the making of a better world. So, aged twenty-three, as a budding doctoral student of anthropology, I set off for India.

I chose to go to the other side of the country than to where I had roots, to a place where distant aunts or uncles would not inhibit my movements out of a sense of protection or social decorum, to the remote forests and hills of the far east of India where I knew no-one. There, in the state of Jharkhand, I lived for two and a half years with the Munda Adivasi tribal people in a village of a hundred mud houses that had no electricity or running water.

It was one of the poorest and most remote parts of the world and seemed to be a good base from which to understand, from the grassroots, the virtues and limits of the various attempts at addressing poverty and inequality—whether it was by international development agencies or by grassroots social movements. I wanted to know how different attempts at social transformation, whether initiated by the state or by non-state organisations, were experienced and engaged in by India's Adivasis, some of the most marginalised people in the world.

In Jharkhand I saw how development funds were syphoned off by the local elites before they could reach the poorest people. I saw how NGO workers came to the forest villages in their Land Rovers, spoke to the local elite to fulfil their 'participatory community development' mission, and then rushed back to the city under the 'safety' of the daylight hours, while the poor tribals hid in the forests until the outsiders had gone. I saw too how on election days, votes were bought and voting boxes stolen by the goons of the strongest parties, and how the poorest tribals wanted to keep the state away from their lives. And I saw the corporate officials of international management consultancies, exploring the mining potential of the region for multinational corporations, being greeted with garlands of marigolds as they landed at Ranchi airport to figure out how to overcome the problems of land acquisition from Adivasis.

It was not until the end of this period in Jharkhand that I first stumbled upon the Naxalites. Their forest armies were expanding in the area and they were recruiting my village friends.

'They are just criminals,' said my research assistant then. She was a middle-class, upper-caste girl from Ranchi city.

On the surface of things, it appeared that she was correct. Indeed, that is how I wrote about them in my first book, *In the Shadows of the State*: the Naxalites as protection racketeers, taking over the local markets of rent-seeking. In exchange for introducing them to the villages, they were offering my friends protection with their guns to syphon off some of the money that came into the area as development funds for infrastructural projects such as the building of roads, dams or bridges. This was money that usually went into the pockets of the locally powerful people—the politicians, the state officials, the contractors and the village elites.

But, my doctoral supervisor, one of the world's finest professors of anthropology, came to visit me in the village where I lived in Jharkhand, and asked in his characteristically understated manner, 'Are they really just a bunch of thugs?' The question kept bothering me.

I had to return to London to write my PhD thesis but I kept track of news about the Naxalites from afar. Although life back at home took over—I became a university lecturer, I had students to teach, I got married—I became increasingly drawn to what the Naxalites were trying to achieve. They had come together, or so they said, to overthrow one of the most powerful and unequal states in the world in the hope of creating a more egalitarian future for everyone. They seemed to be immersed in the lives of the communities I had left in central and eastern India, living as I had once done, as one of them. As Indian economic growth rates were rising, their underground armies were reported to be swelling. Yet, internationally, at the time there seemed to be a conspicuous silence around India's war within. Unlike movements such as that of the Zapatistas in the Chiapas in Mexico, the Naxalites remained largely unknown to the Western intellectuals and students who came to revere other similar faraway indigenous peoples' struggles in their own anti-capitalist movements. I knew I had to get back to those forests of Jharkhand to understand how and why the Adivasis were taking up arms to fight for a different world.

That's how, when the global financial crisis hit between 2008 and 2010, ten years after I had first gone to Jharkhand, I found myself living for a year and a half in a village in an area the guerrillas called their 'Red Capital', Lalgaon. I could not have predicted that the Indian government would launch their military might to eliminate the guerrillas exactly when I stepped back into Jharkhand.

'Operation Green Hunt' began in the autumn of 2008. Trainloads, busloads and truckloads of troops poured in from all over the country and made their barracks across the plains of central and eastern India in schools, hospitals and any other public building they could find. Although surrounding the Adivasi hills where I lived, they did not dare to climb up into the forests unless they were in a force of 500 or more. On those patrols, drivers were sent ahead to scout in tanks and bulletproof vehicles, but the troops all came on foot as the land mines the Maoists had laid under those tracks were targeted at blowing up the vehicles. The road to Lalgaon, where I lived, was thought to be the most mined road in India.

Journalists were prohibited from going into the guerrilla areas unless accompanied by the security forces. Sympathetic journalists and human rights activists defending the rights of India's low castes were jailed. The police tapped the few existing phone networks out of the guerrilla strongholds. When I realised that I couldn't call my husband back in England for weeks on end, for fear of being discovered as a foreign voice speaking a foreign language dialling a foreign land, I wondered what I was doing in that wilderness. But I was already too immersed in trying to understand the lives of my new sisters and brothers, aunts and uncles, nephews and nieces.

Then, at the peak of these counterinsurgency operations, in February 2010, came this long-awaited invitation for an interview with a Maoist Central Committee leader whom I had not yet met. I left my mud hut in Jharkhand to travel to the neighbouring state of Bihar for what I thought would be just a two-day trip.

PART TWO

PRASHANT, THE KID AMONG THE GOATS

4

MEETING THE GUERRILLAS

The security force vehicles had passed but my stomach was still churning as we waited in the hardware shack on the dusty roadside, tucked away from the market stalls. A younger man in blue denim appeared from the side of the shack, as though he had also been waiting.

The man with the squint had been given only enough information to bring me from the bus stop to this shack. He had no idea about what was to happen next. This kind of secrecy—of people being given only the necessary information, no more, to perform a well-defined task—was crucial in a context of war. It would make it difficult to be stalked. Moreover, if one of us were arrested, we would have only very limited information about each other's movements to give to the police under torture. I had not spoken to the man with the squint, but simply following him had transformed him into a familiar, reassuring figure in this unknown terrain. I was nervous as I watched him leave. Bidding farewell to the man with the squint, I followed the man in jeans.

We soon left behind the noise of the market. In front of us lay open rice fields. In the distance, mud houses marked a village.

Still further were the hills—our destination, I guessed. To our right, across the flat plains, the tops of the armoured carriers and tanks were moving off along the road towards another village.

We scrambled down into a parched riverbed with dry scrub and bushes on either side, and followed it away from the market village. The man in jeans said it was a longer route than walking across the rice banks, but in the riverbed we were less visible and would meet fewer people.

We stopped twice. Each time because I needed to vomit. Embarrassed to slow us down, I was happy that no fuss was made about it. The man in jeans simply stepped aside until I was ready to move on. He did, however, switch on his mobile phone. He was making a call for a motorbike. Alarmed, I stopped him and said we should continue as planned, afraid of the extra attention and delay that stopping and searching for a motorbike might cause.

At dusk, we entered the empty courtyard of a mud house at the edge of a village. The young man told me to wait there and disappeared. I sat on the doorstep, resting my back against the padlocked door of the house. The step was coated with the customary mix of mud and fresh cow dung, making it as smooth and shiny as a dark brown chocolate slab. Twenty minutes later it was getting dark, the young man had not returned, and the arched crescents marking the fingertips of the person who had plastered the step that morning eerily jumped out at me. I drew in the sweet smell of the mud and dung to calm myself down.

I became fixated on watching the second hand of my wristwatch turn. But time works in a completely different way in rural India. People would wait for six or eight hours on a railway platform for a delayed train, without becoming angry or frustrated. Or, if a bus were held up for a few hours with a puncture, passengers would wait without making a fuss. Young men could spend hours simply watching time pass. I tried to remind myself of the hours of waiting I had already done over the last year and a half in the 'Red Capital' where I had made my home in the forests of Jharkhand. I needed to be patient.

The young man returned half an hour later. He said we should continue to the last village before the hills as the 'Green Hunt' patrol had returned to its base. The security forces had completed their daytime show of power and the nights, he said, always belonged to the Maoists.

We walked for another half hour, past the last mud house, and towards the hills whose dark contours stood out against the blue midnight sky. Suddenly, in the moonlight, a tall and sinewy silhouette approached us with an AK-47 slung across his shoulders. Out of the shadows behind him appeared at least ten more men.

'*Lal salaam, Didi* (Red salute, sister),' he said, as he put his hand out to shake mine and then raised his fist in the air in the customary Naxalite greeting.

'I am Prashant,' he said.

His voice was unexpectedly sweet and melodious. The name 'Prashant' was a *nom de guerre*. Guerrillas were always given a new name, usually that of a recently fallen soldier who could be collectively remembered through the renaming of a guerrilla. The change of name was important to protect the identity of the guerrilla and their families outside of the movement. Most of the younger Naxalites, however, would not be confident enough to introduce themselves by name, even if they had prior knowledge of the person they were meeting. There was something very generous and welcoming about the way Prashant presented himself to me.

I wanted to introduce myself in return but could not recall what name I had been given for this journey. It had changed so many times.

When he came up close, I saw Prashant could not have been much older than thirty. Smartly dressed in the guerrilla olive-green uniform, he held a green cap in one hand. Silky dark brown hair flopped across his forehead, framing a chiselled face with a fine nose, high cheekbones, and flawless, light, glowing skin. His broad open smile immediately put me at ease.

Prashant rolled out a mat under a *peepul* tree. He said the 'Green Hunt' patrol had caused some confusion. Half of the guerrillas were waiting for us at another village. They would soon be with us.

He opened his rucksack and pulled out a stainless-steel beaker. Reaching into his pocket, he extracted a tightly folded, small, newspaper-wrapped packet and unravelled it, revealing a white powder. He poured the powder into the beaker with water, stirring the mixture with a twig. It was salt and sugar. It had already been relayed to him that I was unwell and he had got the necessary ingredients for rehydration. I drank the mixture and lay on the mat.

I knew there would be a lot of waiting ahead, much organising, and more walking that night, but there was no longer any need for me to be alert. I was in their hands. I closed my eyes, drifting in and out of sleep. It was then that I also drifted from the 'overground' to the 'underground' world that belonged to the guerrillas.

* * *

A soft grey light was spreading across the sky although it was still quite dark. It took me a minute to get my bearings. I was under a tamarind tree. Birds were singing and people talking. Sick and tired the previous night, I had barely noticed guerrilla leaders arriving, soldiers milling around me, and decisions being taken about how far we were going to proceed towards our destination before laying our heads down to rest.

The cold iron barrel of a battered rifle that looked like it hadn't been used in years was staring at me. It separated me from a small, hunched body under a coarse brown blanket. The only exposed part was a peacefully sleeping golden wheat-coloured face, deepened in tone by years of being in the sun. It was Gyanji, a senior Maoist leader whom I had first met in Jharkhand more than a year earlier and who had arranged this trip to Bihar.

Gyanji opened his eyelids and smiled at me, the wrinkles deep around his warm and playful eyes. He sat up and stretched his arms out, yawning, and asked if I had managed to get some sleep. Remarking that it was a crisp and cold morning, he pulled on the olive-green jumper that he had used as a pillow. He picked up a pair of thickset, black, plastic-framed glasses lying next to him, placed them on the bridge of his nose, and rapidly combed what little hair he had with a small, pink, plastic-toothed comb. A shock of white roots peeped out from beneath the arch of jet-black hair that framed his balding head. Clearly the dye was of poor quality and Gyanji had not had time to apply it recently. But it revealed to me that despite his spartan lifestyle, Gyanji cared about his appearance, and this was a humanising quality.

Carefully folding his blanket and bedsheet, he unzipped a neatly packed blue rucksack and slipped the bedding into place. Maoist guerrillas on the move always slept fully-clothed, only removing their shoes, so within seconds they were up and ready to go. I looked at him feeling very dishevelled, for I knew that he had only two pairs of clothes and probably had not been able to bathe in days, but he was so immaculately dressed that there was not a single crease in his olive-green uniform.

To Gyanji's left, flanked by a boulder, another senior leader was awaking. Upon seeing him, I recalled that it was this leader who had brought us to our sleeping spot when it was decided that it was too late to reach our destination the previous night. The earth was flat between the boulders and the leafy tamarind tree had attracted him for the warmth it would provide during the night.

Other guerrillas were scattered across the hillside around us, amidst the rocks and the bushes. Everyone was getting ready to move. Folding up bedding, straightening uniforms, putting on shoes. There were about twenty of us altogether.

Under a nearby guava tree I could see Prashant rubbing his eyes, rolling up the blue plastic sheet on which he had slept. I told Gyanji how warm and kind Prashant had been the night before. Gyanji nodded his head and said that Prashant was one of the finest of the younger generation. Intelligent and loyal, he was respectful of and respected by young and old alike. He was an inspiring teacher to the lower-level cadres and one of their best soldiers. They had high hopes for him, Gyanji said.

* * *

Prashant and I became friendly over the next few days. I learnt from him that he was born into a family of small farmers in a mud hut not far from the rice fields of south Bihar that surrounded us. These were the territories that in the 1980s had become infamous as India's 'flaming fields', where the Naxalites built their strongholds then.

It was a time of revelry and excitement for poor village children, Prashant remembered. The guerrillas had started recruiting supporters from not just the lowest castes but also from among the small farmers of the middle castes, like those from Prashant's community who were traditionally cattle herders. They moved from village to village with their guns, rallying people to fight for their rights. They brought their cultural wing to sing songs and beat drums. And they held secret meetings with villagers at night to plan armed action.

At that time, Prashant was bored at school. The teachers rarely showed up. If they did, they taught by rote, endlessly regurgitating facts and figures that had little relevance to their young lives. Prashant regularly skipped class to graze his family's goats in the forest. It was there that he ran into the guerrillas and watched with curiosity as they went about their daily routine. Fascinated, he went to look for them every day. The Naxalites got to know him as the bright-eyed kid among the goats.

The guerrillas let Prashant hang around as they cleaned and polished their weapons, sometimes allowing him to help. He watched them practise military drills, read and write propaganda, wash clothes and cook food. Mesmerised by their songs of revolution, he wanted to learn how to use their guns.

One winter's day, as his brothers were out grazing the buffalo, cows and goats, and his mother and father were irrigating and weeding the mustard fields, Prashant ran into the forest where the Naxalites were based. He went with nothing but a brown, woollen shawl. He said he wanted to stay.

He later learnt that his mother stopped eating and cried day and night for two weeks after he left. His uncles scoured the forests looking for him. His father sought the help of an educated neighbour to write to the Naxalites, asking them to send his son back home.

Three weeks later Prashant returned home. He said his mother clung to him, kissed him and stroked his hair until her tears ran dry. She fed him chicken curry and milk as a treat. Prashant remained quiet throughout, but when the meal was over and his mother had calmed down, he touched her feet as a sign of respect, and told her that he was prepared to do anything for her apart from one thing. He said he would not leave his new Naxalite family to return to his village. He was not yet ten years old.

Like many children who come to the Naxalites, Prashant became a part of their cultural troop, a non-armed wing of the movement. There he learned to compose songs, read and write. Having grown up knowing only the local dialect of Bhojpuri, in the guerrilla armies he learned Hindi and picked up a smattering of English. *Kranti, Vidroh and Samyavadhi*—Revolution, Revolt and Communism—became his mantras. Marx, Engels, Lenin and Mao, his gods.

The excitement of this new life must have been palpable. Prashant met American comrades from the Revolutionary Communist Party, activists from Nepal, soldiers from the Communist Party of the Philippines and heard about revolutionary struggles across the globe. He watched as the Americans ate awkwardly with their hands, and the Nepalis made bombs with pressure cookers. He was amused that the Filipinos commenced their morning exercises by rotating their heads; in India, they always began the routine with the feet.

But in the 1990s, when the high-caste landlords escalated their retaliation against the Naxalites and their supporters, the Ranvir Sena burnt Prashant's cousin's house to the ground. Soon the house in which he was born was also reduced to embers. Angry, many of his cousins, who had previously only been sympathisers, joined the Naxalite armies. Prashant himself, by then sixteen years old, was ready to become a full-fledged Naxalite soldier.

5

THE CITY IN THE FOREST

Led by Prashant, we climbed further into the rocks, descended into a forest single file and stopped by a stream. The water was no more than a few centimetres deep, barely a trickle between the rocks, but it was more than enough for our purpose.

Gyanji gave me a bright blue and yellow used polythene packet with a picture of potato crisps. 'Lay's', it read, 'India's Magic Masala'. The packet had been neatly snipped at one end to make a perfect spout when full of water. Everyone was pulling out similar packets that had once contained mustard oil, sunflower oil, peanuts or crisps.

It was a stop for a communal '*do number* (number two)' to attend to the call of nature, empty your bowels, and clean yourself with water.

As the guerrillas dispersed behind various trees, bushes and rocks, Prashant placed a bar of soap on a rock for everyone to use when they were done and then helped me to fill my packet with water. I nervously took the packet away, holding it by the spout to stop the water from spilling. Finding a thicket of bamboo to crouch amidst, I soon discovered that the packet would balance perfectly when laid to rest against a rock.

Fifteen minutes later, we were all set to move off. This synchronised 'call of nature' both amazed and amused me. Going to the toilet was not an invisible and private bodily function, but recognised as a daily communal need along with eating food or quenching one's thirst together.

We walked on, still in single file. The terrain changed rapidly from the green forest to the rocky hills. Gyanji was in front of me as we picked our way through the craggy landscape. It was as though a large granite mountain had crumbled there some centuries before. Acacia trees and thorny bushes sprouted from the cracks between the rocks. It was not yet the dry season but already the landscape felt barren.

After an hour and a half of walking, a young man dressed in an olive-green uniform, with an old rifle slung across his shoulder, appeared among the bushes. Behind him were five similarly dressed men, several metres apart. The first sentry post to our destination, I suspected.

'*Lal salaam, lal salaam* (Red salute, red salute),' we greeted them one after another, as they shook our hands and raised their clenched fists in the air. The last soldier was wearing a printed black T-shirt bearing the legend, 'I'm unreliable, inefficient, unpredictable, unorganized, undisciplined, immature, but I'm fun!' A message in stark contrast to the disciplined line that the soldiers had formed to greet us, it made me smile.

We walked on passing two more sentry posts, and then we plunged back into forested terrain. Suddenly the early morning light burst through a clearing in the trees. I blinked my eyes in disbelief. In front of us, bathed in sunlight and framed by the granite hills on three sides, lay a colourful spectacle of interwoven trails reaching out like a spider's web. Carved out of the shrubbery, the trails were lined at waist height by garlands of rainbow bunting. Crepe paper, carefully cut into triangles, neatly glued onto jute rope by dozens of hands. The trails led from one large tent to another.

THE CITY IN THE FOREST

I had met the Maoists in their camps many times in the forests of Jharkhand but nothing could have prepared me for this. It was a small, festive city in the middle of the hilly forests. I felt as though we had stumbled upon Lindon of Gil-galad, haven kingdom of the elves in Tolkien's *Lord of the Rings*. A far cry from the dazzling skyscrapers and shopping malls of Gurgaon erected to permanently tower over New Delhi, it was equally impressive for its grandeur and impermanence. It could be taken down within a couple of hours and not a trace of it would be detectable to the unfamiliar, untrained eye.

The tents housed the various sections of the guerrilla army. There was also a medical tent, a tailor's tent and a 'computer room' consisting of a dirty, battered, chunky Dell laptop and a bashed up grey printer all wired to run off a tractor battery. At one end lay a series of small-tented cubicles. Pits dug for latrines; one even had a white porcelain squat lavatory seat.

In the centre of the web stood a large bright red and yellow tent with a green roof. Seating at least a hundred people, this was the central meeting room. Seven framed black and white photographs hung on one wall of red cloth. Marx, Engels, Lenin, Stalin and Mao Zedong all in a line. Below these international gurus were Charu Majumdar and Kanhai Chatterjee, the two Naxalite leaders of the 1960s whom these Maoist guerrillas now commemorated as the instigators of the Indian struggle. All the photographs were garlanded with marigolds. To one corner of this wall of photos, someone had pinned a rudimentary hand-made drawing of a person holding a gun to the head of Prime Minister Manmohan Singh. Next to this was a similar portrait of Sonia Gandhi, the Italian-born president of the Congress Party, who had married into the Nehru-Gandhi dynasty that had, with the exception of a few years, presided over Indian politics since the country's separation from British rule.

At one edge of the camp, there was a large open space—a field—where at least 200 young men were gathered. One group was running around the field in an anticlockwise direction, side-stepping every 10 metres. Another group was doing the same but running in the opposite direction. Those in the middle were in ten disciplined lines, throwing themselves into the air in a synchrony of star jumps. This was the People's Liberation Guerrilla Army performing their daily morning exercise drills.

The kitchen was perhaps the most striking because of its organisation. Sacks of rice and lentils stacked high on top of each other formed two demarcating walls, while a trickling stream was a third boundary. To provide clean drinking water to the camp, a well had been ingeniously dug into the side of the stream, fortified with large rocks, and was worked by a pulley system. In the middle of the kitchen three trenches of varying lengths had been dug. Each had roaring fires with large aluminium vats atop. Rice and dal or potato curry on the boil, I suspected. Young men were sitting cross-legged on the ground, rolling out chapattis for those who would not eat rice.

We had walked into the conference of the State-level Committee of the Maoists, a meeting that took place once every five years, and which brought together all the guerrillas from the neighbouring districts of the states of Uttar Pradesh and Bihar. For some it had been a fourteen-night-long trek to get here. It was hard to know how many of the total People's Liberation Guerrilla Army were at this meeting, perhaps about 400. I was told that similar conferences were simultaneously taking place across the country in other parts of Jharkhand and across the forests of central and eastern India in Chhattisgarh, West Bengal, Odisha and Andhra Pradesh.

At each conference, the Maoist activities of the previous years would be analysed and evaluated, future plans generated, and solutions to problems found. This was the place where crucial decisions would be collectively discussed, with exhaustive debate, to eventually be put to the vote with the majority decision bind-

ing on all. That was the theory of it at least. Germinated in the
Paris Commune, it was called 'democratic centralism' by Lenin,
who used it to build the Bolshevik Party.

The conferences were also where the Maoist practices of criticism and self-criticism unfolded. These were the elaborate public
confessions and denunciations of mistakes that each soldier had
made; an attempt to reinforce group cohesion and discipline used
by many Maoist-inspired parties, from the Zimbabwe National
Liberation Army to the Khmer Rouge. The conference was also
where promotions were decided and political and military training delivered to the cadres.

Above all, for the Maoist leaders, it was a space in which to
redevelop the feeling of a community and commitment to the
cause that united the guerrillas, to renew solidarity. Dispersed
fighters, working in various parts of the country and sometimes
in isolation, came together for a few weeks, ideally to strengthen,
form and reform bonds between them. The hope was to create a
casteless, classless microcosm of the future utopian community
that they were all fighting for.

In contrast to the surrounding caste-divided villages of India,
in the guerrilla community caste names were eliminated—every
individual became a comrade, born with a new name. While
respect for elders was to be shown by calling them '*dada*' or '*didi*'
(elder brother or elder sister) or by adding the suffix '*ji*', material
differences were to be erased. The idea was that people came to
the guerrillas with nothing and were given everything deemed
necessary for their existence. One uniform and a set of plain
clothes, one blanket, one bedsheet, one plastic sheet, one rucksack and a bar of soap. The division of labour according to the
caste, class and gender hierarchies that existed in the world outside was also to be eradicated. Cooking rotas were to involve all,
men and women alike. And while lower-level cadres were to
learn to read, leaders were to dig the toilet pits.

I realised that this was not going to be just a two-night stay. Prashant showed me to a relatively small but spacious tent in which the four other women in the camp slept. Two of the girls—they were not much older than eighteen—immediately took me a short way into the forest amid the privacy of some mango trees. A bucket of water was waiting for me.

A girl with dark skin covered in foam was washing her hair nearby and smiled at me. Around her breasts, she had fastened a black underskirt that reached down to her knees. I followed suit, unwinding my sari, knotting my blue sarong around me, soaping myself under its folds. Fortunately, over the last year and a half, I had already mastered the art of bathing fully clothed. The girls gathered around me, laughing and teasing. 'Can we soap your back for you, *Didi* (sister)?' they asked. 'Is Lifebuoy soap sufficient or do you need Dove, *Didi*?'

I was intrigued by the assumptions they made about my class background. No matter how long I lived in the jungles, it seemed my status would remain inscribed on my persona—on my body, the way I walked, the way I talked. They weren't supposed to know about my history so I could hardly tell them that I had lived amongst the Adivasis for several years and that in fact I preferred the black silt they found in the banks of rivers to wash my hair.

6

DRESSING AS A MAN

When we had washed and dressed, one of the girls offered to take me to the kitchen for breakfast. We passed a tent where several men were resting and reading. My eye caught the cover of a book about the Russian communist revolutionary, Alexandra Kollontai, lying on top of some bags, but then I saw Prashant. He was sitting on the ground with his legs stretched out straight in front of him, deeply immersed in a moth-eaten paperback with stained yellow pages. Reluctant to disturb him, I nevertheless ended up catching his attention.

Smiling, Prashant joined us. I asked him what he was reading. He had several books on the go including some romantic poetry by Tagore and *Green Poems* by Gulzar. The one he was reading, however, was a book on basic medicine. 'Green Hunt' had made it very difficult to get fellow comrades to hospitals or doctors and he wanted to learn how to treat at least basic illnesses and wounds so that they were less dependent on the 'outside' world, he said.

In the kitchen, we were surrounded by young men, all in uniform, cooking, eating and joking. It did not take much to realise that Prashant was one of those ever-cheerful, gregarious and charming people who talked to everybody and seemed to be loved by most. He brought over a plate heaped full of a mixture of chickpea flour and onions and a raw green chilli to spice things up. He was also carrying a small bowl with a slimy green paste. Chilli and garlic roasted on the fire and ground into a paste with a dash of mustard oil, it provided flavour when there was nothing else to eat with rice. 'Bomb chutney,' he called it and asked if I would like to try it.

My tongue felt numb as we walked to a nearby clearing in the forest after we had eaten.

'What kind of a name is that?' asked a spindly but confident and assertive old man with piercing eyes. He was sitting cross-legged on the ground in a sunny spot wearing just a *lungi*, a sarong, around his waist. Two boys were standing on either side of him, massaging his back and arms. The dark folds of skin glistening across his torso revealed he was at least seventy years old.

'It's a man's name,' he said, 'not fit for a woman. Find another one.'

I had been introduced as 'Durga' after the fearless, invincible and inaccessible Hindu goddess of power, responsible for the creation, preservation and destruction of the world. I liked the name as I felt in need of her strength.

He looked me up and down. The tight jeans and fitted *kurta* top that I had changed into suddenly felt far too revealing. He called Prashant to get some new clothes for the 'guest'.

'Yes, Bimalji,' replied Prashant. I realised then that this was the man I had come to interview, the oldest veteran of the struggle in this part of India. I protested that I had other clothes that were drying but Prashant had already disappeared through the trees.

I watched the two boys place a shoulder each under Bimalji's armpits to help him get up and walk. How had he survived as one of India's most wanted men in a guerrilla army that was constantly on the move? As though reading my thoughts, Bimalji laughed, 'There's no retirement from revolution.'

In the male leaders' tent, Bimalji began his story. It was 1969, two years after the initial Naxalite uprising. He had been posted as a teacher in a poor village school, not far from where we were sitting, when he met a comrade who was editing a journal for the revolutionary cause. Attracted to this leader and his message, the young Bimalji wanted to join their fight against the exploitation of the landless labourers and small landholders by the feudal high-caste landlords in Bihar. The revolutionaries were looking for eager youth like him and, within a few years, he left his teaching post to carry out their underground work in the agricultural plains of Bihar. By the 1980s he was sent to the city of Dhanbad, often referred to as the Coal Capital of India, where for twenty years he worked with industrial workers and the trade unions, and helped in editing and publishing a magazine called *Lal Chingari* (Red Spark).

Upon hearing the name of the journal, I realised then that he was one of the handful of leaders who had begun the Maoist Communist Centre (MCC), reputed to be the most ruthless and violent of all the Naxal groups. For many years, the MCC had been fighting the group that some of the other leaders I knew had belonged to. The founders of the MCC—Kanhai Chatterjee and Amulya Sen—had kept their distance from Charu Majumdar. They had criticised some of Majumdar's policies—such as the annihilation of those individuals belonging to groups they labelled as 'class enemies'—and, from their early days, had sought to prioritise the creation of base areas from which the state should be kept out. And although the Communist Party of India (Maoist) now resurrected both Charu Majumdar and Kanhai Chatterjee as its leaders, for years the MCC had been at loggerheads with those who claimed the heritage of the Communist Party of India (Marxist-Leninist) à la Majumdar. In the late

1990s, as they found themselves engaging in turf wars in Bihar, the battles between the various Naxal factions were intense and killed so many people that the Maoists now called that period their 'Black Chapter'.

I looked around me at the four other men in the tent—two were busy on a laptop, one was reading and the other sleeping—who had once belonged to warring factions. Tonight, Bimalji would be sleeping next to men he had once ordered to be killed. How did it feel? I was about to ask him about these inner-party differences. How could men who had tried to murder each other now work together? But, perhaps sensing my uncomfortable questions, he changed tack.

'Forty-two years of history cannot be recounted just like this,' he said. 'We need to begin much further back, with the 1962 war with China, in fact.' His tone had transformed and suddenly I found myself being given what seemed a well-versed lecture on the official history of the Naxalites, as was to be told by a Communist Party of India (Maoist) leader. Perhaps he realised that his tale had begun with too personal a history, that he had said too much, that I might ask too many difficult questions, but, as his monologue continued, my exhaustion took over and, I am ashamed to say, I fell fast asleep.

It was eight hours later that I awoke to the streaks of hot pink and orange light. Bimalji had apparently dissuaded the others from waking me. The setting sun was beaming into the tent.

Prashant was waiting with his arms outstretched, holding a cloth bag. '*Didi*,' he said giving me the bag, 'You like red, don't you? The clothes you were wearing were red.' I opened the bag and found an embroidered cotton salwar suit. I went out to try it on behind the trees. A full deep red skirt flowed from a tight lime green and gold bodice that clung to my torso, pushing my breasts up. The *churidar* trousers were more skin-tight than my jeans. What would Bimalji say to Prashant's purchase? I draped the green chiffon *dupatta* (scarf) across my chest as a mark of my modesty and returned to the tent.

* * *

Although I had come to meet Bimalji, I found my formal sessions with him long and tedious, and it was difficult to get beyond the well-trodden histories that I already knew. He always seemed on guard and I could never get a word in edgeways to ask a question that might get us beyond the official histories and positions that the Maoists were keen to propogate. But, as is so often the case with long-term open-ended ethnographic research, formal interviews are frequently the least revealing and the most interesting things happen when you cannot possibly anticipate them.

Two nights into my stay at the guerrilla camp, I realised that Gyanji would be walking from Bihar, with a platoon, back to Lalgaon in Jharkhand where I had come from and where I had lived for the previous year and a half. There, in the surrounding forests, a similar State-level Committee meeting for that area was to be conducted. The only safe way to travel across the country was on foot under cover of darkness, marching in military formation with the protection of a platoon, company or battalion. To protect themselves and their wider movement, the Maoist soldiers were instructed not to take public transport or private vehicles. The guerrilla armies would cover long distances—often several hundred kilometres—walking continuously at night, sometimes even for weeks, from one part of the country to another, in order to get to 'safe zones' or to where they had been deputed.

I asked Gyanji if I could return to Lalgaon with him in the platoon. I wanted to experience what it was like to be continually 'on the move'. Short of becoming a 'professional revolutionary', as they put it, joining them for this march back to Jharkhand would mark the last piece of my research.

The Maoists had often taken journalists on tours that lasted several days in their forest strongholds and I had walked with them many times in the forests in their 'Red Capital' in Jharkhand. But my request that night in January 2010 was to go on a journey of a different sort, one on which they would never normally include an outsider.

As I overheard conversations in the camp, I realised that their reservations about letting me go on the nightmarch reflected my own apprehensions. It was a very long distance, about 250 kilometres, depending on which route was taken. Not only would we march from Bihar to Jharkhand across at least four districts, we would also have to cross two major rivers and two busy highways. We would drink from whichever waterholes we found and eat whatever the local people could provide for us. The pace would need to be maintained at over 30 kilometres most nights. Hunted ruthlessly by the state, we had to march in the safety of darkness—all under cover of night and without the light of a torch to avoid drawing attention to ourselves. I would be the only outsider and the only woman.

Above all, there were security concerns. We would traverse territory that the Maoists did not control. 'Enemy zones' that were riddled with the military barracks of 'Operation Green Hunt' and its frequent patrols. Areas that were controlled by a mercenary gang, called the Tritiya Prastuti Committee (TPC), which the Maoists said was covertly backed by the Indian government. The Maoists themselves often hesitated to make the journey because there was little room for slowing down, falling sick or making mistakes. It took Gyanji three days and much consultation with the other leaders to respond to my request.

Then, one morning, Prashant presented me with a grey cardboard box. I opened it and felt a rush of heat through my body. There, wrapped in white tissue paper, were green running shoes. I had foolishly come with only a pair of sandals, unaware that a two-night stay might turn into a three-week journey. I realised that my proposal had been accepted.

DRESSING AS A MAN

The camp tailor stitched a uniform for me on the day of departure. Olive-green shirt and trousers, too large for my waist, were held by a belt. Would Bimalji approve of this attire that drowned my femininity? I tucked my hair into a green guerrilla cap. Moving with an all-male platoon, Prashant said, I would draw less attention and be safer if I could pass as a man.

Prashant introduced me to my bodyguard, someone who would look after me and stay by my side always, even when I had to wash. A young man, not much older than sixteen, stepped forward and shyly held out his hand. He smiled at me, his brilliant white teeth standing out against his dark, almost black, shining skin.

As with some of the others who were to join our platoon, I recognised him immediately from the villages where I lived back in Jharkhand. He was an Adivasi—from the Oraon tribe—and over the course of the last year I had come to know his family well. His father was the only Adivasi to own a teashop in the village and I had spent many hours there. This young man had often served me tea. I had not spoken to him much more than to ask for a drink or a snack or the bill, but had noticed that he was always quiet, polite and deferential.

Prashant introduced him as 'Kohli' although I knew his name to be different. Oraons are often finely built but, even so, Kohli was small for a sixteen-year-old. The rucksack on his back loomed wider than him and the butt of the INSAS rifle, slung across his left shoulder, came all the way down to his calves. The rifle was lighter and better than the one Gyanji carried, but how quickly could Kohli manoeuvre it in battle?

I recalled, though, how he and the other young Adivasi boys I knew wielded with incredible precision their homemade bows and arrows and catapults cast out of thick rubber bands strung across branched twigs. I had seen them playfully practising their shooting skills, smashing small rocks into pieces from a long distance, and even hunting down birds and rabbits in the forest for an evening meal.

Prashant reassuringly told me that I would be in good hands and that Kohli would look after me. He asked me to give my navy cloth bag to Kohli but I declined, keen to carry my own weight. It contained not much more than a notebook and pen, a mike and recorder, a bottle for drinking water, my Lay's plastic packet to fill with water for the call of nature, one change of underwear, a jacket which doubled as a pillow, a sleeping bag, a thin scarf which I could lie on or use as a towel, a pair of flip flops and the embroidered red salwar dress that Prashant had brought for me for easy escape from 'underground' to 'overground'.

The farewells lasted half an hour. The sun was low in the sky. We were in the field at the edge of the camp. Rising out of the martyr's memorial erected in the centre of the field, a red flag with a white hammer and sickle waved high in the sky. A crowd had gathered to say goodbye. They created a large outer ring in the field. They were singing revolutionary songs in Hindi. The socialist anthem, the 'Internationale', rang through the forest, sung at the top of their voices. Other songs about comrades departing on a journey followed, urging us in their melodies to take care with every step. Songs that warned that the enemy surrounded us. Our platoon lined up on the inside of the circle facing everyone else. There were thirty of us.

'Lal salaam, lal salaam, lal salaam,' I shook at least two hundred hands. The final hand I held was Prashant's. It was the last time I would see him. I did not know then how short Prashant's life would be.

PART THREE

GYANJI, AN AGILE MIND

7

NIGHT ONE

The rules of marching had to be learned fast. Always walk in single file. Keep the gap between you and the person in front of you as small as possible. Follow the orders of the platoon commander. The platoon was divided into three sections, each with a section commander. Follow your section commander and stay with your section, even when you sleep. Keep your weapons by you, ready for action at any time.

Everyone, except for me, had a gun. Three AK-47s, some INSAS rifles, several .303s, some Sten guns and the rest police rifles. They had all been stolen from the police, as was the case with most of the Naxalite weapons. The lead section, Section A, had the best weapons and soldiers, and was to fight in the event of attack while Section B, which housed the leadership, would retreat with Section C. I was in Section B with Gyanji, his bodyguard and Kohli.

Communication from one end of the platoon to the other took place via designated runners. Section commanders carried walkie-talkies but their use was restricted to emergencies for fear of interception by the security forces. At the front of the platoon, a scout who knew the route was to lead. Bringing up the rear, a sweeper brushed away footprints, erasing the traces of our presence on dusty or muddy paths.

I was told more rules: at the beginning and end of each stage of the journey, pay attention to the roll call. Know the rendezvous point—RV for short—for the next stretch of the march, should we lose each other. At night, when it was difficult to distinguish friend and foe, always use the code questions when approached by anyone. For the first night, it was: 'Who are you?' The response, 'I am a Shankar. Who are you?' To which the reply was, 'I am Krishna.'

After walking for two hours, we stopped on a hillock outside the village where our section commander had grown up. Like Prashant, he was from a family of small farmers who had once been cowherds and went by the surname Yadav. In the 1980s the Naxalites had driven away the high-caste landlords who owned large tracts of land from this village and redistributed their lands amongst small farming families like that of our section commander. The village was therefore full of people whom the Naxalites could depend on, which is why the guerrillas considered it a 'safe' zone.

Gyanji said the area we were in was also safer than the terrain that lay ahead because we were by the border between the state of Bihar and Jharkhand. Borders were regularly used by the guerrillas to evade the security forces. If chased by the police from one state, they crossed over into the next state to escape further pursuit. The state police forces rarely coordinated with each other and it was unlikely that the Bihar police would cross into the territory of their Jharkhand counterparts or relay information in time for the Jharkhand police to intercept the fleeing guerrillas on their side of the border. Such inefficiencies and lack of coordination amongst the ruling elites must be used to guerrilla advantage, said Gyanji.

NIGHT ONE

Although it was a 'safe' area, following guerrilla best practice, we waited for darkness to engulf us before descending into the village for our dinner stop. The sky was full of bulbuls, starlings and thrushes fluttering and dancing in the air in circles, chirping loudly before they returned to their nests for the night. Soon after, bats flew out of their roosts, their darting and sharp manoeuvring markedly different from that of the birds. When smoke was rising from most of the huts as their hearths were lit, we climbed down.

Two 'runners' from the platoon had been sent ahead to request one plate of food from thirty different houses in the village. It felt strange to be at the receiving end of this hospitality. Over the previous year, in Lalgaon, I had become used to taking a plate of rice to the guerrillas when they stopped by with no time to cook for themselves. Somwari, the Oraon tribeswoman in whose house I lived in Lalgaon, and whom I called my 'sister', insisted that the plate was heaped so full that rice fell off it. She said the boys would be tired and weary and needed to eat well. We gave them a share of whatever we had cooked for ourselves: rice and usually one other preparation as accompaniment. Perhaps a lentil dal, a spinach broth, a tomato chutney, or, if there were vegetables, some curry made from those. Once in a while, though, would come a day when we had only a green chilli with salt to spare.

The platoon broke up as everyone dispersed into the village to eat. I retreated into the foyer of a house with my bodyguard Kohli and our section. Staying in the shadows, I followed the rules we had agreed upon to draw as little attention to myself as possible. But Kohli and the young men who were looking after me found it difficult to remember that I was supposed to be a man. '*Didi* (sister), are you okay?' they asked. '*Didi*, can I fill your water bottle? There is a hand pump here,' they said.

A decision had to be taken about how far to proceed that night. To continue much further would have meant leaving the safety of the forested areas and of the border zones, and marching across the exposed agricultural plains, across a busy highway, and traversing more rice fields before safer territory could be reached again. The journey would take another six hours. Perhaps eight.

I felt everyone's eyes on me, wondering whether I would make it. Would I last the whole journey? Gyanji had carefully plotted all the points at which I could safely be sent out, transiting from 'underground' to 'overground' by motorbike or bus.

I thought about what I knew of Gyanji's own physical challenges. He was an intellectual with an agile mind but his body was not made to trudge through the forests of eastern India. Although he never talked about it, over the course of the time I had spent with him, I discovered that he suffered from a sharp abdominal pain. I had seen him collapse flat on the ground in the middle of a meeting of guerrillas, gasping to recover from the pain. Kohli said that it was a gift born of his inability to eat on time, to get two meals a day.

Years of wearing the polyester olive-green uniform in the sweltering heat without washing for days on end had given Gyanji an itchy body rash. Sometimes there was no time to wash for eight days in a row, he had confessed. Two days ago, I had overheard Bimalji trying to convince Gyanji to give up the polyester uniform and wear cotton pyjamas in the platoon. But Gyanji insisted that he did not want treatment that privileged him above the rest. I had also learnt that he suffered from a bad ankle. After several hours of continuous walking it would simply give way and make him fall.

Thinking of Gyanji's fortitude despite all these ailments, made me determined to walk the whole way, to try not to falter on a single step, and not be the reason for any delay. I told Gyanji I was prepared for what lay ahead. He raised his eyebrows at me. I could feel his eyes gently asking me whether I was sure. But he turned around and told the platoon commander we were ready to go.

NIGHT ONE

As it turned out, the platoon commander, Vikas, was not ready himself. Of the platoon commanders I had met, he was the one I liked the least. I had come to think of him as 'the interrogator'. The first time I had met him was one night six months into my stay in Lalgaon, when, with a different platoon, he passed through the hamlet where I lived. I took a plate of rice and spinach from our house to the bamboo grove where his platoon was resting, curious to see them as they were said to have come from afar.

When they had eaten, he returned my visit by sending two of his armed guards to Somwari's house where I lived. They led me back out into the village and to a nearby disused room with crumbling walls where Vikas was waiting in a dark corner, sprawled out across an old charpoy. Arrogantly throwing questions at me, he asked who I was and why I was there. He appeared to have no interest in my responses and instead went on to talk at me, recounting stories of spies who had entered the forests but were never seen again. 'Do you know what we do to them?' he asked. 'We cut them open and throw them in the gutter, pumping their bodies with bullets till they look like a sieve.'

When he let me go, I tried not to let on that I was shaking even though I knew it had been just a show of power. A few days later, when more senior leaders called me to the guerrilla camp in the forest where he was staying, he looked down at his feet and blushed. But I was left with the bitter taste of that first meeting in Lalgaon.

Everyone was now ready to march on and cross the flat rice fields, but Vikas argued it would take several hours for all of us to be fed. He said it would be 10:00 p.m. before we could continue the journey again. We would reach our destination only by four in the early morning provided we walked nonstop all night. Vikas persuaded Gyanji and the section commanders that it was not a good idea to persevere that night.

We found a grassy area with several *mahua* trees to rest under, a half-hour walk from the village. Although I knew that a *mahua* tree had many uses—wine was distilled at home from its small yellow flowers, cooking oil was pressed from its seeds—what I did not know was that the Naxalites considered it to be the very best to sleep under because its large flat leaves trapped the air beneath it, preventing the daytime warmth from escaping into the sky at night.

Sleeping positions under the trees were mapped. Sentry rotas agreed. Mats and blankets were rolled out. While some of the soldiers tossed them out hastily, Gyanji took great care to clear the patch of earth on which he would sleep, laid out a mat, and stretched a pressed bedsheet perfectly across it. A very luxurious bed, he joked. No matter how rough or rudimentary the conditions, it was still possible to differentiate degrees of comfort.

He was not what I had expected of a leader. Although he could be firm, Gyanji was soft-spoken, had none of the oratory skills of other charismatic leaders, was small built, and had a quiet and almost reticent demeanour. Even though he considered the war against the state and the need to train new soldiers necessary, it seemed to me that he was uninterested in the techniques of making landmines or in the plots to loot guns. He would rather watch the dance of starlings and read late nineteenth-century European and Hindi-Urdu poetry, short stories and novels, alongside Marx.

There was soon a chorus of snoring men around me. Somebody was complaining that his neighbour had selfishly cocooned himself in the one blanket they shared, without leaving any cover for his freezing friend.

I had too many thoughts to be able to sleep. The moon was very bright that night. It made me pensive. What were the emotional costs of living underground for a leader like Gyanji? With Kohli and Gyanji's bodyguard asleep between us, I told Gyanji that I could never contemplate joining them. It was not just the difficulties I had with the cycles of violence they were caught up in. Nor was it just the question of whether their methods and programmes were appropriate or not. The first and insurmountable barrier was that I could not withstand leaving behind my beloved family and not see them again. I could never break their hearts, I said.

I didn't ask how his children lived with a big question mark about who their father was. There were many families in India where the man would send money home from Dubai or Doha and visit his loved ones only once a year. However, this migration is perhaps easier for a child to comprehend than having a father who has taken up armed struggle in the wilderness in the heart of the country.

Gyanji, I could see, was staring at me, but I could not read his thoughts until he spoke. 'Don't you think that we all have the same concerns?' he asked. He had not seen his mother for the last two years and even if he wanted to, he could not. He said, 'Do you know, I've been told she is so worried about me that she cries herself to sleep every night?'

A little agitated, he continued, 'You know our wives, many of them live like widows. Do you think we haven't broken all of their hearts?'

I felt remorse for what seemed to be an insensitive reflection on my part. Gyanji carried on and he told me about his best friend Paresh, killed in an encounter in 1992, and of the pain of visiting Paresh's mother who could only see in Gyanji a reflection of her son. He told me about Nimesh, another close friend, who in 1999 went in search of his kidnapped fiancée and fell into the trap of a gang sponsored by the state. The gang made him watch his beloved being raped, before killing them both. Gyanji said he went to visit Nimesh's mother at their mansion in a wealthy suburb of Delhi to find that, after the murder of her son, she had become both deaf and dumb.

By the time I met him, Gyanji had been underground for more than twenty years. As a young man, he had more or less broken off links with his parents and siblings to create a new family with the rebels underground. Many young guerrillas— men and women—turned to him as a pseudo-father. He was reputed to be kind and gentle but also firm and derived immediate respect from those he came in contact with. I was already so used to seeing him as a father figure in the underground army that it was easy for me to forget that it was at the cost of him breaking ties with his own family.

Gyanji soon joined the discord of snoring men. But I lay awake, gazing at the dark patches on the moon, reflecting on the things I had learnt about him.

A phone was ringing. I had been drifting off into sleep but was jolted wide awake by the sound. Its shrill tone seemed so out of place amidst the silence of the night that it made me tense. It was late, perhaps past midnight. Who could be calling at this time? Usually there was no phone reception in these areas and one had to climb hillocks or ask the local people where the network of a distant cell phone tower could be accessed. Moreover, we were under strict instructions not to use our phones during the march unless absolutely necessary for they could be intercepted or tapped or triangulated by the Indian police; it was an easy way for them to discover our whereabouts.

The phone abruptly stopped ringing and I heard Gyanji whispering that he would call back. I watched him get up and disappear into the distance. Who was it? Whom did he need to call at this hour? But I didn't like to ask.

The night was so clear and the sky so bright that I could see Gyanji's silhouette pacing up and down on the dark outline of the nearby hillock. Clearly something was up, he seemed to walk faster and faster. Five metres paced in one direction, five metres the other way, back and forth, again and again.

He returned after what seemed like an eternity. His shoulders were slouched; his upright bearing and customary poise had disappeared. From within my sleeping bag, I whispered to ask if he was okay.

It was his wife, he told me in English, clearly not wanting the others to hear him. She was crying because their son was having trouble keeping up with classes at school. She wanted him to leave the forests to meet them. He could not do that. They had had an argument.

I was surprised. I knew that Gyanji was married. He had told me that his wife was a 'professional revolutionary' too. But 'going out' meant going 'overground', away from the protection of the forests and the underground army. It was a lot to ask.

Gyanji was a highly wanted man. The police had promised a reward for anyone who brought him in. One lakh rupees (£10,000) in cash. Special security teams had been developed with the specific aim of hunting him down. Gyanji said that arrested comrades had, under torture, been interrogated for information about him and had a recording of his voice played back to them. Athough the police had somehow managed to get his voice recording, they did not yet have a picture of him.

'I thought she was with you, with the Naxalites,' I said.

She was once, he said sombrely, but she had left. It had been against his wishes, but she was determined to support their three boys and give them a better and more stable upbringing than what they could provide with a nomadic lifestyle. Now he rarely saw any of them, except very occasionally, perhaps once in six months, whenever they could arrange to meet in a safe house in a small town or when she was able to come and visit him in a jungle where he was based. However, as the security forces grew stronger, it had become increasingly dangerous to make the passage from 'underground' to 'overground'.

Settling back under the blanket between his bodyguard and Kohli, he said he didn't know what to do because they were under strict instructions not to venture out of the safety of the underground armies. I could hear the anguish in his voice. He fell silent and I could sense his retreat into something deep within him. I didn't know how much more to ask and then heard his soft snoring.

'Chai?'

It was still dark, but I looked up to find Gyanji standing next to me, holding out a stainless-steel beaker, full of piping hot syrupy-sweet tea.

'Five-star treatment!' I groaned, climbing out of my sleeping bag and rolling it up. The milk smelt like honey.

'It's my only weakness,' Gyanji confessed with a mischievous look in his eyes.

He was clearly in a better mood and had slept well. I, on the other hand, had kept thinking about his wife and what it must be like to be married to a man you rarely saw and could not discuss with friends and acquaintances, who would not be around for your children when you needed him. Would Gyanji indeed break the rules and leave the forests for her? Was his need for tea the only weakness that Gyanji felt he had?

8

SACRIFICE, RENUNCIATION, LIBERATION AND VIOLENCE

Gyanji represented a generation of people who became 'professional revolutionaries'—that's what the Naxalites called them, 'PRs'—who had been underground for more than twenty years. They came from a very different background—a much more privileged one—than that of the Dalit 'untouchable' landless labourers who had been attracted to the Naxalites in the plains, or of the Adivasi tribal youths who later joined the guerrilla armies in the forests and hills.

The elderly and middle-aged male professional revolutionaries (women were rare), like Gyanji, came from well-to-do middle-class families, from the dominant castes of their ancestral villages, often the highest castes. They had usually been well-educated in the big cities. Many held postgraduate degrees and could switch, as Gyanji did, from rustic Bhojpuri in one sentence to fluent English the next.

Gyanji's own family once owned large tracts of land in Bihar. His father had been a government engineer, a prized and coveted job for a family like his. He had provided for and encouraged his four children to get university degrees, move to the city and secure jobs that matched his own.

Like others before him, it was at university that Gyanji said he was 'politicised'. In the seventies and eighties, a whole generation of youth was awakened in radical politics within the colleges and the universities of India's large cities—Kolkata, Delhi, Mumbai, Patna, Warangal, Hyderabad. Gyanji's inspiration, like that of his friends, came at first from a dynamic teacher in college.

He joined a group of students who put aside their formal learning for their university degrees and set up radical reading groups. In the daytime, they studied for the most technical and scientific of degrees—mathematics, as Gyanji was pursuing; or chemistry, engineering, biology or physics, as others were. But at night, they cast aside their equations, algebra, formulae, regression charts and graphs, and morphed into revolutionaries, discussing how to bring 'heaven on earth' and create a communist society. Reading world history and debating its conjunctures, they discussed how they could remake it.

Interspersed with poetry, they began with the basics: reading Marx, Lenin and Mao Zedong, Charles Bettelheim's history of the USSR and William Hinton on China. They covered a lot of ground. They thought about the virtues and limitations of Sartre's existentialism, watched Foucault from afar and progressed on to the Marxist debates of their day. Paul Sweezy versus Maurice Dobb; did capitalism develop from the internal contradictions of feudalism or was it an external force that overrode feudalism?[1] What was feudalism? Was India capitalist or feudal?

Reading books, however, was never enough, Gyanji had said, recalling Marx: 'Philosophers have hitherto only interpreted the world in various ways, the point is to change it.'[2]

They felt that they were part of a world history of student mobilisation, linking hands with the protestors against the Vietnam War, the participants in the uprisings in Paris and the rise of the American Black Panthers. Fired by the passions of those before them in faraway places who had taken to the streets, fought abuses, prejudices and inequalities, and challenged their governments, Gyanji told me that they cycled to the slums at the edge of their cities. There they saw the face of poverty, exploitation, oppression and repression. Moved by the injustices around them, they fought for basic human rights and equality, and wanted to mark themselves apart from the general middle-class apathy, insensitivity and wilful blindness to the poor.

After completing his degree, Gyanji began preparing for exams for entry into the Indian Administrative Services where the cream of the country sought to serve the government of India. It was here that he thought that he would be able to fight for the disenfranchised poor. He now spent his nights preparing to join the Indian state. During the day, however, like many others who came to join the Naxalites, Gyanji worked for the human rights movements.

For a few years, he went on 'fact-finding' missions to expose the atrocities committed by high-caste landlords against their low-caste labourers. They uncovered and publicised the stories of thousands of poor men and women cheated, thrashed and raped by their employers. He wrote about people who were worked into the ground for the benefit of others who then, when they could no longer use and abuse them, discarded their bodies as they would animals'. He found story after story of police collusion and the perpetration of similar crimes within police offices and stations.

The more he worked for the local branch of the civil liberties movement, the more he lost faith in the Indian parliamentary process, and the more he realised that the idea of India as a democracy was a farce. He said he began to see that the state was corrupt from top to bottom and despite measures to include marginalised populations it preserved the interests of India's elites. He concluded that even the most sincere government servants made little difference; they could not act in isolation from the overall system and were either forced to compromise themselves and their principles or were completely side-lined by others.

Working with the civil liberties movements to call the state to account and agitate for reforms began to have clear limitations for Gyanji. What was needed was a revolution to change the entire social system.

It was at that point that Gyanji abandoned his ambitions of serving the government and pleaded with his university teacher that it was time for him to be introduced to those who had taken up arms. He wanted to accompany those fighters to the country-side and live with the rural poor to mobilise them in a struggle against their oppression. He was ready to take the oath to become a 'professional revolutionary', a PR.

In the villages of Bihar not far from Patna where Gyanji was, those who had been released from jail after the repression of the initial Naxalbari struggle were trying to rebuild their revolutionary parties once more. Gyanji was embraced into the fold of one—the Communist Party of India (Marxist-Leninist) Party Unity.

Like those who joined the Naxalites alongside him, by virtue of having committed himself for so many years to the revolutionary party, Gyanji slowly rose into the upper echelons of leadership to develop the new communities of revolutionaries from the later generations. It is these older revolutionaries, the students of the 1970s and 1980s who broke with their families and the worlds they had grown up in, who have led and sustained the guerrilla struggle to what it is today. Many—such as Gyanji—married within the party; some left their wives and husbands for new ones underground; others remained single. Having children was not encouraged during the war but they adopted new generations of youths such as Kohli as children of the revolution. Trying to live their ideals, they broke with their past rooted in their erstwhile families and created new families and new worlds underground.

* * *

One early evening in Lalgaon, about six months before I embarked on the march, I was returning home from a nearby village when I crossed a hill where Gyanji's platoon was based. Seeing me pass, Gyanji sent his bodyguard to invite me for a cup of tea. Poking the twigs to reignite a fire, Gyanji seemed rather melancholy. As I sat down on the ground beside him, he said, 'When we began, we all thought that the revolution was just around the corner. Who would have thought that decades later we would still be here, fighting against the odds?'

Over time, he said, they had all realised that they would not see the fruits of their struggle in their own lifetime. The world had changed rapidly and an equal society on a global scale became an ever-distant vision. But, he went on, 'We have to keep this dream alive. If not for our children, then for the generations that will follow.'

I asked him if he had ever considered leaving the Naxalites. He looked at me intensely but was silent. 'Once,' he eventually replied, 'in the late nineties.'

I waited, not wanting to ask more than he wanted to reveal. But he said no more. It was only later, as I tried to piece together Gyanji's life history, that I realised from what I had learnt from others that Gyanji had left when there had been a major disagreement amongst the Naxalites about the correct interpretation of the Indian economy. It was a question about the extent to which India was 'semi-feudal' or 'capitalist', and the period went down in Naxalite history as 'the two-line struggle'.

Although, as any anthropologist ought to, I learnt the language of the people I was studying, the local dialects of Nagpuri and Sadri in this case were clearly not enough. I wasn't trained in the language of these communists and it took me several more years to understand the vocabulary of political economy and what they called 'the modes of production'—terminology that was so important to the Naxalites and over which they seemed to have so many disagreements, over which splits and factions were allegedly formed. For instance, I became more familiar with the debates over what exactly made an economy 'semi-feudal' or 'capitalist' from their point of view. Was a feudal economy one in which land was colonised by just a rich minority with the rest of the population working for these landowners, partly bonded and indebted to them over generations? Was the presence of people selling their labour for a wage a sufficient condition to say that the economy had transited to a capitalist one, or did farmers also need to be accumulating and investing and reinvesting the surplus they generated from agricultural production to deserve this title for its economy?[3]

How the economy was classified mattered to the guerrillas because it was the basis of the strategy they would use in their war. It determined the extent to which they would work in rural areas, as opposed to the cities. Whether they would fight a protracted Maoist, clandestine, rural-based war, or whether they would take on nonviolent open mobilisation of people in the cities, in preparation for a final insurrection, as proposed by Lenin. It also determined the extent to which they were willing to use the formal procedures of elections within the Indian parliamentary process or bypass them altogether. If they analysed the economy to be semi-feudal, they would fight an underground rural war. Whereas if capitalism was concluded to prevail, they would first pursue nonviolent mobilisation using parliamentary elections.

I learnt from several people who left the revolutionaries that, in the 'two-line struggle' of the late nineties, not only were there internal disagreements about how to analyse the Indian economy, but also that democratic norms of discussion and debate within the party had been flouted. Despite research which showed otherwise, certain powerful leaders maintained that the country was semi-feudal; the analysis remained the same and therefore nothing changed. I imagined that Gyanji—then a sensitive and idealistic young man—was so disappointed in and disillusioned by how the debate was handled, that it temporarily broke the movement's spell over him.

But years later, as I sat with him in Lalgaon, he reflected more generally that indeed there were many frustrating problems within the movement. They faced them daily. Everywhere there were individuals who sought to make their name or fortunes, he said. People who wanted their names to be recorded in history, their egos to be pampered, their deeds and thoughts to be recognised as heroic achievements and their lives to be remembered as a unique story. When he looked around him, however, he said that he saw no better alternative.

There was no other movement or organisation in India, Gyanji said with a conviction that seemed hard to question, that had men and women who were more sincere, more honest and more committed in seeking to bring about change collectively for a better world. These were people, he said, for whom it was enough to simply keep alive that hope, that dream of a different, more egalitarian, future. They sought no individual returns or personal recognition for devoting their lives toward this end. For them the individual was, as it should be, he said, just a point in history. According to Gyanji, these were people who have erased themselves from history, who have sacrificed themselves for the cause.

That day, Gyanji went some way towards answering a question that had always perplexed me: what drove intelligent men like him to callously sever all connections with their pasts for what was just a dream, perhaps even a fantasy? What gave them the strength to withstand loss after loss and keep on fighting, committing their lives so fully to a different future that might never materialise and for which they would never get individual recognition?

Clearly, outrage at the forces of inequality, the regimes of exploitation and the deep discrimination that surrounded them was not enough. Many of us who are overcome by fury about these very issues are often left despondent rather than hopeful about ever being able to take on and change the world. A conviction that theirs was *the* correct ideological path wasn't the answer either. As was so clear from Gyanji's own doubts, there was much internal debate about how to analyse the Indian economy and what path the struggle should take. What then compelled their intellect to strive for a utopian human community, devoting their lives to fight together, when the circumstances were so clearly set against them?

* * *

As Gyanji had implied, one idea that seemed crucial to keeping alive the dream of an ideal human community was sacrifice. Once seen as a means of appeasing and obliging the gods, by the end of the nineteenth century some scholars said sacrifice was about much more than the giving of gifts to deities. Though considered primarily in religious contexts, sacrifice became seen as a crucial means for people to enter an imagined world that is sacred, that is 'other-worldly', and bring its influence to bear in the world of their everyday lives, a world that was prosaic, transient and ordinary.[4]

Through this lens, the idea of sacrifice can be a supremely creative force. It enables people to transcend and overcome the ordinary world they live in, to join forces with the imagination of a different world, the world of the extraordinary, in order to create and breathe life from that ideal world into the here and now. People offering themselves in sacrifice can create new solidarities between themselves based on the idea of that extraordinary future world, which in turn would help build the utopian human community of their imagination in the present.

Naxalite leaders like Gyanji were born into fairly affluent dominant-caste families and were enmeshed in perpetuating the very systems and ideas that the revolutionaries condemned. These were families that owned large tracts of land and were steeped in long histories of exploitation and oppression of the low-caste labourers who worked for them. They were families who valued education as a means of bettering themselves, whose younger generations secured salaried government or corporate sector jobs, building city apartments and houses served by multiple servants. Some even sent their children to study in the US and the UK, often to get MBAs, work in New York and London, and sometimes returning to India with new ideas of how to make more money, comfortably sliding into the top echelons of a deeply segregated country. While there were exceptions, increasingly, these families lived in a world that celebrated the values of individualism and material accumulation, reproducing the inequalities of the world. Bearing this burden of the baggage bestowed by their privileged backgrounds, cutting ties with their families, crushing their personal histories and destroying their past personas were crucial measures for the Naxalite leaders to engender a new world.

Across the world, most acts of sacrifice take place through symbolic violence—for instance mutilations of the body, the killing of animals, or the consumption of food—where the body part, animal or food is a representation of the human participants making the offering. Such rituals represent people metaphorically crushing their everyday mundane worlds and symbolically killing themselves in order to participate in creating an immortal moral world which conquers, transforms and encompasses the world of the present. A central creative force in sacrifice, this rebounding violence negates the everyday world allowing its participants to reach out to something that surpasses it and then colonises it with the ideas of another world.[5] Not innate to people, this violence is a symptom of their attempt to create a world beyond the one in which their everyday lives are trapped.

Superhuman goals like that striven for by Gyanji and his fellow leaders—the creation of an ideal world with an equal and democratic human community in the here and now—are so set against the values of the everyday world that surrounds them that they come at considerable human cost. Indeed, like many of the leaders I met, Gyanji fully expected a brutal end. Not in battle—as face-to-face battles in guerrilla wars were rare—but in police custody. Many of Gyanji's comrades had been picked up in the cities, brutally tortured for information, and then killed extra-judicially to be presented in one of India's infamous 'fake encounters'. Gyanji said that in the eyes of the police, he was far too important a leader for them to let him live as they were determined to 'cut off the head of the movement'. However the guerrillas ended up dying, for any revolutionary cause, the greatest sacrificial force is the giving of human life itself: human sacrifice. When revolutionaries sacrificed themselves and thus the world around them to create a world of their dreams, their death and destruction would regenerate life itself to become creative forces.

The direct opposite of sacrifice, its antonym, is suicide. Commenting on a friend who had hanged himself from a ceiling fan, Gyanji once scoffed, 'What an individualistic selfish act! It is for nobody. It does not contribute, create or construct anything. The struggle against self-seeking individualistic thinking is harder than the struggle against the enemy.' I think that Gyanji saw suicide as the consequence of an individual leaving one moral world but with no other world to create.[6] A place of torment caused by insatiable passions and limitless desires that can never be fulfilled, because there is no creative project to make and contain them.

That is perhaps why the rituals of martyrdom, celebrated in the month of November in an annual festival in villages across their strongholds, were the most important celebration for the Naxalites. Martyrs' Day marked the death of people who had sacrificed their lives to create a new moral world, transforming them into immortal celestial bodies leading the path forward, passing on the dreams of an imagined future society, entrusting others to realise them. Martyrdom transformed the emotions provoked by the brutal deaths of comrades in the struggle from being a sentimental weakness into a powerful creative emotional force.

Moreover, although their lives may have taken all sorts of complex twists and turns, and even though only after death is the person's real name publicly revealed for the first time, in death a perfect legend was created in the myths of martyrdom. Stories of martyrs all had a common theme: courageous men and women sacrificing themselves for the people, living simply amongst the poor, taking up their struggles. Every martyr was valorised as representing the virtues of generosity, kindness and selflessness, as a person who had no space for the creeds of self-interest, caste or class. Martyrdom enabled the creation of the perfect revolutionary, fighting the cause of the oppressed, representing the future utopian world, the abstraction of an ideal to lead the revolutionary struggle.

Perhaps this was one of the reasons why, for men like Gyanji, the burden of the blood that the thousands of martyrs of the movement had shed weighed so heavily. The dead comrades represented not only the loss of people one knew as individuals, they also became the anchors that grounded the future imagined world into one's everyday reality. Martyrs gave the life-transcending permanence that was necessary to penetrate the present world with ideas of the extraordinary future world the guerrillas wanted to create. The burden of the martyrs contained a legacy; it was the means by which those in the movement sought to constantly improve themselves; it was the essence of what it means to be the perfect human.

'Living martyrs?' Is that what marked out men like Gyanji who had renounced their lives and broken the bonds of their pasts in order to create a world that was more equal and more democratic? Suspended between the living and the dead, waiting for their own deaths, they already marked the new egalitarian future and tried to live as and embody its ideal human subject.

* * *

The more I had dwelt on the uniqueness of these Naxalite leaders, the more I found myself reminiscing of the Sunday afternoons when I had tagged along with my grandfather to the ornate marble Jain temples of Nairobi where I grew up, to pay respects to the deities amidst the monks. On some occasions, we went to the Digambar temple where I was always reduced to staring at my feet because the Jain monks there had left behind everything—*everything*—in their search for liberation. Symbols of enlighten-ment in a conservative society, it was always rather shocking as a child to be exposed to their nudity. Only a few days before setting out on this trek with Gyanji, on the bus ride to the Naxalite ter-ritory in Bihar, I had passed a line of naked monks marching on the highway. They would only eat food that was offered to them and they carried absolutely nothing with them.

Was there a continuity between the figure of the communist revolutionary and a long history of renunciation for liberation in India?

As it turned out, I was not that far off the mark with the comparison between renouncers and revolutionaries. Like several of the other leaders I met, Gyanji had once been on the Hindu path of renouncing this world of hierarchy, waiting for his indi-vidual liberation. Coming into his teens, he had turned vegetar-ian. Rejecting everything but the very basic items of clothing and food to live on, uninterested in girls, he proclaimed celibacy. He said he spent his time reading Vedic texts and gazing into the setting sun on the banks of the Ganges, hoping to one day be enlightened by God. He was waiting as a yogi to be shown the path of escape from this world and its endless cycles of rebirth, a liberation that would take him into another world of equality—Nirvana.

The figure of the yogic renouncer has played a special role in the Hindu cosmos.[7] While their numbers are small, and it is generally men of higher-caste origin who are found renouncing, any person (from any caste or gender)[8] can become an ascetic. At one end of the spectrum there are the naked or semi-naked monks with shaven heads or ropes of uncut, matted hair living austerely on alms only and meditating in complete solitude for hours on end;[9] at the other end there are the human-flesh-eating, excrement-consuming, prostitute-fornicating ascetics, such as the Aghori of Banaras, who proclaim a radical equality in which there is no distinction between the Brahmin and the untouchable.[10] These ascetics all seek to acquire the transcendental knowledge that will liberate them individually from time and the endless cycle of suffering and rebirth, into another world of equality.[11]

But Gyanji said he realised the selfishness of seeking liberation only for himself—as desired by the renouncer—because of the influence of his university teacher and the political mobilisation around him. In seeking to attain equality outside of this world by himself, the renouncer ensured the endurance of hierarchy in the very world that he renounced.[12] Gyanji turned from the path of renunciation, which aimed to liberate the individual in a different world, to one liberating for communal ends in this world, with his first political task as a Naxalite being to distribute a pamphlet on 'the Death of God'.

The stark social hierarchies of Indian society have come hand-in-hand with a long tradition of putting renunciation to work for political purposes. Gandhi, clad in his white loincloth, is perhaps the obvious example. Although their political purposes were different, like Gyanji, some of these historical renouncers had turned away from seeking their individual liberation through departure to another more equal world, and instead sought to question the inequalities of the present. They had subverted the religious monk ideal of extinguishing the future and leaving the world for their own personal freedom and had instead committed themselves to creating a liberated world for everyone.[13]

In the case of Gyanji and his comrade friends, this path of liberation meant working with others to create a world of radical equality in the here and now, marking a new future in the present, generating a parallel, more equal world. And, it also meant fighting for a better world for the whole of society (not just for a few individuals).

So perhaps the alleged difference between India's yogic gurus, renouncers preaching non-violence such as Gandhi, and the high-caste Naxal leaders who renounced their worlds to create a new liberated society underground wasn't as vast as I had thought at first. 'Gandhians with Guns', they were called.[14] Revolutionary violence was a sacred calling. Perhaps it was the long history of renouncing the social hierarchy of Indian society that partly explains why contemporary India both exports yogic gurus and continues to produce armed communist insurgents.

On the one hand, Hindu, Buddhist or Jain monks renounce the hierarchies of their society to liberate themselves individually from the endless cycles of rebirth to reach an eventual future world of equality. On the other hand, India's Naxalite guerrillas break with their pasts to commit to a casteless and classless community, seeking to liberate the whole of society for a more equal future to be fought for in the present. Whereas one seeks emancipation for the individual in the future, the other works for the ideal of liberation for communal ends in the present.

But both involve a conviction and commitment, a faith in the means to an end, which, like following a religious doctrine, is hard to shake. They are both willing to sacrifice everything, including themselves, to attain their ideals of liberation. Taking up arms is then merely one of the means to this end. Whether one agrees with these revolutionary methods or not, the hierarchies of Indian society have themselves produced some of the world's most committed pursuers of a more equal society.

Gyanji, I knew, would not think much of my musings. To suggest the homology between violence, sacrifice, martyrdom, renunciation and revolution to him and his comrade leaders would be perceived by them as the equivalent of Marxist blasphemy. It is not just that they are too close for comfort; such comparisons are also the antithesis of the Naxalite understanding of the utterly secular world that they are producing, in which there would be no place for religion and which should only be analysed through the mantra of class analysis. But it was this closeness between renouncers and revolutionaries, turning revolutionary violence into a sacred calling, that meant that men like Gyanji, who were once chided by their friends for not being able to harm an ant, or so I heard, were able to take up arms.

* * *

I was compelled to question my own position on revolutionary violence from the time I first met Gyanji in December 2008. He was in the middle of what they called 'a cooking lesson' when I arrived, in a forest clearing in Lalgaon where they had set up camp for a couple of nights. A circle of fifteen young men in uniform were seated on the ground around an older man who was a Central Committee member, and another man they called their 'chemistry teacher'. The older man had a weighing scale in front of him and was measuring out flour, mixing it with butter and sugar. 'How much flour?' he asked. 'Eight ounces,' someone responded.

Interrupting the lesson, a flustered young man rushed in, dripping with sweat as if he had been running a marathon. His arrival was met with raucous laughter. He had apparently spent the day running from village to village but failed to return with the one crucial ingredient he had been sent out to get: 10 litres of cow's urine. Cows were abundant, but the young man had been too embarrassed to ask their owners whether he could collect their pee in a bottle.

I was confused. The purpose of the lesson only became clear to me when we descended into a ravine to test the 'recipes'. Some did not work. Others were considered mediocre. The best concoctions hurled the large boulders, under which they had been placed, high into the sky and blasted them into little pieces.

Flour, butter and sugar were all code words for substances such as potassium chlorate, nitric acid, methanol and sulphur. The cow's urine was needed to make ammonium nitrate. All the ingredients had been placed into a small plastic container with a detonator and linked to a camera flash via a long wire. The clicking of the flash triggered the detonator, exploding the contents of the container. The men were making and testing the infamous Naxalite manual landmines, the main deterrent keeping the security forces out of these guerrilla strongholds.

The bombs tested that day each weighed no more than 250 grams, but the final landmines would be anything between 4 and 20 kilograms, depending on the type of vehicle that was to be attacked. They would be laid beneath the dirt track where the vehicle would pass, either in a triangle shape or, for maximum impact, in a 'W' formation. The aim was to kill the government soldiers but to keep the weapons inside the vehicle intact. Four kilograms of gelatine was enough to blow up a jeep while ensuring that the weapons could be retrieved. Eight kilograms would destroy the weapons as well.

'What's your stand on violence?' the Central Committee leader, Arunji, whom I was also meeting for the first time, asked me later that evening as we sat around a bonfire in the clearing.

I knew this was a test to understand to what extent I was friend or foe. I found myself floundering. The truth was that I really didn't know.

Violence, Gyanji told me later, is simply a means to an end. No significant revolutionary change has taken place in the world without violence, he said. No change of regime, no change of state power: the English Revolution, the French Revolution, the Cuban Revolution, all the anti-colonial revolutions; he could have gone on.

'Our violence here is not indiscriminate or anarchic; we do not condone terrorism,' he clarified. Their targets, he explained, were very specific. In the feudal areas, their violence was against the landlords. In the tribal-dominated hilly forests, they targeted mainly the Indian security forces. He said they let the government teachers, the health workers and the development workers carry on their activities. They only attacked the police and forest guards. Civilians were out of the question. Their methods, he said, were very different from those of the suicide bombers responsible for the 9/11 attacks. Those, he said, were acts of terrorism, for they killed innocent people.

He said that the Indian government and its representatives only drew the public's attention to the Naxalite arms. 'But,' he said, 'look at the everyday violence inflicted on the people here by the ruling elites. Sixty years of what they call independence from colonial rule, but they have brought only poverty. They have looted the people's land and forests and given them nothing in return. No sanitation, no electricity, no running water. People are dying prematurely of disease and are reduced to living like animals. In fact, worse than animals. The ruling classes pamper their poodles but thrash their servants.'

His language was emotional but I knew that to some extent he was correct. A farmer killed himself in India every half hour because he was in debt, a child under five died every fifteen seconds hungry and sick, and people were regularly killed or imprisoned for fighting against low wages or for trying to protect the small pieces of land they had. Meanwhile, the number of dollar billionaires kept rising. Gyanji said it was easy to focus only on the guerrilla guns and forget this wider 'structural violence', the violence inherent and endemic in the social and institutional structures that prevented people from satisfying even their basic human needs.

The violence of the oppressed is often seen as a response to the violence of the oppressor.[15] But over the time I lived in Lalgaon, my reservations about these binaries grew. The oppressed were never just one homogenous group of people. What about those who were co-opted by or turned to the other side? Or those whom the Naxalites shot dead as police informers, betrayers or traitors?

I had already heard stories of the men in Lalgaon—there were at least three—who over the years had been killed by the Naxalites as police informers. The most talked about had been a contractor who was reputed to corner the contracts of development programmes from the local state office but kept all the money for himself. He had two wives, was rumoured to have a mistress as well, and was deeply unpopular, for he was said to care only for himself. The Naxalites suspected him of selling information about their movements to the police and eventually held a 'people's court' to decide what to do with him. The villagers administered him with 200 lashes, but when his punishment was meted out it was said that he was so strong that his body didn't even flinch. Eventually the guerrilla squads put five bullets through his head and left his body at the riverbank as an example to potential renegades.

Gyanji said that killing was an extreme measure, only to be used against those people who couldn't be brought into the fold. But, I wondered, who was it who decided if this was the case?

Was it justifiable to take anyone's life in this way? Would it not evolve into a reign of fear amongst the people and never-ending cycles of violence whose primary victims were 'the oppressed'?

Moreover, were the Adivasis being pitted against each other through the spread of this insurgency in ever more sophisticated ways? The Indian government had taken lessons about counter-insurgency operations against guerrillas from other parts of the world. Poor Adivasi youths from areas neighbouring the guerrilla strongholds were being used to front the anti-Maoist security forces to fight their Adivasi brothers and sisters.

I realised the significance of the state using Adivasi youths when one evening the security forces climbed up into the hills, as they did every three weeks on their combing operations, occupying the Lalgaon school and turning it into their barracks. On such occasions, I usually left the village as I was concerned that if the state forces knew I was living there, in the name of my own security, they would ask me to leave and not allow me back in unless I was accompanied by them. But it was already late afternoon by the time their armoured vehicles crested the hills that day and it would have been an arduous eight-hour journey back to Ranchi city, one that I would have had to undertake mostly at night. Moreover, I had been in Lalgaon long enough to think that if I didn't venture out of the house and kept a low profile, I would be safe and could leave undetected early the next morning. In fact, I had become so complacent that after 7:00 p.m., when the security forces were supposed to be confined within the school, I was enjoying the evening breeze by the front door, which I had left ajar, and was seated on the floor in Somwari's house teaching her seven-year-old daughter to read by the light of a kerosene lamp.

A shadow fell across our doorway. I was stunned to see two young men dressed in army gear. '*Didi*, do you have some?' they asked, not specifying what. I could barely breathe but was quick to realise that they had come searching for *mahua*, the wine that Adivasis distil from the *mahua* flower. I went into the interior room of the mud house to fetch Somwari, hoping that I would be able to hide in the kitchen while she dealt with them. But the men realised that something was amiss. I heard them speaking Nagpuria, the language spoken in my doctoral research site, a day's journey away. They were asking each other whether I was really Somwari's sister, as I had claimed.

I knew I had to find the courage to talk to them. Although I was shaking inside, I walked out confidently. Somwari stood by staunchly, her arms crossed, as though she were my bodyguard, or so I later teased her. In my clearest Nagpuria I authoritatively asked the young soldiers where they were from. They were taken aback that I could speak to them in their own dialect. As it happened, they were new recruits who had joined the security forces just six months ago, and I knew not only the villages they were from but also a doctor for whom one of them had previously worked as a chauffeur. Establishing myself as their village elder sister, I reprimanded them for breaking the rules and coming out of their barracks at night in search of booze. I told them what they knew very well, that they might lose their jobs if the superintendent of police found out what they were up to.

And so we became complicit in each other's transgressions, and I rested assured that they would not reveal my presence in the village to the superintendent. In the process, I fondly came to see them as Adivasi youths, just like the ones I lived amidst. Those young men had been recruited into the Jharkhand Jaguars, a unit specially formed to fight the guerrillas with their own tactics. They were to be in the frontline of operation, and were those most likely to die in encounters with the guerrillas.

As is so often the case with war, the poor were now being used to fight the poor. Targeted recruitment of Adivasi boys into the police and the security forces had begun. In neighbouring states like Chhattisgarh, the police had armed Adivasi boys as Special Police Officers and armed Adivasi vigilante groups, recruiting from the very communities the Naxalites lived amidst, pitting the poor against the poor to kill each other.

Over the year that I came to know Gyanji, I relayed my concerns to him. I said that in the end they would never get rid of the politicians who collaborated with the multinational companies and created government economic policy that generated inequality; instead, the Naxalites would kill the hundreds of young Adivasi soldiers who were being used by the state armies.

Gyanji said it was true that the young men who fronted the security forces would be the Naxalites' first casualties. In an attempt at justification, he said that when these men worked for the state, they became an arm of the state; the Naxalites would never target the same men when they came back home to their villages, off-duty, to visit their families.

I wasn't convinced by this response, but other thoughts were also pressing. 'Is it not often the case that the power flowing from the barrel of your gun will reproduce the very systems that you are trying to extinguish?' I asked.

Gyanji looked away at that point and his thoughts seemed to be elsewhere. Eventually he said, 'It is one of the biggest problems that a clandestine underground movement faces.' In that moment, he was talking about the Naxalites as if they were an abstract entity.

He added that state repression of the kind being generated against them dangerously reduced their revolutionary activities to military strategy alone. In the face of this despair, it was hard to keep hope alive, making it far too easy to start replicating the violence of the oppressor.

This state repression, he continued, gave them little space to work with the people. It did not allow them to develop political consciousness, political education or mass mobilisation. The danger, he said, was that people joined the Maoists without sharing their vision and imagination of a different world. And in that context, the gun became just a means of accelerating their upward social mobility within the very systems the Maoists sought to crush.

By the time he finished I could see that I had touched a raw nerve, so I put the conversation on hold.

9

MORNING ONE

Behind Gyanji, Kohli, wrapped in a shawl, was squatting in front of the curved aluminium pot in which tea was boiling. The makeshift cooker was a small fire burning within a triangle formed by three large stones. As he added twigs to stoke the fire and occasionally crouched down to blow at it, the warm orange flame lit up his smooth dark face.

I squatted next to Kohli and copied him as he warmed his palms at the hearth, gently turning them towards his body and then the flames. It was always nippy at this time in the morning, before the sun rose, but the heat of the fire and the tea soon warmed me up.

Gyanji was talking to the soldiers nearby. Section B (which included Kohli and Gyanji's bodyguard) had men he knew intimately, but the rest of the platoon (Sections A and C) had soldiers from a different part of Jharkhand to the areas where he generally worked. Their gentle banter was disrupted as Vikas, the platoon commander, went over to them.

I heard Vikas say, 'But we do have time. We can't start walking until late afternoon anyway. It'll be a nice treat for *Didi*.'

I could not quite hear Gyanji, but he seemed annoyed. I asked Kohli, who was still next to me, what was going on, uneasy that my name might be being used as an excuse for something I did not understand.

Kohli said the problem was Vikas. He was insisting that we get a chicken from the village and cook it for breakfast, proposing the very things that Gyanji detested. Kohli said that Gyanji abhorred this kind of behaviour because it marked the Naxalites as being a cut above the villagers; chicken was expensive and most villagers would only cook it on special occasions. The case would be different, Kohli explained, if there were a village celebration, a ritual, or a commemoration, when everybody would have chicken. But to slaughter a chicken on an ordinary morning like this, Kohli explained, tarred the guerrillas with the same brush as the state and forest officials who rode roughshod over the villagers and their livestock.

Eventually Gyanji came over to us and sat by the fire. He turned to Kohli, who was looking gloomy, and asked merrily, 'What's up, the revolution must be fought with a smile!' But he seemed to be talking as much to himself as he was to Kohli.

Vikas and the section commanders had decided that we would stay in this forest for most of the day and then start walking before dusk. Gyanji told Kohli that it was probably a good time to take my uniform to the tailor in the nearby village. Despite the belt, my trousers kept slipping down; I had to stop every 50 yards or so to roll down the waistband and was worried that I was slowing everyone down. Screened by a clump of bushes, I changed into my red salwar dress—the one that Prashant had brought for me—and gave my uniform to Kohli.

The morning light was shining through the trees. Those not on sentry duties had broken twigs off a nearby acacia tree to use as toothbrushes and were huddled in groups scrubbing their teeth intensely. Like all cleaning rituals, brushing teeth was a communal task. Every so often the men stopped to spit out the fibres, chat a little, and then scrub their teeth again in a cycle of brushing, spitting and talking.

It was a skill. My grandmother had taught me to use those sticks when we lived in Nairobi. Despite the availability of tooth-brushes, and the fact that acacia sticks were sourced all the way from the Great Rift Valley and brought to our house in the city, she preferred to brush her teeth as she had done in the villages in Gujarat. The ritual took time and the intense concentration it required was curiously meditative. One edge of the stick was chewed to moisten it and split the fibres, creating a brush like tip. Teeth were scrubbed over and over, up and down, and finally, when the twig was so soggy that it could bend in half, the curve was used to clean the tongue. The used twig could be discarded anywhere to disintegrate without polluting the environment. I looked at my modern plastic toothbrush. It didn't have quite the same effect and certainly was far from eco-friendly.

When the teeth were done it was time to attend to the guns. Everyone was given rifle training. But would any of these guer-rilla fighters ever use their guns in battle? The Naxalites avoided meeting the state forces in face-to-face encounters and focused on guerrilla warfare—ambushes for selected killings, seizure of weapons, and keeping the state forces out of their strongholds through the planting and detonating of landmines.

Perched on rocks and under the trees, the guerrillas dismantled their weapons. Some soldiers had wrapped oil-soaked cloth around the twigs and deftly cleaned the inside of their gun barrels. Others were polishing their receivers with scarves or towels, paying atten-tion to the nooks and crannies, until the metal shone.

This was another communal cleaning ritual, more dangerous than the last one. I had met a soldier who had injured his hand while cleaning a gun that happened to be loaded. He was lucky, he said; others had died through such careless mistakes.

I walked over to Vikas who was brandishing his AK-47. 'Every rifle has its own story,' he proudly declared.

Most of the rebels' rifles had been hijacked from the police and from wealthy rural elites known to keep arms. During my sojourn in another Adivasi area of Jharkhand ten years ago, one into which the Naxalites had wanted to expand then, I knew that the first action of the guerrillas when they entered an area was to disarm it. They attacked remote rural police stations to steal their arsenal and twisted the arms of the rich rural elites into handing over their guns. It was a tactic that not only gave them weapons but also the monopoly on violence in the region, crucial to forming a parallel state there.[1]

I had heard first-hand about the looting of weapons from my friend, an elderly Austrian lady who had once lived with her high-caste Gujarati husband, a retired teacher, in a rural idyll in Jharkhand that had long been home to a community of Anglo-Indians. One night, in 1992, the Naxalites had kidnapped her because her husband had denied that he had two guns when an armed squad had visited them a few days earlier. In fact, her husband had heard about Naxalites seizing guns from other rich neighbours and had deposited his two weapons at the police station for 'safe-keeping'. The guerrilla squad had walked my Austrian friend a few hours into the forest, given her lunch and dinner, and at night found her a bed to sleep in in one of the huts in a nearby village. She said the incident made them leave their beautiful home amidst the birds, deer and the forest and take up a high-rise flat in a gated compound in the safety of the city. But she was struck by the respect with which the Naxalites had treated her, calling her 'aunty', insisting she ate one more roti, even finding milk (which was a luxury in the area) for her to drink, and explaining how they needed the guns to fight the war for the poor. As soon as her husband retrieved his rifles from the police station and handed them over to the squads, they delivered her home.

Vikas wanted to tell me the story of his weapon so I listened. He had got it two years ago from the state of Odisha, he boasted. It was part of a Maoist operation that had acquired legendary status amongst the guerrillas and had been widely reported in the Indian press. In Nayagarh in 2008, Maoist guerrillas had simultaneously attacked the district armoury, the police training school armoury, the police stations and several police outposts.

Three platoons had marched from Bihar through the forests of Jharkhand and into Odisha for that mission, Vikas said. It had taken them two weeks and they had met cadres from all over the country who had travelled equally long distances to get there. There were, in total, 360 guerrilla fighters. They synchronised their raid to first disconnect all communication lines into Nayagarh, disrupt its power supply and block all the entry points into the town. Then they rode into town in trucks, buses, jeeps and motorbikes and seized all the arms they could find. Fifteen police personnel and one townsman died in the process, but they recovered a huge cache—1,200 weapons and more than 100,000 rounds of ammunition. There were so many guns that they had not known what to do with them. They stashed some of the weapons in a nearby wildlife sanctuary, hoping to go back for them at a later point. Even carrying two or three rifles each, they couldn't take them all back, he said smugly, caressing his AK-47, which was one of the 400 guns that had made it back into the guerrilla squads.

In comparison to Gyanji's police rifle, Vikas's rifle was slick. Its rounded magazine and polished barrel stood out against the wooden buttstock and pistol grip.

Such weapons had surrounded me for at least a year, but it was still hard not to feel uneasy around them. As I watched Vikas carefully polishing the butt, I recalled Gyanji's haunting remarks to me some time before, about how the barrels of these clandestine guns could reproduce the violence of the oppressors. At that moment, the journey that lay ahead seemed to hinge on purifying the pollution that could creep into the revolutionary firearms.

PART FOUR

KOHLI'S HOME AWAY FROM HOME

10

NIGHT TWO

The rustling of feet through leaves on the forest bed cut the silence of the mid-afternoon. Alert, I closed my notebook, threw it in my bag, slipped on my shoes and jumped up. We had been resting under the trees, waiting to embark on our first full night of walking towards our destination in Jharkhand.

Guerrilla soldiers emerged one after another through the bushes. I counted twenty-five young men. It was another platoon. The villagers had told them that we were in the vicinity, their platoon commander said. Like us they were also on their way back home from the State-level Conference but were heading back to the borders of Chhattisgarh where their regular areas of operation lay. Gyanji said we could walk together for a few hours until our paths diverged. They split up into small groups. One lot joined me under the canopy of trees where I had been writing. The rest joined the sentries in their various positions.

Two hours before sunset, the whistle blew. I took my position behind Kohli as we assembled in six rows for the roll call. As yet unused to the routines of life in the platoon, I hesitated when it was my turn. I was grateful when Kohli shouted out 'fifteen' on my behalf. Each soldier rapidly relayed his number one after another, until the last one declared 'fifty-five'.

I concentrated on following Kohli's footsteps. Darkness would soon engulf us and I thought it would be easier to walk if I could intuitively fall into the rhythm of his pace.

Clambering down the steep granite face of the hills, meandering around towering rocky outcrops, we began the descent into a gorge. Below us lay a forest of acacia and *plas* trees in full bloom covered with large bulbous crimson flowers. I was taken aback to find myself in a long line that looked like an army of ants, weaving through a carpet of bright red towards the rice fields that stretched out as far as the eye could see up to the horizon marked by the blue hills of Jharkhand.

Those were the forests and fields of the *Jungle Raj*—as the Adivasis who lived there often called it—that undulated over thousands of square kilometres and into the states of West Bengal, Odisha, Chhattisgarh, Maharashtra, Madhya Pradesh and Andhra Pradesh. The landscape would change dramatically over the year. In a month's time, in March, the sweet scent of the small white flower of the *sal* trees would float across the air making one feel intoxicated and light-headed; it was a time when romances blossomed, the forest dwellers said. Soon after, the ground would be parched and pock-marked with black patches where forest fires were deliberately spread in a controlled manner to clear the undergrowth for the easy collection of the pulpy flowers that were shed by the *mahua* trees during the night, forming a yellow carpet.

These magical moments would then be swept away by the hot winds, called *lat*, that relentlessly blew day and night over the bleak landscape as though a hairdryer had been permanently switched on, and the temperature would soar towards 50 degrees Celsius. There was no relief from this heat. The trees lost their leaves and were reduced to spindly sticks reaching out to the sky.

Forest hideouts, in which the guerrillas could remain camou-
flaged, would now be few and far between. The ground water
levels would sink so low that only pits dug deep into dry river-
beds could produce water. The security forces used the adverse
conditions of these months to scale up their patrols. It would feel
as though everything had been left bone dry, gasping for the
first rain of the monsoons when the rivers would flow fast again,
curtailing easy access by the security forces to the guerrilla
strongholds; the jungle and the fields would turn lush and green
once again.

How many more platoons would be making their way towards
various parts of those forests? Although the Naxalites had not yet
formed guerrilla bases anywhere in the country, they regularly
crossed from one zone that was a stronghold to the next.

Halfway down the gorge, the path forked. It was time to
part with the other platoon. The two platoons stood facing
each other for the ritual goodbye. A shake of hands followed by
raising the right fist with a '*lal salaam*'. I watched the platoon
walk westwards and disappear through the trees. I wondered
what obstacles they would face on their journey. When the last
of them was gone, we headed south, towards the *Jungle Raj*, the
terrain that had been deemed inhospitable for centuries by
many outsiders but a place that the Naxalite guerrillas considered their home.

Crossing a rocky outcrop, a high-pitched buzz rose above the
sound of the wind whistling through the trees. Bees. The intri-
cacies of the architecture of the hives were magnificently dis-
played on the underside of the rock.

Gyanji turned around, his eyes brimming with mirth. 'Do you
recall the passage about bees in Marx's *Capital*?' he asked.

'A spider conducts operations that resemble those of a weaver,
and a bee puts to shame many an architect in the construction of
her cells. But what distinguishes the worst architect from the

best of bees is this, that the architect raises his structure in imagination before he erects it in reality,' Gyanji recited.[1]

Imagination is indeed what makes us different as humans to these other living creatures. These words of Marx, emphasising our ability to imagine another world and to set about building it, appeared to be the crux of Gyanji's commitment to the Naxalites for the past twenty-five years. They enabled him to endure the never-ending hardships, disappointments and tragedies of life underground, while preserving his optimism for creating a different world, keeping his hope alive and nurturing new recruits like Kohli to achieve this end goal.

'*Didi*, let me carry your bag now,' Kohli said, turning around. I had lost count of the number of times Kohli offered to relieve me of my bag. We had only just begun a long journey and I did not feel comfortable being given special treatment, especially in a society of people where the norms of the division of labour were to be broken down and everyone had to pull their own weight.

Darkness fell rapidly as it always does in this part of the world, so close to the equator. Soon the big orange ball of the sun that had dropped behind the trees would disappear completely for ten hours. With the loss of daylight, the contrast between Kohli's black hair, black belt and green uniform was erased; he became a charcoal silhouette.

The landscape came alive with night sounds: the chirping of crickets, the occasional buzzing of a mosquito and the croaking of frogs and toads. The hum of a whole new community of creatures made me acutely aware of these nocturnal beings which, like the guerrillas, were now busy creating new worlds under cover of night.

Although Kohli earnestly recommended that I use my torch, as none of the thirty guerrillas in the platoon had one in hand, I was reluctant to inadvertently draw attention to our presence with a light in the pitch dark. Apart from marching guerrillas, there were few circumstances that would produce a line of moving lights in this remote landscape. But Gyanji said that one light would make no difference for it could be a stray villager walking around.

I reached into my bag for the cheap but reliable black plastic torch I had bought in a local bazaar in Jharkhand. It had replaced the posh metallic, purple-coloured, heavy Maglite torch sold to me in London's Covent Garden for its refined optics, power and durability, but which had inexplicably stopped working within a month of being in rural Jharkhand. I flicked on the switch. Before I knew what was happening, I found myself floundering and on my knees. The light was blinding and I had lost my footing.

Kohli grabbed my arm and crouched down. He told me to take it easy and not try to stand up immediately. He asked whether I had twisted my ankle and wanted to make sure I was okay before I rose. His soft concerned voice was soothing.

Embarrassed, I picked myself up feeling gauche and clumsy. Would I ever learn to move as nimbly as the rest of this platoon? Gyanji held out my fallen cap. I twisted my hair back under its green canvas, conscious of keeping the platoon waiting. Kohli gently insisted that it was time I gave my bag to him. I looked at him reluctantly. But Gyanji agreed.

We carried on. Kohli suggested that I might in fact find it easier to walk without the light and that my eyes could easily adjust to the low visibility. Taking my torch away, he told me to follow the back of his trainers and place my foot exactly where his had been. The most important rule, he said, was to steer clear of dark patches.

As my eyes grew accustomed to the dark, a white trail miraculously appeared before me. That was the path I needed to take. The dark patches were uneven ground, holes that could sprain one's ankle. In the light of the torch, the trail disappeared. It took some time to find it again. Kohli was right. Once you learnt how to see your way, it was easier to walk in the dark.

We marched on but drew to a halt at the edge of the gorge from where the treacherous journey across the open rice fields would begin. We waited there for the two 'runners' who were sent ahead to scope out the terrain to return with intelligence on the movements of the Indian security forces.

Everyone took turns to go off into the bush—'*ek number*', that is, number one for a pee, and '*do number*' or number two for more. It would be our last stop for a few hours.

'All men to the right-hand side and all women to the left,' Kohli announced. He was repeating the rule with a tactfulness I found rather endearing. He did not wish to make an issue of the fact that I was the only woman.

The temperature dropped rapidly with the fall of the night. As everyone dispersed, Kohli laid a fire. The twigs were soon crackling merrily. Reaching into his bag, Kohli brought out a battered Bisleri mineral water bottle, half full of white liquid—a mixture of milk and water. Kohli knew what Gyanji craved. Amazed that we were going to have tea, I gazed at the long thick eyelashes that framed Kohli's almond-shaped eyes, as he bent over the fire. Why exactly had he left Lalgaon to live his life amid these fighters?

The two runners reappeared, panting. They reported that a 200-man column of the security forces, on a patrol to comb the area for us, had spent the day occupying a school just half a kilometre away. Fortunately for us, they had just returned to their main camp 15 kilometres further south. It was safe for us to move on and cross the agricultural plains to reach the cover of the next forested area.

Gyanji turned to Vikas and said that we must avoid the main security force camp at all costs and asked whether he knew the route through the village of Behra.

Vikas seemed preoccupied and was playing with his mobile phone. There was no reception in these areas unless you climbed a hill. What was he doing? It was a rather flashy device with a large screen and fluorescent green digits that lit up, certainly not the bottom-of-the-range Nokia device that everyone else carried.

Vikas insouciantly assured Gyanji that he was certain of the lay of the land and that we were in safe hands with him, Vikas, spearheading our expedition. A look of frustration crossed Gyanji's face. Perhaps he was a little disappointed with Vikas's flippancy, but he was trying not to show it. He told Vikas to put his phone away, that it was late and we should get going.

I took my place behind Kohli once again when the line formed and we marched on. The terrain changed rapidly. When the trees disappeared, a midnight-blue sky heaving with stars unfurled above us, revealing a vast patchwork of rice fields in front.

The new challenge was to learn to balance oneself walking on the bunds, the narrow raised banks that divided the fields and retained water during the monsoon. Like the forest tracks, in the dark the bunds appeared as a white trail. Every muscle in my body was tense. Outside of the forests, it felt different. We were clearly very exposed on the plains.

Cutting through the songs of the insects echoing in the night, the harshness of a motorised rumble grew steadily louder into a reverberating drone. In the distance a halo of bright white light appeared. It loomed increasingly larger, like a UFO that had landed in the middle of the fields.

Above the deafening sound, Gyanji raised his voice at Vikas. 'Why are we going this way?' he asked. I realised that the halo of light was the Central Reserve Police Force barracks and the noise, the generators used to power the camp. Although the surrounding villages were without electricity and shrouded in darkness, the camp was floodlit. Soon the lampposts skirting the camp rose into the sky. At this pace, we would be at the barbed wire fence of the barracks in no time. Around 3,000 security force men were camped there. I did some quick arithmetic in my head: a hundred of them for every one of us.

Furious, Gyanji told Vikas that it seemed he didn't know where he was going. He was supposed to be familiar with every tree and undulation of the land here. 'What are you doing all day? Are you only wining and dining with the contractors?' Gyanji barked at Vikas.

'Stop!' someone cried out behind us.

Several people were huddled together on the ground about 10 metres behind us. Kohli and Gyanji ran towards them. A young man was lying flat on his back.

Gyanji told everyone to be quiet and to take position. He asked the section commanders to turn off their walkie-talkies. Here, so close to their barracks, the security forces may have mechanisms to intercept them.

Gyanji knelt by the young man who was shivering. His name was Bildeo. I had noticed him when we had stopped at the end of the gorge as he had been vomiting. A few days ago, Bildeo had suffered from malarial fevers and Gyanji and some of the other leaders had been concerned about him joining the march, but Bildeo was determined to return to his home in Jharkhand.

Kohli extracted a large white plastic kit from his rucksack. Unzipping it, he shone his torch inside. It was stuffed with medicine, syringes and bandages.

'Don't worry, it is going to be okay,' Kohli said tenderly to Bildeo. 'We're all here to look after you.'

Gyanji felt Bildeo's forehead, neck and hands and took his temperature, handing over the thermometer to Kohli, as it was too dark for him to see. Kohli said it was 42 degrees Celsius. Gyanji asked Kohli whether he had some glucose and quinidine and reached into his own bag for his orange, floral-printed bed-sheet. This he gave to Vikas, instructing him to get two men to build a makeshift stretcher.

Meanwhile, Kohli filled a syringe, turned up Bildeo's sleeve and injected his arm. Gyanji later told me that although Kohli was young, he was very bright. He spent all his free time learning to read and had quickly picked up basic healthcare.

Two men appeared with a couple of long strong branches and fastened the orange bedsheet between them. Bildeo was lifted onto the sheet and four men hoisted one end of the branch onto their shoulders. Gyanji told Vikas to move to the rear of the platoon and assigned a young man from the area in Vikas's place to lead us towards Ambla village, 4 kilometres to the west of the camp. With Bildeo on the stretcher, we were ready to march on.

We skirted around the military camp. The generators were deafening. It felt as though we were circling around a Venus flytrap that would devour us, its poisonous light to be avoided at all costs.

The pace was very fast. About forty-five minutes later we reached the first house of the village. It was too close to the security force camp to stop but we knew we were now on the right track. Another two hours of trudging followed. Every half an hour there was a quick changeover of the men carrying Bildeo. We marched in total silence until we covered the 15 kilometres between the camp and the safety of a forested area.

As the sky disappeared and the darkness of the canopy of trees engulfed us, I immediately relaxed. It was amazing how quickly one could grow accustomed to perceiving one's environment from an entirely different perspective. Once places of danger and mystery in my imagination, now the very same forests had turned into a zone of safety.

We marched on and finally arrived at the outskirts of the village where we could seek some medical help for Bildeo and he could be moved to the safety of the houses of some sympathisers to be looked after by a doctor. We stopped and assembled in three columns. When the roll call was over, Gyanji told me to take a break with the rest of the platoon. He disappeared into the darkness with Vikas to make arrangements for Bildeo.

Exhausted, I sat under a *sal* tree, rested my back against its wide trunk and stretched out my aching legs. I was relieved that we were taking time out and, as I relaxed, I could feel the knots deep within my shoulder blades and under my neck slowly loosen, and the tension dissipate.

'Child soldiers,' I thought, looking at the contours of several of the young fighters who stood in formation around me; that's what they were called in the media. The words conjured a picture of children forced out of their homes, some even abducted, and then indoctrinated into the rebel cause. It was an image that was global in its production and reach—from Sierra Leone to Nepal, into the offices of the Save the Children Fund, and through our letterboxes. I had heard of the reports from the Indian police chiefs about coerced conscription of children by the Maoists. These were the reports that were being perpetuated amongst India's chattering middle classes, which got picked up by Amnesty International and eventually made it into the UN secretary-general's annual report on children and armed conflict. They meant well, but how much did the evocation of 'child soldiers' explain about the lives of these youths and how they had ended up in the rebel armies?

Kohli, as attentive as ever, offered me some water. Touched by his constant care, I asked him the question that was at the forefront of my mind, 'Kohli, what happened, what made you join this *Jungle Sarkar* (the Forest State)?'

Kohli stopped smiling and looked down at the ground. Even in the dark, I could sense a shadow cast over his face. I had clearly touched a raw nerve. Should I have been so bold?

11

EGALITARIAN IDEALS, HUMANENESS AND INTIMACY

Kohli's father had hit him for spilling milk on the floor. It was only a small cupful but Kohli was smacked across his face. In response, Kohli threatened to run away. That was when he first tried to live with the Naxalite squads.

I knew Kohli's father, Mangra Oraon, well. He was a jolly, kind and generous man. His teashop was my favourite haunt to soak up the village gossip as many people stopped by. Under two brick walls and a corrugated iron sheet, open on either side to the elements, Mangra had built three mud stoves fired with wood and had set up wooden tables with long benches on either side for customers to pass time comfortably with cups of his steaming brew and snacks. One stove was dedicated to a constant supply of sickly sweet milky tea. On the other two, Mangra fried samosas stuffed with potatoes, dry fruit and peanuts—*singaras*, they were locally called—and floury onion *bhajis*, all served with a deliciously tangy tamarind and chilli chutney. There was always an Indian sweet or two on offer too. On special days, like the weekly village *haat* (market), when people came from neighbouring villages to sell their produce and meet each other, he deep-fried *rotis* made from rice and lentil flour and served them with a hot chickpea curry.

It was unusual for an Adivasi to have a teashop. Most Adivasis survived by farming, grazing their animals, and foraged for fruits, roots, flowers and leaves from the forests. Needs not met by these subsistence strategies were fulfilled by working as manual wage labourers, carrying heavy loads on heads or across shoulders in the vicinity of the village, or by migrating as labourers to other Indian states for six months of the year. Small enterprises or busi-nesses were normally run by local Hindus and Muslims. Kohli's father was the only Adivasi in the region to try his hand at one.

The tea-shack, though, could barely make ends meet and relied heavily on the assistance of Kohli and his siblings. Kohli's youngest brother, only six years old, following in his father's footsteps, was also enterprising. He set up a fried eggs stall in front of his father's shack. The boy took pride in perfecting the eggs, seasoning them with chilli, onion, salt and pepper, and only reluctantly left the stall to go to school.

I remonstrated with Kohli that surely a father's transient annoyance was not reason enough to join the Naxalite armies. Kohli agreed with this, adding that at the time his father had good reason to be stressed. It had been the start of spring and the Adivasi festival of *Sarhul* that hailed their New Year. People from nearby villages had converged in their hamlet, so the tea-shop was doing brisk business. *Sarhul* was held on different dates in different villages so that they could all attend each other's ritu-als and celebrations. The ancestral spirits of the Adivasis that inhabited the forests and rocks and trees were appeased to ensure a fruitful year ahead and there was a special ritual sacrifice in the Adivasi *Sarna*—the sacred grove. On this day of spiritual celebra-tion, Mangra was overwhelmed with the rush of customers at his stall and was understandably tense.

Kohli had never wanted to work in the tea-shack anyway and his recalcitrance on this busy day was the final straw for his exhausted father. The previous year Kohli had run away with his older brother to work in a brick kiln in West Bengal for six months. Kohli's angst stemmed from his resentment towards his father's incessant parental supervision.

What about school? I asked Kohli. School, he declared, was a waste of time. I knew this was true because I used to teach there myself, for a few hours a day, whenever I could spare the time. I was usually the only teacher at the school, although, on the books, there were four teachers in all and a headmaster. There were no benches to sit on. The textbooks, ordered eight months before, were yet to arrive. The headmaster, apparently a paedophile, was said to have raped four girls. The school was a front for rechanneling funds received as salaries and money and materials allocated to cooking free midday meals, to add to the black money reserves of the building construction contractors. The midday meal scheme, a government initiative to discourage child labour and encourage literacy by supplying free meals to school-aged children, and consequently to increase school enrolment, was in fact notorious in these areas for feeding the black-market supply of kerosene, rice and dal. The traders and contractors responsible for distributing the subsidised fuel and oils meant for the schools sold off the provisions for a profit.

Although school buildings were now being erected everywhere as part of a central government scheme funded by the World Bank, UNICEF and the UK's Department for International Development (DFID) since 2000, their purpose was unclear. In a village in the high forests of Lalgaon consisting of fewer than a hundred households, there were two separate schools simply because the village's two hamlets fell into two different revenue villages. Neither school had any teachers on site, but no contractor would refuse to build a school as money could be syphoned off the whole way through the construction process, from the foundations to the finishing.

While building schools seemed, above all, to be a good source of black money for the unscrupulous, they had increasingly become convenient places for the security forces to host their barracks. Most of these barracks in schools were temporary but some new school buildings—there was one 9 kilometres from where I lived—were in fact constructed with the dual purpose of serving as army bases. These new schools were the only buildings in the entire area erected in fortified compounds, usually two storeys high with police sentry outposts on the rooftop and window-holes through which soldiers could open fire on any perceived threats.

Kohli went on to explain that on the evening that his father hit him, in the midst of all the singing and dancing of *Sarhul*, the Maoist zonal commander of their area, Parasji, a close friend of his father, had visited their home. Kohli had pleaded with Parasji to take him to the squads, but the Naxalite leader refused. Kohli said he should have known that Parasji would never go against his father's wishes.

However, early the next morning, when Kohli had gone into the forest for his morning ablutions, he had passed the guerrilla squad that his sister Anju had joined, and decided to stay with them. That same evening, when Anju's squad went to provide support for a platoon from Odisha, camping out in the Bhiwandi forest, he saw Parasji again. Anju's squad commander had insisted that Kohli be taken to Parasji who was addressing a meeting with the platoon in the forest.

Kohli was apprehensive about meeting Parasji face-to-face. Deeply embarrassed, he had just stared at Parasji's feet. He fully expected Parasji to send him back home but, to his surprise, Parasji said, 'I see, you came anyway.' With a rueful expression on his face, Parasji told Kohli that his father would be very upset, but patted the boy's head. Kohli knew then that all would be okay.

There were five other boys who had joined the guerrilla squads at around the same time. I had met all of them. One—a fourteen-year-old Kherwar boy—had been sent by his parents. His father had caught him drinking by himself at home on several occasions and eventually asked Parasji if he could take him into the guerrilla armies and try to instill a modicum of discipline in the lad. The second—a sixteen-year-old Birhor boy—had just come back from the brick factories in Odisha where he had gone with his parents. He had become very sick in Odisha and so, when he returned home, he decided to go and live with the squads. When I met him, he had been with the squads for six days although he said he had spent a month-long stint with them earlier. The third was a boy who had come to the armies because he was upset that his step-mother, whom he lived with, gave more food to her real son than she did to him. There was also my neighbour's son, an Oraon boy. One of six children, his father was a construction labourer in Chennai. He simply wanted to be with the 'jungle police'. The last boy was from a village high up in the hills—where the two non-functional schools had been built. His father had worked hard to save money to buy him a bicycle to go to the school near where I lived, but instead the boy cycled to the bazaar and spent his time watching the men there play cards. His parents, deeply disappointed when they eventually found out, were naturally angry with him. In a fit of sulks, the lad moved out of his parents' home and went to live with his neighbours. When his parents, in the hope that their son would return home, convinced the neighbours to stop encouraging the boys' defiance by feeding and sheltering him, the teenager decided to join the guerrilla armies.

Kohli's story of running away to the guerrilla squads to escape parental pressures was quite common, one I had heard many times in all shapes and forms. Moving in and out of the squads seemed like the most natural thing to do for the Adivasi and lower-caste youths who joined the guerrilla armies in these parts of India. While parents and grandparents would hide the guerrillas when necessary and provide them with a plate of food when asked, it was their children and sometimes grandchildren who joined the armed squads. What struck me was that almost every story of Adivasi and low-caste youths joining the guerrillas in these forests and hills had a similar beginning to that of Kohli: a fight with a parent or a sibling, a love affair forbidden in the villages but accepted in the Naxalite armies, a desire to leave home and see another world. Despite their individual twists and turns, what was significant in all these stories was how, for those who recounted them, the Naxalites had come to be another home.

Kohli's sister, Anju, a year younger than him at fifteen, had also run away from home to join the guerrilla armies to be with a boy in one of the platoons who had declared his love for her. Her parents did not find him a suitable match. He was from a different tribe—a Munda not an Oraon—and in any case an Adivasi girl was not supposed to choose her own husband. She followed in the footsteps of Tara, her older cousin who had earlier joined the squads and married a man in the guerrilla armies.

Anju's fourteen-year-old cousin, Lila, followed suit. In awe of her older cousin, Lila wanted to go where so many other young people had gone, fascinated by the excitement of life on the move. With a voice like a nightingale, Lila soon became a driving force of energy, singing and dancing in the Naxalite cultural division. Lila flourished in the guerrilla armies, but Anju's fate was different. After six months, her parents convinced Anju to return to the village and marry a man they had chosen for her. Mangra laughed when he told me about it, 'She's done her revolution; now it's time to start life.'

Adivasi weddings are usually simple affairs. But Mangra had spent a fortune on Anju's wedding. Somwari, in whose house I lived, criticised Mangra. She said he was getting too influenced by his Hindu neighbours. Outside his mud house, Mangra erected a regal wooden stage draped in red and yellow cloth, decorated with colourful flashing lights, and with a centrepiece of two golden thrones for the bride and the groom. He hired a generator for electricity, erected marquees to house all the guests and made enormous vats of curry. He even travelled to Ranchi city to buy makeup for Anju. Since nobody used such products in the village, I was given the responsibility of dressing Anju. Unzipping the bag of cosmetics, I was amused to find pale pink foundation for Anju's almost black skin, bright red lipstick, several shades of green eyeshadow, powder, bindis, bangles and safety pins. There was even men's eau de toilette for Anju; Mangra had only basic literacy and clearly hadn't understood the label.

My artistic efforts were in vain. The mascara streaked Anju's face as she cried her way through the night of ceremonies. Mangra and his wife regretted having forced Anju to marry a boy she did not care for. Much later, I bumped into Mangra in distress in the village. He had received a letter from Anju, who now lived with her in-laws in a village about 30 kilometres away. Mangra confided that Anju was unhappy in her new home and wanted to return to the forest armies.

* * *

Boys and girls like Kohli and Anju joining the Naxalites often marked a kind of adolescent rebellion which had a longer history in the area. Kohli had alluded to it. It was hard not to resist comparing Adivasi youths running away from home to live with the guerrilla armies and Adivasis escaping home for six months of the year to carry bricks in the kilns at the peripheries of India's growing metropolitan cities.

A few years ago, in the spring of 2002, I had travelled overnight by train to follow several Adivasi friends from another village in Jharkhand, the village in which I had lived then, to one of the thousands of brick factories on the banks of the River Hooghly outside Kolkata. There, on the shores of that murky grey vastness, Adivasis came to do all the work that the local Bengalis considered too demeaning to do themselves. They broke their backs carrying bricks in and out of kilns. Men shouldered wooden poles weighed down with hampers of bricks at either end. The women balanced a plank of wood on their heads upon which were stacked two columns of eight bricks. Line after line of workers, moving brick after brick. Unregistered, unprotected and undocumented, it was on the backs of these invisible armies of low-caste labourers that a brand new India was being forged.

I lived with my village friends in the dismal slum that the brick kiln owners called 'housing' for just over a week, marvelling at the fact that they would have to live there for twenty-four more. The mud houses in the villages were like palaces in comparison. In the same way that the Central Reserve Police Force camps seemed to devour the darkness of the villages with their floodlights, the brick kiln was surrounded with lamp posts and lit throughout the night while the labour camp adjacent to the kiln was shrouded in darkness. In the slum camp we ate, drank and slept in tiny rooms with galvanised tin roofs so low that you could not stand upright. They absorbed the sweltering heat to such a degree that during the daytime the ceiling was too hot to touch. Six people, barely able to squeeze into the room, slept side-by-side and were savaged all night by mosquitoes. Three taps served 500 people with drinking water. There was no sanitation, just the riverbank for both bathing and defecating.

Adivasis going to the brick kilns were almost always duped by the contractors and employers who hired them, returning home with meagre savings, if any, to show for all their hard work. Despite these horrific conditions, the youths perceived their own participation in this migration as a temporary space away from the constraints of village life. Freedom from parents, freedom to live out their fantasies with prohibited love affairs and an opportunity to see a different world.

There were, of course, important differences between migrating as construction labour and joining the guerrilla armies. Differences that led Kohli to join the Naxalites. Although at first sight, living with a guerrilla squad may seem a more dangerous proposition than working in a brick factory, everyone knew that the construction industry was responsible for large numbers of deaths and serious injuries. Indeed, according to a report by the UN International Labour Organisation in 2005, there were 40,000 industrial fatalities in India per year (so annually about sixty times more deaths than those reported to be a result of the Naxal conflict).[1] Moreover, in the guerrilla armies there was the opportunity to learn to read and write, acquire medical skills, and operate new technologies—mobile phones, computers and guns. And although the guerrillas were not paid, there were also no contractors who swindled them. On Anju's wedding day, exasperated by her attempts to tighten her petticoat, Lila succinctly summed up the differences between staying in the villages and migrating as manual labour, versus living in the guerrilla armies: '*Didi*, can't you see—all those who stay with the *Jungle Sarkar* get fat!'

Perhaps life for Adivasi youths was indeed more comfortable in the Naxalite armies than going out to work but what struck me was how, just as the opportunity to migrate to distant places for six months of the year had become part and parcel of the social fabric of Adivasi life in the hills and forests, so too had the ability to join the Naxalites.

* * *

Like so many guerrilla insurgencies, the Naxalites aimed to follow Mao's proposal, made famous by Che Guevara: 'the guerrilla must move amongst the people as a fish swims in the sea.' But given the long history of Adivasis keeping outsiders at arm's length in this region, how had the Naxalites befriended the Adivasis? Why did the Adivasis come to treat the guerrilla armies as a home away from home?

Sometime during the start of my stay in Lalgaon, Kohli's father, Mangra, had talked to me about the arrival of the guerrillas. It was an October evening and I had walked to their house at the edge of the forest, just five minutes away from where I lived with Somwari.

Their courtyard was a very busy place. A room was being erected to the side of the main hut and the new mud walls glowed golden brown in the late evening sun. A neat pile of tiles lay in front of the room. Painstakingly hand-moulded by Kohli's parents, the clay had been slowly baked over three days in an oven they carved into the earth. Eight men were laying the roof, an intricate framework of bamboo poles on which the mud tiles tightly clasped each other. These homemade tiles were far better than any of the factory-manufactured ones that had become fashionable in the local towns. Like the mud walls, the hand-made terracotta tiles kept the house cool in the summer and warm in the winter. And when the rain fell on the tiles, it rang through the house like a dancing melody.

Somwari and her husband had been there since early that morning, helping to build the room. Everyone offered their labour for free, knowing that Kohli's parents would do the same for them. This form of labour exchange, a common practice between Adivasi households, was called '*madaiti*' (help). Adivasis built each other's houses, sowed each other's fields, and harvested each other's crops without getting paid—just with the goodwill that the other would do the same for them when needed. At the end of the day, the person whose work was being done always threw a party to mark their appreciation of this solidarity.

Arriving towards the end of the building activities, I went to help Somwari stitch together *sal* leaves into plates and cups for the party, using the veins of discarded leaves as thread. Adivasis in Lalgaon lived off the nature that surrounded them, creating things that were biodegradable. Their forested homes had barely been touched by the waste generated by the world of consumerism. It was rare to find polythene bags or plastic bottles in Adivasi *haats* or plastic utensils or furniture in their houses. They took great care of both their houses and their surrounding environment, wrapping their shopping in leaves, cloth baskets, or pouches they had made in the folds of their saris or *lungis*. Winnowing baskets, fishing nets, pots and pans, bows and arrows were all made at home or by nearby craftsmen from local materials. It was also a rare case that, no matter how poor the inhabitants, one found a house that was not spotlessly clean.

Kohli's mother had prepared a simple meal of rice and spinach broth to feed all those who had come to help build the house. But what everyone was gasping for at the end of a hard day's work was the rice beer she had been brewing over the previous eight days and the fresh *mahua* wine she had distilled the night before. With the last of the mud tiles placed on the roof, the atmosphere was jovial. Laughter echoed over the clank of the nearby hand pump as the water gushed out and people washed the mud off themselves. Soon the merry crowd was seated around the courtyard relaxing and drinking. Kohli's mother served fried spicy pork alongside the beer and the wine. Somebody began beating the *mandar*, a local drum, and soon several men and women were holding hands, dancing in a circle.

As the party sang and whirled into the night, Mangra began to talk of the guerrillas. He said that in the beginning all the Oraon Adivasi families I could see around me viewed the guerrillas with the same suspicion as they did the forest guards and the police, and gave them a wide berth.

Although the Naxalites wore a slightly different uniform to the state officials, their leaders were also of high caste, light-skinned and tall. Like other outsiders, the Naxalites seemed at first to court the very people whom the Adivasis mistrusted. These were the middle-caste Sahu traders in the village market from whom Adivasis bought their kerosene, oil and spices. A few of these traders doubled up as contractors controlling the trade in forest products from the region and for whom the Adivasis scoured the forests for *kendu* leaves to make the Indian *bidi* cigarettes, *mohallan* leaves for leaf plates, *sal* seeds to make oil and soap, and truffles and other delicacies that got a high price in the market. These traders gave Adivasis a pittance for their labour, piled their Tata trucks high with the valued goods, and thundered out of the forests, leaving behind a cloud of dust.

Over time however, Mangra said, the Naxalites won them over. How? I asked. Mangra flicked his torch on and asked me to follow him.

We walked across the rice fields and into the centre of the village. A stone's throw from his tea-shack, Mangra pointed to a ruin. A pile of concrete rubble stood out amidst all the mud constructions. I had noticed it before. It was the Forest Rest House. The Naxalites bombed it and then set fire to the seven trucks that were parked outside, which the contractors used to take away logs. The forest rangers had been threatened by the Naxalites before, but after that action they never returned. Mangra said that that was when they first began to refer to the Naxalites as our *Jungle Sarkar*, our Forest State.

The next attacks, Mangra said, were on criminals who had long roamed the forested regions. A highwayman, who held up trucks and public jeeps to rob the people on board before disappearing into the forest, was apprehended about 40 kilometres away but brought back to Lalgaon to be killed. Three bullets were fired into his head and his body was left at the river crossing for all to see.

Then, Mangra said, the *Jungle Sarkar* got rid of the contractors who had won state tenders to collect *kendu* leaves from the area.

The *kendu* leaf collection was the region's most lucrative trade and until then had been dominated by a few Brahmin families from the agricultural plains who controlled both the formal economy and the black market in leaves. The *Jungle Sarkar*, Mangra said, had not only replaced these crooks with men from the village but had also raised the wages for the leaf collection.

At first it reinforced the similitude in my mind between the Naxalites and the Sicilian *mafiosi*. A group that muscled in, shoved out the big boys, and replaced them with their own. The Naxalites seemed to be a protection racket, albeit one that incorporated the local people on more agreeable terms and perhaps with a greater threat of violence than their predecessors.

But Mangra said that the *Jungle Sarkar* also established schools and free health camps. They built and funded four schools in the vicinity, although if you visited them you would think that they were run by a private group, an NGO. They also schooled the youths who joined the guerrilla armies. Mobile health camps were held in the local villages at least thrice a year. The guerrillas brought in doctors from outside the region and provided medicines for free. I later saw one of the health camps in operation in Lalgaon. It had attracted hundreds of people from all the nearby villages. In an area where there were no doctors or functioning healthcare centres and where the fees of unregistered medical practitioners and witchdoctors could plunge households into serious debt, I began to see why, for people like Mangra, the Naxalites had tried much harder in serving them than the state had.

Mangra, however, was not done trying to explain to me the reach of the Naxalites. Most importantly, he said, it was those imperceptible little things that you couldn't easily measure—the small things—that counted. I asked him what he meant.

* * *

Mangra began by recounting his first meeting with Parasji. When the guerrilla leader appeared in their courtyard, Mangra was eating his supper. He usually hid whenever an outsider was thought to be poking about in the village, leaving his wife to make excuses by saying he wasn't home and that he had gone into the forests. But that evening Parasji surprised them. He came after dark—most outsiders would make sure to leave the forest areas by dusk—and caught them off-guard. There was no time to escape so Mangra decided to take control of the situation.

He sent Kohli to borrow a neighbour's chair but Parasji insisted on sitting on the floor on an old jute sack, just as everyone else did in the villages. Mangra said he looked weary, as though he had been hunting in the woods. Parasji, addressing Kohli's mother with great respect as *chachi* (aunt), asked her whether there was any leftover food. The request threw her into a panic. That night, as there was absolutely nothing else in the house to eat, she had only made a meagre corn meal, *ghatha*, which they would never serve guests.

Parasji seemed to sense the woman's distress and said that just a little bit of *ghatha* would do. He forestalled her, however, from fetching milk from the village to serve with the *ghatha*. When Kohli returned with the pale pink plastic chair, they were taken aback that Parasji gently refused it saying that they should never bring one on his account or for any other Naxalite.

It was a cold winter and Parasji spent the night with them, sleeping in the front room. He was running a fever, so they covered him with all the blankets that they could find. At dawn Mangra brought the local quack—the only kind of doctor in the vicinity—who had a quick look at Parasji, gave him some malaria medicine, and advised him to rest. Within a few hours a Naxalite squad came by and took Parasji away.

Mangra said Parasji returned a few days later to thank them for looking after him and to reimburse them for the quack's fees.

That was how their friendship began. After Parasji, the family also met Gyanji, Ashokji, Ganeshji, Madhusudanji and other Naxalites. But it was Parasji, Mangra said, who held a special place in their family.

Over time they understood these men as fellow human beings and started to differentiate between them—that some Naxalites were 'soft' and others 'hard'; some easily lost their patience and others were peacemakers; some were shambolic and others, perfectionists; some were full of energy and others were lazy lay-abouts. They sought out Gyanji for advice on all kinds of decisions—into which school to enrol their child and into which family to give their daughter's hand in marriage. They teased Sureshji for his tedious orations saying, 'everything has a price but Sureshji's speeches were free.' Nonetheless, be it Parasji, Sureshji or Gyanji or any one of the other Naxalite leaders, *ji* was a local affix of respect which was curiously used by even the local police for the rebel leaders—there came to be, over time, a big difference in the way the villagers treated the Naxalite guerrillas and the way they treated other high-caste outsiders.

Security and conflict experts have debated whether people are coerced, or whether it is 'greed' or 'grievance' that leads them to throw in their lot with rebel movements such as the Naxalites. In the absence of adequate reporting and research, the situation infamously referred to in Guatemala as 'caught between two armies'[2] became known in India as the 'sandwich theory' where people were sandwiched between the fire of the state and that of the Maoists.[3] Slowly, first-hand accounts of these regions emerged, giving more agency to people's involvement with the guerrillas.

Just as the debates on the Vietnam War had drawn attention to the rational cost-calculating economic peasant who participated in revolution only to improve his future position,[4] and others have more recently emphasised the role of 'greed' in their econometric analysis of worldwide civil conflicts,[5] in India some analysts have stressed the significance of utilitarian benefits in joining the rebels. The Naxalites were marauders whose financial predation and indiscriminate looting drew angst-ridden youth and poverty struck tribals to them. The most explicit of such perspectives mapped the Maoist spread onto mining areas to show that the mines served as a cash register for a loose confederation of militias whose local commanders were in it for the money alone; it was no coincidence that the rebels were found in India's mineral-rich areas for it was the prospect of extortion from that wealth which explained their proliferation.[6]

Rejecting the role of 'greed', others stressed the role of 'grievance' and the significance of the 'moral economy' in granting people the agency to participate in the insurgency.[7] They focused on the significance of extensive poverty, low literacy rates, limited employment opportunities, social oppression and human rights violations, which moved people into rebellion; those on the margins of survival joined the guerrillas because the insurgents addressed their grievances.[8] An extreme version of the grievance argument turned revolutionary mobilisation into a politics of identity, and in recent years spotlighted the dispossession of Adivasis from their land and forests by mining developments, turning the Naxalites into an Adivasi movement.[9] A spontaneous uprising of India's last original inhabitants came about as a result of this dispossesion, consisting of Adivasis who had nothing left but to take up arms to fight for their land to prevent their own annihilation. The 'politics of communism' was, thus, superseded by the 'politics of indigeneity'.

Clearly the Naxalite effort to set up health camps and schools, and their attempts at mobilising people around land rights or forest rights were important in winning support. But over the time I lived in Lalgaon, I realised that, regardless of the success or failure of their programmes and campaigns, the much deeper appeal of the Naxalites was the respect and dignity with which they treated the Adivasis, looking upon them as equal human beings.

What mattered the most in winning over Adivasis was the Naxalite ideology of egalitarianism which guided their humaneness and nurtured easily overlooked subtle interactions between people. The Naxalites paid attention to how one was spoken to, the tone of voice that was used, the terms of respect with which they addressed people. They paid attention to the way a house was entered, whether they left their footwear outside the door or not, whether they sat on the floor or on a chair above everyone else. They made it a point to share food, drink and even eat from the same plate. They joked and teased the villagers with the ease of familiarity. It was these, the 'small things' as Mangra had said, that enabled the guerrillas to win local people's hearts and minds.

The Naxalite ability to develop relations of emotional intimacy, based on their egalitarian ideals, is why boys like Kohli felt comfortable joining the guerrilla armies and had faith in leaders like Parasji or Gyanji. In the armies, over time, new recruits could get enthused about the Naxalite political struggles for better wages, land and forest rights, or calling the state to account. Some became interested in preserving their tribal languages and creating a written script, as the Naxalites had encouraged in the Gond tribal areas of Chhattisgarh. A few Adivasis even became interested in communist history and ideology, in debating the necessity of revolutionary war against the Indian state, and in the vision of a wider global march to a communist society. But in attracting Adivasis to their armies, the humaneness of the rebels was perhaps more important than the material grievances they addressed.

The egalitarian values that led them to treat others as equal human beings also explained why Naxalite armies were considered a sanctuary for society's misfits. There was, for instance, Sureshji, a Naxalite zonal secretary, who was the son of a Dalit mother and sired by a higher-caste man whose identity he did not know. In the villages of the plains where he was born, not only was Sureshji ostracised for being a Dalit and a bastard, but he also suffered from leprosy, a disease highly stigmatised in India. He had a BA in History and had worked for an NGO, but it was only when he joined the Naxalites that he felt that he was treated with dignity.

Jitesh was another kind of misfit: an Oraon who had ended up working as a servant for an Indian Administrative Service officer since he was twelve years old. A school teacher had got him the job, to cook the officer's food in return for an education. He served the officer for six years in Delhi and Rohtasgarh. Meanwhile, back at home in Lalgaon his brother was accused of murdering his neighbour and Jitesh's name was filed in the case as a collaborator. His brother joined a Naxalite platoon to evade capture and jail. Jitesh, upon his return from Rohtasgarh, went to live in his mother's natal village. There he fell in love with a girl from a different tribe and before they knew it, a child was born out of wedlock. Now that he had to provide for his daughter and her mother, he had no option but to bring his new family back to Lalgaon where he had a house and some land. Haunted by the murder accusations wherever he went, he too joined a Naxalite platoon. His parents were distressed; one son with the Naxalites was acceptable, but two was too much. What if they lost both sons? Although he eventually decided they were right and went to work as a manual labourer in Gujarat, the Naxalites had provided a safe haven for him when he could not fit back into village life for fear of being incarcerated for the murder.

As more and more Adivasis spent time with the Naxalites, and married men and women in their armies, the guerrillas became a part of the kinship networks in the area. Whereas for high-caste leaders, like Gyanji, joining the movement had meant breaking with their past and their families, for the Adivasi youth who formed the rank and file of the movement, the Naxalites represented a continuity rather than stark rupture from the life they lived, a home away from home. While the Indian government keenly represented the guerrillas as terrorising and coercing Adivasis into the movement, Adivasi youth moved freely in and out of the guerrilla armies, almost like they were visiting an uncle or an aunt.

Ideology and politics, often treated as abstract theoretical concepts or ones associated with people in high places, are inscribed into our everyday lives—in the ways we behave towards each other and the relationships we forge. It was the ideology of the Naxalites—the priority they gave to developing egalitarian values—that generated their daily efforts to supersede the deep hierarchies of caste and class that mark Indian society, thus creating an affinity with the Adivasi communities they found themselves amidst. Imagining and attempting to create a more egalitarian world, they nurtured bonds of emotional intimacy and familial networks running between the villages and the guerrilla armies, such that Adivasi youths moved in and out of the squads as though they were another home. And though the same bonds eventually also came to undermine rebel support, it was the development of these kinship relations between the armies and the villages that enabled the guerrillas to move amongst the people as a fish swims in the sea.[10]

* * *

As the years went by, more Adivasi children went to live with the Naxalites and the guerrillas' presence became ever more pervasive in their day-to-day lives. They had become, after all, 'our *Jungle Sarkar* (Forest State),' Mangra said.

After getting rid of the forest officials, police, thieves and contractors, and establishing their own schools and mobile camps, the Naxalites took up redistributive measures. They filled the ponds with little fish for communal fishing. People fished together with mosquito nets and village-made fishing baskets and shared the harvest.

Although the Naxalites did not take away anyone's land for redistribution—they said that here in the hills everyone was only just about getting by—they redistributed 40 acres that had once been taken by the state for a cooperative farm. The state farm, like many state projects, had never functioned and the Naxalites split the land into two parts. Half the land was to be equally shared between the fifty Kherwar Adivasis who lived in the vicinity and had only small parcels of land. The other half was used to cultivate rice for the guerrilla armies. They also gave disused state buildings—for instance those that once belonged to the forest officials—as homes to poor families whose houses were collapsing.

They redistributed, too, the right to pick *mahua* flowers from the forests. Although some people owned *mahua* trees on their land, the trees in the forest officially belonged to the state forest department though it gave the people of the area the right to use their produce. In April, villagers would sleep under the trees, waiting for the drip-drop of the pulpy small yellow blossom at dawn. The flowers were collected, dried and then distilled into *mahua* wine. In times of need, many households lived off the money earned from selling the dried flowers or the wine. *Mahua* wine was sold at 12 rupees a bottle. My sister, Somwari, usually made five bottles a week, earning her enough to buy spices, soap, kerosene oil, matches and other essentials for the week. The trees were valued not only as a source of wine but also because their seeds could be pressed for cooking oil. However, although the village population had increased, the number of *mahua* trees had not. There was not an endless supply of trees to meet everybody's needs. The Naxalites conducted a survey of the *mahua* trees in the forest and then, over the course of many meetings with all the villagers, re-divided the trees to make sure every household had equal access to them.

Apart from these forms of redistribution, any major dispute in the village, especially those between the higher castes and the

Adivasis, were soon being settled in 'people's courts' set up by the Naxalites. State courts, notorious for taking years to resolve disputes, leaving families crippled in debt and eventually settling in favour of those who paid the most as bribes, had in any case been discarded by most villagers. The Naxalite people's courts gained the reputation of delivering justice fast and at no cost. In Lalgaon, I had seen these people's courts resolve a battle between two brothers over the right to pick the flowers from eight *mahua* trees in the forest, decide whether or not an inter-caste elopement deserved to be reprimanded and even make a ruling on the allotment of a tract of land to enable someone to build a house.

The Naxalites also arranged other activities, Mangra said. In the rainy season there were football tournaments in which teams from all the surrounding villages participated. In 2009, I saw one in operation. Thirty-two teams, each representing a village, had entered the competition and for several days the area behind my house turned into a festival. Bamboo posts were erected as goals, a mike and generator system were brought from the nearest town and stalls were set up around the field selling tea, fried eggs, chickpeas and tobacco. I was invited by the young men to distribute the prizes and found myself handing over a 10-kilogram goat along with a 7,000-rupee silver shield to the winning team. The team that came second got a 7-kilogram goat and a 5,000-rupee bronze shield and the one which came third, a 5-kilogram goat and a 3,000-rupee copper shield. Five gas lamps were awarded to the best players. I was told that 1.5 lakh rupees was spent in total. It all ended with a dance party on the playing field.

In the winter, the Naxalites organised a festival to commemorate the Adivasi anti-colonial rebel heroes, attracting thousands of people to Lalgaon until late into the night. The first time it took place in 2003, 20,000 people gathered for over ten days in Lalgaon. Guests were invited from Ranchi and as far away as Delhi—including journalists, human rights activists and some politicians. Electricity generators were brought in. Dance troupes, music bands and street theatre acts came from afar in a celebration of the revolutionary spirit. A famous sculptor was brought from Rohtasgarh in Bihar to make a memorial of the tribal rebels, 20 feet high into the sky. The villagers criticised the *Jungle Sarkar* for getting an artist from the plains whose sculptures of the legs of the rebel leaders were made as though they were those of people from the plains; they complained they were so fat that they looked like they had elephantiasis. An Adivasi artist, they said, would have created more lifelike Adivasi tribal rebels. However, despite these minor quibbles, the festive spirit was fondly remembered and resurrected annually, albeit on a smaller scale, and the memorial left a lasting impression on the Lalgaon landscape.

The guerrillas expended the most energy on their protests and rallies. Daytime marches, torch-lit processions and road blocks— the villagers participated in all of them, Mangra said. Under banners protesting privatisation, liberalisation and globalisation, they demonstrated against inflation, agitated for employment under the National Rural Employment Guarantee Act and picketed against the corruption in the Public Distribution System of food for the poor. They burned effigies of Prime Minister Manmohan Singh, Deputy Chairman of the Planning Commission Montek Singh Ahluwalia, responsible for many of the trade and liberalisation reforms of the Indian economy, and Home Minster P. Chidambaram. Mangra chuckled as he recalled the exaggerated potbellies of the effigies, made by the villagers to reflect the politicians' insatiable appetite for the food and resources meant for the poor.

The local agitations were followed by several other rallies to escalate their grievances to the district capital, to Ranchi city, and even to Delhi as part of a wider open mass organisation of the Naxalites formed to protest the displacement of Adivasis in the name of national development—displacement by dams, steel plants and power plants.

Mangra said, 'Before the Naxalites arrived, many of us weren't even aware what a "minister" was. We didn't know that the National Rural Employment Guarantee Act was to ensure us work. We had no idea that we were entitled to Below Poverty Line cards to get subsidised rations. Most of us had never left the region to even venture to Ranchi city, let alone Delhi. The Naxalites educated us on what was due to us from the state; in fact, on what the state was supposed to be.'

* * *

But the more involved the Naxalites got in their lives, the more the problems that emerged, Mangra said. Some people felt left out of the organisation of the festivals and the tournaments. Some accused others of not turning up to the rallies. Parents didn't always like the people that their children had become after being with the guerrilla armies and were worried that they would lose them altogether. Some people were left unhappy about the decisions taken in the people's courts. Some people were tried in the people's courts for allegedly being police informers and those judged guilty were shot dead, creating fear amongst everyone. And then came the violence of the security forces of the state into the hills.

The state security began climbing into the hills in a force of 500 or more and used the local school and the disused primary health centre as barracks. They had no qualms about being brutally oppressive towards the villagers or using them as human shields to enter the forests and track Naxalites.

On one occasion, during my sojourn in Lalgaon, the rebels blew up the health centre in an attempt to prevent the security forces from occupying the building. Open firing between the two sides followed and the next morning the villagers paid the price.

Women recounted how the security forces had torn down their doors, pulled them out by their hair and accused them of harbouring 'terrorists'. One woman was so scared that she fainted. Another woman died of a heart attack as she watched her son and husband being mercilessly beaten.

In a neighbouring village, in April 2009, at the time of the elections for the lower houses of parliament, the Central Reserve Police Forces arbitrarily killed five villagers, claiming they were Maoists. The guerrillas had blown up two Central Reserve Police Force soldiers who were part of a polling party going to man the electoral voting booths, and the security forces were retaliating. People from Lalgaon left in truckloads on a rally to protest the killings of the villagers.

Everyone was now afraid whenever the security forces crested the hills, terrified of getting caught in a crossfire with the Maoists. Moreover, they said, the guerrillas could escape into the woods, but those left behind in the villages had to face the brunt of police brutality. Those who could fled to the houses of their relatives in other villages when the state forces came to the villages. Others considered joining the guerrilla columns. Still others wanted to abandon the area entirely.

12

NIGHT THREE

Although we were one man down, I felt a new spring in my step.
I knew I had no choice but to place my trust fully in the guerrillas.
I was completely in their hands and would have to let go of all my
fears to concentrate on mastering the art of night walking.

A tinkle of water echoed in the darkness. Soon a small stream
appeared in front of us as a black ditch. A soldier from Section
A was deputed to stand at one end and shine his torch steadily
across it. We forded the brook one after another. I had learnt
that the gleam of one solitary light in the dark would pass unno-
ticed whereas twenty-nine torchlights switching on and off
might raise alarm.

As soon as we all reached the opposite bank, Vikas rounded us
up. He said a highway lay ahead. It was unlikely to be busy so
late at night but, if it was, we were to split into our sections and
go across in small groups, taking care to duck behind the bushes
and not get caught in the glare of a headlight.

We had walked for less than ten minutes when we heard what
sounded like crashing waves. Rolling in one after another, they
got louder and louder. It was the sound of mammoth trucks

hurtling down the highway. From behind a bamboo thicket, we watched them thunder past. They were travelling in a convoy, 20 metres apart from each other, going at about 50 miles an hour. It seemed dangerously fast for the potholed road they were on. Their headlights beaconed out like antennae, lighting up the rear of the truck ahead of them. Curiously enough they were not honking, which is usually the first indication of vehicles on the road in India, even when there is nothing to beep at.

They were conveying coal in their open backs, Gyanji whispered, wondering why they were on a diversion from the major highway artery that they would normally travel. These were beasts on a silent mission, tearing through the country in the darkness of the night.

Like the security force camp that we had crossed a few hours ago, the coal trucks seemed like they were on an alien hunt, aloof from the rest of the environment. They were the latest face of the 'development' mission that for centuries had been looting the forests, land and water from the Adivasis. The new growth gurus had promised that if the mining development across the country were accelerated, it could create 6 million jobs.[1] But they never talked about sharing the profit with the locals, nor did they guarantee that local people would get the best of the new jobs.

Mining operations in Jharkhand had historically seen the influx of outsiders who took away the benefits; Bihari or Bengali high-caste middle-class men and women who had, over the last century, settled in cities such as Ranchi, Dhanbad and Jamshedpur to occupy the new housing, the new schools and promenade in the newly manicured parks, whether they now belonged to Tata or the Central Coalfields. In Jamshedpur, popularly dubbed 'Tatanagar', even the name of the Adivasi village, Sakchi, on which Jamshed Tata built his steel plant, was erased. The Tata Group went on to become India's largest multinational conglomerate and is now operating steel plants in the

UK as well. Meanwhile, the Adivasis who lived on the land of the original steel plant can be found trying to eke out a living by scouring the waste for iron discarded in the smelting process.

The latest mining developments promised barbed wire fences, security guards and mining mafia rising around the new migrants to keep the locals out. The few locals needed as collaborators could perhaps penetrate these new internal borders but most Adivasis would have no other option but to live on the margins of the mines, towns and cities, scavenging for a livelihood on the fringes of the developments, reduced to abject poverty. With their autonomy over their lives taken away, they might, if lucky, seek a daily-wage job carrying coal or iron ore, becoming another silver-lipped dark face on a Sebastião Salgado photograph. But it was just as likely that they would be displaced entirely from the region, forced right out, enabling the mining companies to crow in jubilation, as they have in other parts of the country (such as in Odisha), that they have reduced levels of poverty.

For the moment, however, there were some hiccups curtailing the expansion of the mining companies. They couldn't easily access the land. The Adivasi rebellions of the late 1800s against the colonial government taking over their land had, with the intervention of some Christian missionaries, eventually resulted in special protection being granted to Adivasi lands. Only an Adivasi could buy the land of another Adivasi. These protection measures were constitutionally reinforced and other laws were added—such as the need for the consensus of at least 80 per cent of the local people to buy their land. Although Memoranda of Understanding had been signed between large multinational corporations and the government, it wasn't easy to acquire land.

Human rights activists had claimed that this was the real reason behind 'Operation Green Hunt'. In the name of fighting the guerrillas, the government was covering the rich mining areas with military barracks to make life brutally unpleasant, accusing locals who did not comply with them of being Maoists so that eventually they would either be forced to leave or could simply be arrested or killed. It was a slow clearing of the ground, a slow purging of the people.

The last of the trucks sped past. We counted at least fifty of them. In front of us lay a bare tarmac road and then the rice fields again. The coast was clear. We ran across, one after another. The paved road beneath felt cold and hard.

It was past ten o'clock when we finally reached the outskirts of the village where we were to have our dinner. We had been walking for at least five hours. Two runners had been sent ahead of the platoon to ensure one plate of food was kept aside from thirty different houses so that all the fighters could eat. Once again we congregated in the forests by the village, waiting in the peripheries while it was decided who would eat at which house.

'Now you've truly become a guerrilla; it's the trademark of a soldier to be able to fall asleep anywhere anytime.' Gyanji's chuckle woke me up. I seemed to have learnt the art of taking short power naps, shutting my eyelids at any opportunity and entering deep sleep at the drop of a hat.

Food was ready. I followed Gyanji to a house in the middle of the main hamlet. I was sorry to awaken the residents of the house who had already gone to sleep.

'*Lal salaam* (Red salute),' greeted the old woman who opened the heavy wooden door to the mud house, holding a kerosene lamp aloft.

Laying out jute sacks on the floor for us to sit on, she brought out the steel plates on which food had been kept aside for us. Gyanji was very apologetic about the lateness of our visit, but she said it was no trouble at all. She fetched a stainless-steel jug of water. Gyanji and I sat in the front room of the house while Kohli and Gyanji's bodyguard remained outside to keep watch.

I wondered whether Gyanji knew about Kohli's reasons for joining the Naxalites. I knew the story the Naxalites liked to tell—and which their supporters in New Delhi liked to hear (those who revelled in the fact that there were still remnants of a leftist agenda being played out somewhere in the distant hinterlands of the country). It was that the Adivasis had little choice but to take up arms to defend themselves against the land grabs by mining operations and development projects instigated by multinational corporations in collusion with the Indian state.

Yes, sighed Gyanji. Boys like Kohli are wonderful, he said. The problem is that they are too innocent. That's how the Adivasis generally are, he said. 'They just come and go as they please, moving back and forth between their villages and the guerrilla armies.' When they went for a short time, it was no cause for concern, Gyanji said, for although the Naxalites did not permit alcohol, the boys needed to quench their thirst.

I bit my tongue. I didn't like his high-caste prejudice—the flip side of the image of the wildness, savagery and barbarism of the Adivasi was an idea of their innocence, vulnerability and gullibility. Despite their egalitarian ideals, which seemed to have won the guerrillas some success in attracting Adivasis to their movement, it seemed hard for even the most sensitive leaders to overcome these deep-seated high-caste stigmas towards India's tribes.

Our views about alcohol were also not in sync. The Naxalites forbade any form of alcohol consumption in their guerrilla squads. They were even against its production in the villages. It was a sore point between Gyanji and me and we had argued about this issue before. My perspective was that homemade alcohol and its consumption by Adivasis in villages like those of Lalgaon was a crucial part of Adivasi sociality and the guerrillas ought not to interfere. Rice beer (*hadia*) and *mahua* wine were sacred and men and women together equally partook in their consumption. Guests were usually welcomed with *hadia* or *mahua*. There was even an old saying that only enemies were given one cup, friends were always served two or more.

The Adivasi culture of drinking was very different from most Indian households, in which men would rarely admit publicly that they consumed alcohol but in fact spent fortunes on expensive Indian-made spirits such as Royal Challenge whisky or Old Monk rum. These were imbibed behind closed curtains, without women present, and often consumed quickly and guiltily. I had told Gyanji that his own prejudices about drinking alcohol were based on such high-caste masculine cultures of drinking and that this Adivasi custom was very different and ought to be valued.

I couldn't help myself. 'I understand that you can't have drunken soldiers in times of war when the enemy is at your threshold, but perhaps every now and again, you should brew alcohol in the armies—Adivasi-style—for special occasions, and let everyone just have a bit of fun,' I suggested.

'You can't mummify your Adivasis as they are,' Gyanji retorted. It was no use valorising and preserving what they have right now, he said, they had to change. 'Whether you like it or not, it is inevitable that their cultures will be obliterated with development.'

There was a fundamental difference between our perspectives. For a movement so keen on building an egalitarian world, ultimately their path seemed to be based on ignoring the forms of egalitarianism that were already alive and well in Adivasi communities. It was an issue that had divided the communist movement. There were people still debating what Marx and Engels had really thought about the Russian *mir*, a form of early common ownership of land, and whether it could pass directly from that peasant form to higher forms of communist common ownership, or whether it was necessary for Russia to go through the same process of historical development as England had and which included the spread of capitalism.[2] But this was neither the time nor the place to argue about the stages of the revolution versus the virtues of working with revolutionary utopianism, so I let Gyanji's comment pass.

The problem, he said, was that young Adivasi men often went away from the squads and did not return. It was then that the Naxalites felt they had failed in delivering a political education. People came to them from very different backgrounds, he said, but they needed to be educated to recognise the violence and inequities around them, and to want to change the world. They needed to be prepared, he said, to take on not just the world around them but also the structures and injustices that they could not see. They needed to understand the Naxalite programme of long preparation to seize power and commit to it. But this is where we often fail, Gyanji said. It was one of the reasons that he felt they needed to start recruiting from the universities and colleges again.

'If there is only continuity rather than the ability to imagine change and act towards it, we might just as well all be bees,' Gyanji said.

We rinsed our plates outside and returned to rest in the front of the house to wait for the others to finish eating. The silent act of pouring water from the jug for each other seemed to have washed away some of the tension between us. But I was full of questions I knew Gyanji would not like to hear. Might the Naxalite ability to provide a home away from home for the Adivasi youth not only be a strength but also represent a weakness, an Achilles heel?

As though he had read my thoughts, Gyanji, who was playing with a mobile phone, exclaimed, 'I knew it!' He showed me the phone, flipping through some pictures. A pale-skinned woman with long dark hair, a pouting mouth and a slinky black top which barely covered her breasts was staring at us. There was another picture of a semi-naked woman. Then a man and a woman kissing. I couldn't make out whether they had any clothes on or not. It was soft porn.

It was Vikas's phone. 'I took it from him. It is just as I suspected,' Gyanji said. At that very moment Vikas walked through the door to say that everyone had eaten and that we should leave. He took a step back when he saw Gyanji holding his phone out to him. 'What is all this?' Gyanji thundered. Vikas looked sheepishly at the ground. He said a local contractor had given him the phone and that the data chip was already in it.

The Naxalites viewed pornography as part of the spread of a feudal imperialist culture that used sex as a weapon to divert the youths from the problems and struggles of society. Gyanji seemed upset not so much about the soft porn itself but what it meant in relation to the circles of influence—the kind of men—that Vikas must have been moving amongst outside the guerrilla armies.

But before Gyanji could confront Vikas further, Gyanji's bodyguard walked in with Kohli. I looked at all of them. If he stayed long enough with the guerrillas, what would happen to Kohli? Had Vikas once been like Kohli? Or would Kohli turn into another Gyanji?

PART FIVE

VIKAS, FRANKENSTEIN'S MONSTER

13

NIGHT FOUR

'Mother-fucker, bring out the terrorists!' The harsh voices of North Indian men grated loudly in my ear. They were banging and kicking at the heavy teak door of the house in which we were staying. 'Bring out the extremists! We'll burn your house down if you don't!' The chopping of the blades of a helicopter grew increasingly deafening, drowning out the shouts.

I awoke with a start. A silver sky, so heavy with stars that it felt one could just reach out and touch them, peacefully stared down at me. It took a few moments for me to get my bearings. I had been having nightmares again. I needed Somwari. At home in Lalgaon, she would calm me down, helping me get rid of the visions that disturbed my night sleep. She concocted a potion of jungle medicine to help me sleep and placed under my pillow a bar of lead, a piece of turmeric and a section of a clay roof tile, assuring me that they would drive away the evil spirits that were taunting me. I tried to go back to sleep.

The high-pitched buzz grew irritatingly louder. A mosquito beating its wings, 800 times a second, they say. The female Anopheles mosquito carrying *Plasmodium falciparum* was responsible for perhaps more deaths in India than the Naxalite-security force encounters. Every year the disease left at least 1,000 reported dead and 2 million people affected. As the deadliest animal on earth, the mosquito was in fact India's greatest internal threat, yet I had never seen signs of a nationwide government programme to eliminate malaria.

In Lalgaon I slept under a mosquito net, encouraging Somwari to do the same. She was greatly amused by my bedtime ritual, which involved probing with the light of my torch across the net, deep into every corner, trying to find the one mosquito that was bound to have somehow found its way in, intent on keeping me up at night. My deep satisfaction on spotting that bugger would be quickly overtaken by the frenzy of trying to kill it. The best way was to clap and trap it between one's palms but one could also try to pinch or squeeze it as it rested on the net. My brilliant white net had rapidly developed red and black blotches where I had successfully managed to target and squash a few.

The incessant buzz was drilling deeper into my head. It wasn't even the monsoons, the breeding season when the harmony of humming filled the night as the parasites tried to find their soul-mates. In fact, I wasn't sure whether there actually was a mosquito in the vicinity or whether my increasing paranoia was making me imagine the malevolent buzzing. I remembered I had forgotten to take my weekly pill of Lariam and reached into my bag.

It had been a struggle to get my travel clinic in north London to prescribe the drug. On their immunisation maps, India was the land of the *Plasmodium vivax*, which, although it caused recurring malaria, was not as virulent or lethal as the *Plasmodium falciparum* and could be treated with a fusion of chloroquine and paludrine. However, having lived in these regions between 1999 and 2002, I knew that I needed mefloquine; it was vital to protect against *P. falciparum*. One monsoon night in 2001, I had awoken shivering uncontrollably under my blanket. I got up to reach for some warm clothes, but my head was spinning and a sea of glimmering stars rapidly swallowed me as my legs crumbled. Crawling along the floor to a phone, I made a desperate call to a friend, a doctor, who took me straight to hospital. 'Brain fever' is what they called it locally. It was *P. falciparum*, and if not treated immediately, it could turn your brain into jelly before killing you. And so, before I returned to Jharkhand, I insisted to the nurse who saw me in Islington that she prescribe Lariam for me.

It was only much later that I came to know that the US Army had developed Lariam in the 1970s to protect their forces in far-flung places but that it had become infamous for the psychosis it induced: the depression, the paranoia and the hallucinations. 'Horror movie in a pill', it had been labelled, and was allegedly responsible for high numbers of suicides in the defence forces. It was even once suspected to be the reason that some soldiers had killed their wives and then committed suicide at the US Army installation at Fort Bragg in North Carolina. Perhaps more American and British soldiers fell victim to the drug's side effects than they did to the forces they were fighting.

Nevertheless, I refused to believe that my recurrent nightmares of being chased by Indian Air Force helicopters as I ran through the villages of Jharkhand were a consequence of taking Lariam for more than a year. I have always had vivid dreams.

Cringing at the thought of its bitter aftertaste, I pushed the big white pill out of the packet and armed myself with my water bottle. The trick was to take a large swig of water and make the pill float whole down the throat without letting it touch any part of the mouth. But the pill was gigantic. Death by the security forces, death by brain fever, death by Lariam? The choices seemed bleak.

I felt a tap on my shoulder. Then another. Kohli was trying to wake me up. He said it was 3:00 a.m. and we needed to get a move on. We had barely rested for four hours. As I sat up rubbing my eyes, I could see the silhouettes of the others rolling up their mats and folding their blankets. Within minutes there were three parallel lines of guerrillas. I packed my sleeping bag and joined Section B's line for the roll call. Soon we were marching again.

Having hardly slept I felt drained. Someday soon the end would be in sight for me, but for young men like Kohli, it could become a relentlessly gruelling life to be on the move constantly. Several older Adivasi men (in their mid-thirties) whom I had met in Lalgaon told me they had been with the guerrilla armies in their youth, but the nomadic lifestyle of the *Jungle Sarkar* was very difficult and they had eventually given up to settle down for a humdrum existence in the village.

All the senior leaders I met had some chronic health problem or other. Gyanji suffered from a severe form of gastritis and a bad ankle. Parasji had spondylitis. Another, who had been hit on the forehead by a test explosion, was gradually losing his vision in both eyes. Others lived with chronic back aches, bad knees and diabetes.

With such a tough life on the move, it was no wonder that it was difficult to retain Adivasi youths in the struggle year after year. Even Parasji, who had been underground for twenty odd years, who usually seemed so resilient and committed to the cause, sometimes wondered whether a period in prison would give him a much-needed 'holiday'—that's how he put it—from the revolution.

When the sky turned purple at dawn, it felt like we had already been marching all day. But now we were in 'safe' territory, amidst villages of Naxalite sympathisers, so we could soon rest to regain our strength and, after four days and nights on the move, have our first wash.

Relaxing in the shade of a spinney on a hilltop, I couldn't help but smile as I observed one of the young soldiers assuring his mate that he would soon look like the Indian Bollywood actor, Shahrukh Khan, as he gave him a haircut.

Kohli escorted me into the courtyard of a house where, under a rusty hand pump, a bright red plastic bucket with a blue mug neatly hanging off its side awaited me invitingly, overflowing with clean water. From behind a wooden door painted blue, two young girls were watching with shy curiosity, whispering and giggling to each other. The only other sound was the cooing of the doves nesting in the eaves of the clay roof tiles. Kohli waited patiently outside the courtyard as I poured jug after jug of water over myself with my blue sarong tied across my chest.

In the sweltering heat, I relished the coolness of the water. It made my skin tingle and my tired body feel alive. Such pleasure one could derive from the simplest things. One bucket of water was not enough. The hand pump groaned and clanked. Four buckets later, I had washed my guerrilla fatigues too. Relaxed, refreshed and reinvigorated, I walked back with Kohli to where the others were soaking in the sun.

'Oil, *Didi?*' Vikas was holding out a heavy square glass bottle. It looked like an expensive perfume. The label across it read 'Bajaj'—manufacturers of Indian motorbikes and auto-rickshaws, Bajaj was now producing the 'Chanel' of hair oils in the eyes of the lower classes. 'Made from real almonds, thick and fragrant,' he recited, sniffing to inhale the fragrance with his flat nose. 'Smell it, *Didi*. It's much nicer than that pungent Engine mustard oil you've got.'

Clearly proud of his bare muscular arms, he deliberately clenched his fists to flex his biceps. They were glistening with the oil as they emerged from the glittery pale pink sleeveless jumper made from plastic fibres. He had put on this garish vest, considered *haute couture* by the young men in the local town, while his olive-green shirt was drying in the sun. The static made the fibres of his jumper stand out from his body like an electrified psychedelic animal and made him look rather like a peacock, showing off his iridescent plumage.

It was a gesture that reminded me of a certain kind of masculinity prevalent amongst the upwardly mobile lower-middle classes in India. Over the months I had known him, I marked not only the rough ways in which Vikas spoke to his juniors, often coming across as an overbearing bully towards younger men, but also the softer gestures through which he tried to build bonds with others, especially with women, towards whom he could be rather patronising.

In fact, Vikas had shown this kind of machismo in the immediate aftermath of our very first meeting in Lalgaon, the one when he had brashly 'interrogated' me. I had met him again, a few days later, at the strange cooking lesson where the Naxalites were making bombs and had watched him ignite the fuses before running to a safe distance to await the explosion. Later that night, I realised I had left my scarf by the explosion site and ruefully thought it had probably become tinder by then. However, Vikas, who had quietly retrieved it, was soon making a song and dance of restoring it, bowing elaborately with his arms outstretched, holding out the immaculately folded white garment to me. He was probably trying to make up for the 'interrogation', but at the time he struck me as a poor parody of a Bollywood hero coming to the rescue.

When Vikas held out the almond oil bottle, that very same macho hero image flashed before me again. I politely declined his offer, fully aware that the cadre's daily needs were to be fulfilled by only the most basic of commodities: Lifebuoy soap, Colgate toothpaste, Engine mustard oil. Like the soft porn on his mobile phone and his attempts to order chicken curry as a treat for me at our first stop on the march, it was mere bombast and no big deal. His airs and graces nevertheless marked him as being similar to most higher-caste young men in the vicinity and therefore far from the ideal revolutionary that the Naxalites were trying to create, or indeed from the Adivasi communities he had come from.

I walked to the grass mat where Gyanji was darning a hole in his jumper. He was keenly listening to the BBC World Service on the small and battered black transistor radio that he carried with him everywhere. This radio seemed far more important to Gyanji than his rifle. With the speaker pressed against his ear, his head cocked to one side, Gyanji was able to decipher, through the crackle of the white noise, current events in New York or London. The little machine not only brought news of the world into the guerrilla strongholds; it also gave crucial information, faster than internal messages could be delivered, about Naxalites in other parts of the country, arrests that had taken place as well as ambushes and attacks. Someone always listened to the news and reported any important events back to the group.

Gazing down from our vantage point atop the hillock, we could see the villagers quietly going about their daily activities. Some men and women were working in the fields, others were collecting firewood, and still others were grazing their cows, water buffalo and goats. In the distance, at least a dozen people were digging up a road, carrying boulders, and laying gravel across it. A motorbike revved up from that construction site, its grating rumble shattering the silence. It curved around towards us, stopping at the foot of the hill.

A smartly dressed man in black jeans, a black leather jacket and a red cap got off the bike and started walking up the path. His urban modern style was written into his confident gait and he looked out of place in this rural setting. He was holding a white parcel and Vikas went to receive him. I could see them talking halfway up the hill. They seemed to be teasing each other, joking and laughing.

Gyanji said the man was the contractor responsible for building the road we could see in the distance. He reached into a trouser pocket to produce what looked like a booklet and asked Kohli to take it to Vikas because he had run out of receipts. I realised what was going on. The contractor was giving the Maoists some funds and in return Vikas would give him a receipt to show that he had paid his 'tax'.

When Vikas returned, his breast pocket was bulging with money and he was holding the little white box that I had seen earlier in the hands of the contractor. Golden syrup was leaking from the package. Vikas untied the red strings holding it together and opened it to reveal at least thirty pieces of *gulab jamun*—a sweet made of fried dough balls of milk powder, coated in a cardamom, rose water and saffron-flavoured sugar syrup.

Vikas said he had already 'tested' the sweets. He said he had made the contractor eat the first *gulab jamun* to ensure they were not drugged. I noticed, though, that Gyanji did not touch the sweets. I similarly refrained when the box came to me.

Gyanji took Vikas aside and they seemed to have a heated exchange. Gyanji looked annoyed. I could not hear much of what was being said, but I could gather that the altercation was about the contractor and money.

Looking despondent after his chat with Vikas, Gyanji returned to the grass mat and picked up his needle and thread. When Vikas joined the guerrillas—some ten years ago—Gyanji said he had been just like Kohli. He was sweet, innocent and respectful. He came from an Adivasi family like Kohli's. His family were blacksmiths—Lohras not Oraons—and their home was at the base of the plateau where Kohli's family lived. To the side of his small mud house, his father had a furnace for smelting, fired with wood from the forests. Anyone who needed a hoe bent, a plough made, or any other tool, would go to him. Vikas's mother worked as a manual labourer and collected fruit, flowers and leaves to be sold in the market. Together, the family made *mahua* wine and sold it to passers-by to make ends meet. Like Kohli, Vikas too left home in a huff after a minor squabble with his parents. When he came to the guerrillas he had apparently shown great promise. As one of the best military fighters, he quickly rose within the ranks to commanding a platoon and soon went on to the Zonal-level Committee of the movement. But now Gyanji was clearly disappointed in him.

Gyanji said he had heard some days ago that Vikas owned a four-wheel drive Bolero jeep and had recently secretly hosted a lavish second wedding, marrying an educated Oraon woman with a master's degree. Vikas kept the Bolero and the Oraon woman away from his village wife and daughter, in a two-storey brick house that he had constructed for himself in Ranchi city, Gyanji said.

'The only reason why Vikas stays in these armies today,' Gyanji added cynically, 'is because he is earning.'

Those who joined the guerrillas did not get paid. 'To earn' therefore meant that Vikas was in some way lining his own pocket through Naxalite activities. He was secretly diverting resources away from the common needs of the struggle and amassing the wealth for his own private use.

14

ACCELERATING THE REACH OF THE STATE AND CAPITAL

Opportunities for guerrillas to 'earn'—to pocket money for personal use away from common needs—arose from the very processes through which funds were generated by the movement. Aside from the daily food, clothing and medical needs of the soldiers, the Naxalites needed funds for the legal battles of their imprisoned comrades, for political rallies, for health camps and village-based agricultural activities, and for buying and making arms. With neither a trade in drugs nor a rich foreign backer, and with all their activities officially banned as 'terrorist', the guerrillas relied on tapping pre-existing black markets in the areas of their operation. In particular, they had three main sources of funds: large-scale corporations (like mining operations); the illicit economy of forest products (especially *kendu* leaves); and the black economy around state infrastructural development projects (such as the building of roads).

I called the Naxalite methods of funding 'protection rackets'. 'Taxation' is what Gyanji preferred, emphasising that it was money that was in any case illicit, already circulating through corruption rackets, or accumulated by exploiting the labour of the poor. He justified their actions by arguing that they diverted these funds from lining the pockets of rich capitalists to fighting the war of the poor, thereby purifying and cleansing the money by putting it to use for the public good. He added that while they took the money of these rich elites as 'taxes', they would not support their 'anti-people' activities.

With the threat of violence affirmed by their clandestine armies, the Naxalites replaced the earlier state-contractor nexus of black markets in areas they wanted to control.[1] They could do so not only because they had disarmed the area but also because the idea that they were a very powerful organisation, with hidden resources and manpower way beyond the region, had spread rapidly. The myth of their legendary power was based on their secrecy, together with the occasional breach of secrecy, which generated uncertainty about their size and spread; they could be anywhere and everywhere. In areas of new expansion it was possible for someone to suspect that someone else might be involved; for this to create the impression that everyone was involved; for that suspecting person to then become involved; and for this to result in further suspicion, setting off a chain reaction as ever more people became involved. The local elites thus became afraid of not cooperating, and this fear became the basis upon which the Naxalites could offer them protection to access the informal economy of black market resources, which included protection from the possibility of their own rebel activities as the most locally powerful force.

As cadres rose in the ranks to seniority within the underground party, the more the responsibility they were given, to collect money from the contractors, keep accounts, and redistribute funds. Middle-level leaders—those commanding platoons like Vikas, in the Zonal Committees, and in the State-level Committees—all had these financial responsibilities. They had to coordinate with the village elites to decide which of the villagers would become the contractor for any given scheme; agree to what level the chosen contractor would implement the project; ensure that the contractor saved for himself from the construction process only the amount that had been agreed with the Naxalites; and they also had to retrieve a predetermined amount of money from the building process for the guerrilla armies. The complex calculations and negotiations involved in collecting the 'taxes' meant that some of the funds could get 'lost' along the way instead of being redistributed within the movement. There was always the excuse that a contractor claimed that costs had been greater than predicted, that some state officer asked for more than their 'fair' share of the commission, or that somebody needed to be given a 'gift' for some crucial information. In the context of the mines, since most were usually outside the immediate guerrilla stronghold, out of the physical reach of the Naxal leaders, it was entirely possible for the more junior Naxal commander responsible for collecting the funds to demand more than was agreed with his leaders and to pocket the surplus. Because of the need to be clandestine vis-à-vis the Indian government's efforts to hunt them down, it was difficult in all these cases for more senior leaders to check up on the claims of their juniors. The upshot of these circumstances meant that there was always the danger and temptation to squirrel away some of this collected money for personal use—to 'earn', as Gyanji had put it.

* * *

The method of access to funding from which these 'earnings' were syphoned was dependent on the source. For large corporations, including mining operations, the Naxalites demanded a 'tax' from the managers in return for not interfering with their operations. So, while on the one hand they held rallies against the multinational corporations behind the mining operations, had open non-violent mass organisations involving a wide range of people demonstrating against the displacement brought about by such business activities, mobilised workers to agitate for better terms and conditions of work in mines and factories, and sometimes set fire to trucks moving out mineral resources from mining sites, on the other hand, they did not destroy the mining operations altogether.

For instance, the easiest bombing target—a 267-kilometre-long Essar pipeline transporting iron ore slurry—was left largely untouched. The pipeline ran straight through the heart of the guerrilla territory in the forests of Bastar, Chhattisgarh. From the Bailadila mountain, where 8 million tonnes of iron ore were processed a year, it carried the ore slurry to the port of Visakhapatnam in Andhra Pradesh where it was made into pellets to be shipped to an Essar steel plant in Gujarat. This tacit co-existence of the Maoists and mining companies made global headlines when, in 2010, Wikileaks released a diplomatic cable sent by the US consulate in Mumbai.[2] The cable quoted an Essar representative who claimed that the company paid significant amounts of money to the underground guerrillas in Chhattisgarh to safeguard Essar plants. Although the Essar group and the Maoist spokesperson from the region both contested these allegations, the police arrested a Hindu contractor and an Adivasi freelance journalist on charges of serving as couriers between Essar and the guerrillas. The contractor was allegedly found with 15 lakh rupees (£15,000), which he was to deliver from Essar to the Naxalites via the Adivasi journalist. Also under scrutiny were two high-caste men running an NGO that was to carry out the 'Corporate Social Responsibility (CSR)' activities of Essar in the area. These 'CSR' reps were alleged to be mediators between Essar and the Maoists.

In the big picture of future development, Gyanji had said that they were not against mining per se as it was crucial for the advancement of any society. What they were against was the way in which private companies exploited the labour force to ruthlessly accumulate all the profits. In a communist society, he said, everyone who worked in the mines would get an equal share of the fruits of their labour. And he added that one of the greatest challenges of the future would be to invest in making mining operations ecologically sustainable.

Entering the black economy of state-led infrastructural development programmes, the Naxalites had to negotiate a complex network of government officers, politicians and contractors. Whether funded or designed by the World Bank, USAID or the UK Department for International Development (DFID), the building of schools, hospitals, police stations, roads, bridges, dams, and community centres constructed by the Indian government have long been subject to a system of percentage cuts that have lined the personal pockets of government officials and their nexus of politicians and contractors.[3]

These cuts were a part of the bribes and gifts commonly requested for getting many jobs done in India—the 'speed money', the *chai-pani* (or, literally, money for 'tea and water'). But they also involved the shaving-off of a percentage of the funds—a 'pc (percentage)' or a 'commission', as it is locally called—of the money coming in for the construction, and that was predetermined by a set of locally agreed unwritten rules about who was allowed what share of the cut at every stage in the construction process. Not only did the government officers implementing the building works expect to earn a percentage of the funds, the contractor also saw it as his right to snag a slice of the pie in the construction process—in fact, it was an essential part of the deal. Moreover, often the contractor also needed to provide a cut for the local politician who had enabled him to win the tender for the contract. So as soon as the contractor had the job, the hope was to syphon away at least 10 per cent of the amount received for the construction by using inferior material, digging to only half the prescribed depth of the foundation, and paying less for labour than was officially recorded.[4]

When the Naxalites came into an area, one of the first things they did was to negotiate their way into these social networks of contractors and politicians and to make their own demands of a share of the illicit funds. Guerrilla soldiers like Vikas would be sent around to the houses of the contractors and politicians in the middle of the night with their guns to strongarm these local big men into giving the Naxalites a cut of the profit that they raked in from their involvement in the black economies. Unarmed, and now fearing the new clandestine armies in their region, it was hard for these local moguls to refuse the terms and conditions of the Naxalites who came to see them.

By gatecrashing the local black markets in this fashion, the Naxalites not only gained funds, they also changed the terms of operation. They introduced their own rules about how fund extraction should take place, how much money was to be taken, and who should be responsible for it. They also set up regulations about how the loot should be distributed—what proportion of the money should be spent on village health clinics, education in the armies, legal fees for political prisoners, and arms.

In Lalgaon everybody knew the rules. Those projects considered to be for the public good were not to be touched; the entire budget amount allocated for construction was to go into the building. This included the building of schools, health centres and all small projects such as the construction of wells and hand pumps. However, other projects—such as the building of roads or bridges—were a major source of funds for the guerrillas.

It was important to the rebels that the construction projects of roads and bridges were never completed to curtail the entry of Indian security forces into guerrilla strongholds. The landscape was dotted with incomplete bridges that would keep these regions entirely cut off from the plains during the monsoons by

1. Marching with the guerrilla platoon from Bihar to Jharkhand, 2010. Photo by Alpa Shah.

2. Maoist State-level conference in a forest in Jharkhand, 2010. Photo by Alpa Shah.

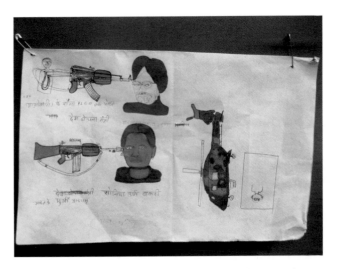

3. Rudimentary drawing of Prime Minister Manmohan Singh, Congress Party President Sonia Gandhi and a helicopter representing government counterinsurgency operations, found pinned to the wall of a tent in the Maoist State-level conference in a forest in Bihar, 2010. Photo by Alpa Shah.

4. Roll call in a Maoist platoon, Jharkhand, 2010. Photo by Alpa Shah.

5. Arriving at a temporary guerrilla forest camp for a 'cooking lesson', Jharkhand, 2008. Photo by Alpa Shah.

6. A Naxalite guerrilla reading a newspaper in an Adivasi house in Jharkhand, 2009. Photo by Alpa Shah.

7. Painting the Maoist flag, Jharkhand, 2009. Photo by Alpa Shah.

8. The collection of *kendu* leaves, used for making the Indian cigarette *bidi*—one of the main sources of Maoist funding, Jharkhand, 2009. Photo by Alpa Shah.

9. The forested hills of the guerrilla stronghold in the Chotanagpur Plateau, Jharkhand, 2009. Photo by Alpa Shah.

10. Burning the effigies of Prime Minister Manmohan Singh, Deputy Chairman of the Planning Commission Montek Singh Ahluwalia and Home Minister P. Chidambaram at a Maoist demonstration in the forests of Jharkhand, 2008. Photo by Alpa Shah.

11. Oraon Adivasis sharing labour to sow each other's fields with rice, Jharkhand, 2009. Photo by Alpa Shah.

12. Oraon mother and daughter drying *mahua* flowers to make mahua wine, Jharkhand, 2009. Photo by Alpa Shah.

13. Walking with Somwari and my neighbours to the Maoist International Women's Day celebrations in a forest in Jharkhand, 2009. Photo by Alpa Shah.

14. Government billboard offering compensation packages for Maoists to 'surrender' with their arms, Sukma, Chhattisgarh, 2015. Photo by Alpa Shah.

15. Indian security force martyrs' memorial, Sukma, Chhattisgarh, 2015. Photo by Alpa Shah.

vast, fast-flowing rivers that the security forces would not dare cross. Year after year, although the roads would have a new layer of dirt and stone chips spread over them, the Naxalites prevented them from being tarred so as to enable the easy planting of land-mines that could be manually detonated from a safe distance when a security force vehicle traversed the gravel road. In fact, the villagers said that one understood that one was in the territory of the *Jungle Sarkar* when the tarred-road ended and the dirt-road began.

In the black market of forest products—a third source of funding for the Naxalites—the collection of *kendu* leaves was the most lucrative. With its dark wrinkled bark, which crackled like a firework when used as kindling, and its wide dark green leaves, *kendu* trees grew in the forests 'owned' by the government. During the months of April and May, the large soft leaves were collected. The government floated tenders for leaf collection and there was money to be made in this official economy. However, there was much more to be made in the black economy of the Tiger Sanctuary, where conservation and national park rules officially prohibited extraction of any kind of forest resources.

In the official areas for collection of leaves, bids for the auction of a region were calculated on the basis of the quantity of leaves declared as collected from the previous year. The richest and most powerful contractors—owners of multiple businesses, mills and factories, and even journalists—lived in the region's cities, and placed their bids against each other. Areas were officially auctioned for as much as 40 lakh rupees (£40,000) a year. But there were always far more leaves to be collected than the esti-mated volume for the government auctions and the contractors stood to earn a significant amount more for each area. Not only did the main contractor accumulate a profit, but so too did the series of mediators he employed—from the person who procured the leaves from the leaf-pickers, dried them and packed them in sacks, to the area-wide collector who transported the leaves to a collection depot in the nearest city.

When the Maoists infiltrated this economy, they once again created their own rules at several stages. On the one hand, they doubled the wages of the Adivasi and low-caste labourers who brought the leaves from the forests and demanded that the contractors provided the collectors rice puffs and jaggery for each day that they went searching for leaves. On the other hand, because they controlled the trade of the leaves through the contractors, in effect, they also controlled the prices and profits, enabling them to get a slice of the funds.

I accompanied Somwari into the forests of Lalgaon to collect the leaves one day. We set out early in the morning, climbed high into the hills and walked deep into the jungle to find the trees that the others had not yet touched, and returned home well after dark. We picked only the largest and best leaves, arranging them carefully in bundles of twenty-five facing one way and twenty-five facing the other. Somwari and her neighbour wrapped the bundles in a shawl and carried them on their heads; each load was larger than they were. Despite the hard work, they said it was relatively well-paid as the Naxalites had doubled the rate for the leaves.[5]

While raising wages for the Adivasi workers, the Naxalites' intervention in the *kendu* economy enabled them to tap one of their main sources of funding. In the government-auctioned sites for leaf collection within the guerrilla strongholds, for every sack of leaves collected by a contractor the guerrillas demanded 70 per cent of the profit.

In the Tiger Sanctuary, a vast conservation area in which leaf-picking was officially prohibited, the stakes for accumulation were higher. It took a great deal of perseverance to understand how the illicit process of accumulation worked there. One evening in May 2009, against the setting sun, I boarded the front seat of a truck going into the heart of the Tiger Reserve to pick up the collected leaves. I was with the two younger brothers of a contractor I had come to know well in Lalgaon, Rafiq.

Rafiq had been given the responsibility by the Naxalite leaders for *kendu* leaf collection in the area we were in. His younger brothers—not much older than nineteen and sixteen—often helped him and the Naxalite leaders with all kinds of odd tasks such as conveying messages, chauffeuring people around, and arranging food and supplies. The young men got a thrill out of riding around on motorbikes, running clandestine errands for the Maoists, and it gave them a certain status among their peers. Now they were helping Rafiq with the *kendu* leaf collection.

After a precarious climb through the narrow forest roads, a punctured tyre and dragging a fallen tree off the track, we finally arrived at the village where the leaves had been packed into sacks. Rafiq's brother (the nineteen-year-old) told the Adivasi labourers to load the sacks onto the truck and, with a pot of green paint, set about the task of writing the name of the village where the leaves had been picked on each sack. Holding the pot for him, I realised that it was the name of a village far away from the Tiger Sanctuary, in an official auction area, rather than the name of the village we were in. I understood then that the leaves, illegally collected in the Tiger Sanctuary, were being made 'legal' because once they left the sanctuary no one would know where these leaves had actually come from. They would earn a higher profit compared to the leaves collected in the official areas because no auction fee had been paid to harvest them.

Everyone worked in silence but the quiet of the forest was broken by the roar of a motorbike steadily growing louder. It was Rafiq. He had come to check that the loading was proceeding smoothly and was soon bellowing instructions at the labourers and his brothers. Surprised to find me there, Rafiq stopped shouting. He came over and handed me a mint as a gesture of acceptance, before revving off to the next village where another truck was being loaded.

The men worked fast but it was well after dark by the time the final sack was stacked onto the truck from the last village depot. Sweat poured down the backs of Rafiq's brothers and the labourers as they took deep breaths and in unison tightened the ropes to tie down the sacks to the sides of the vehicle. In a spirit of camaraderie, the workers chanted a song about loading and tying down ropes, and the truck was piled high, albeit somewhat tilted. I thought it would keel over, but the driver assured me that we could take at least fifteen more sacks. We drove back to the village where I lived. As I hopped off the truck, I expressed my concern that it was late—the sun had set—but he would still have to meander out of the hills and drive into the city to get to the depot. He merely smiled sweetly, saying that the transport of these black leaves was always done in the dark. The government officials had been paid off to let them slip away quietly into the night.

In following this black economy of leaves from the Tiger Sanctuary, I realised that a share of the profits of the collection was given to the villagers like Rafiq and his brothers who arranged their packaging and collection. The rest of the profits would return to the vaults of the guerrilla armies.

* * *

In tapping these illicit funds not only did the Naxalites inevitably engage cadres like Vikas in the capitalist economy around mines, development projects and forest product contracts, they also drew in and involved villagers who previously had no access to these economies. For, as the Naxalites changed the local rules of extortion, they also replaced the historically established contractors with their chosen village men.

The established contractors were Hindu middle-caste and Muslim men who now lived in the cities. Their ancestors had been brought to these Adivasi-dominated areas from the 1800s by the colonial officials who had thought that the natives indigenous to the area were too 'wild' and 'savage' to do anything but chop trees and carry wood and therefore needed these more 'superior' castes and classes to arrange the extraction of timber and other forest products out of the jungles. Over time, when conservation agendas prohibited logging for commercial purposes, these Hindus and Muslims stayed on and sought a living from the black economy of logging or entered the petty trade in non-timber forest products or set up shop as grocers or moneylenders. Those who flourished in this local economy migrated out of the forests and into nearby towns and cities. There, they established larger businesses but maintained control of the most lucrative forest and development resources within the villages by becoming their contractors.

When the Naxalites arrived, they replaced these wealthy town-based Hindu and Muslim elite contractors with the more impoverished of the village middle castes and Muslims who continued to live in the villages. Democratising contract-running in this manner, the Naxalites also nurtured villagers whose compliance and support they could better rely on (than the old elites) because of the patronage they had received from the guerrillas in getting these new opportunities to prosper.

Rafiq, for example, was not much older than thirty. He lived with his mother, wife, two children and two younger brothers in the neighbouring hamlet. Proud to be Pathans or Pashtuns, the highest-status Muslims in the area, his family traced their roots to a regal past when, in the sixteenth century under Sher Shah Suri, their clan had ruled Bihar. Rafiq's great-grandfather had arrived in the forests of Lalgaon in the British era when the forest trade was booming. Skilled in preparing and preserving the skins of wild animals, he was known all over the region for his ability to procure the hides of tigers, lions and leopards.

However, by the time Rafiq's father took over the trade, the forests had been made into one of India's first Tiger Sanctuaries and, in any case, it had become rare to spot wild cats. The family was reduced to poverty. Rafiq's father owned only the land on which their house stood and a small garden plot. He encouraged Rafiq and his brothers to each learn a different trade. Rafiq's oldest brother traded cattle—cows, water buffalo, oxen and goats—that he bought in the villages and sold in the cities. The next brother migrated to construction sites in Odisha as an electrician for nine months of the year. Rafiq himself spent his days in the teashops of Lalgaon, gambling away what little money he had playing cards, and his nights visiting the local foreign liquor den and the two single women who were reputed to survive by selling their sexual services to loitering men.

It was poor, disenfranchised Hindu and Muslim men like Rafiq whom the Naxalite leaders slowly befriended as part of their process of ousting the historically established contractor–politician nexus from the area. At first they made them their village-level workers and eventually allowed them to become contractors. Although they were from poor families and had no qualms about supporting the Naxalites as village-level workers—supplying necessary commodities for the cause, passing messages, being informers—these young men thought the labour of carrying arms on the move was beneath them, fit only for the poor Adivasis and low castes who became foot soldiers. They never considered joining the guerrilla armies, even though the Maoist leadership was predominantly from the highest castes. When I asked Rafiq why, he replied, 'It is not for people like me. Life is hard in the guerrilla armies. Carrying all your possessions on your back, walking for miles, not knowing from where your next meal will come or where you will sleep—whether it will be on a rock, in the forest, or beside a snake. It is the low castes—Harijans[6] and Adivasis—who live like that. Life in the guerrilla armies is the life for the low castes.'

Occasionally, when they found a suitably educated Adivasi youth who could liaise with officials and businessmen in the city and do the books, the Naxalites gave contract opportunities to these Adivasis. Take for instance Birsa, a young Oraon man from Lalgaon who towered above his kin at 5 feet 8 inches. One of the very few educated Adivasis in Lalgaon, he had been sent to Ranchi city for his schooling. He passed both his metric exams (the equivalent of GCSEs) and his intermediate exams (A-Levels) and then enrolled into a BA degree which he never completed. In Ranchi, he had stayed at the Kartik Oraon Adivasi hostel, a hotbed of Adivasi youth politics, where he was radicalised by the various groups fighting against the displacement of Adivasis by the building of large dams constructed by the state and a proposed army field firing range not far from Lalgaon. Some of these groups were associated with the churches and others with the *Jharkhand Mukti Morcha* (the Jharkhand Liberation Front), fighting for the independence of Jharkhand from Bihar. When he returned home to Lalgaon from his city hostel, he was enamoured by the Naxalite leaders who spoke about the same struggles in more radical terms and had taken up arms and were laying down their lives for those causes. So, he went to see what life was like in their armed squads.

Birsa had been living with a Naxalite squad for a few days when they came across a police patrol. Parasji, who was leading the squad, asked his men to shoot at the patrol as they were too close to avoid or evade. In the firing that ensued, one of the squad members was killed and this death affected Birsa so deeply that he did not have the courage to continue in the guerrilla army; he returned home.

Back in Lalgaon, recognising that Birsa was one of only a handful of educated Adivasi young men, the charismatic state-level leader, Madhusudanji, asked him to help in organising the Naxalite rallies and mobilising villagers to come to them. Birsa became a part-time village-level worker of the movement. As one of the few Adivasi youth to have this role, with great gusto he worked alongside Rafiq and the others. He learnt how to use the Naxalite printing press that they had erected in the forests to make leaflets and flyers for their festivals and rallies. During the day, he drew posters and banners under the trees, patiently helping the perfectionist zonal secretary, Sureshji, who was meticulous about design and with whom every task grew tediously long to complete. During the night, he painted slogans as graffiti on the walls of the houses, 'Long live the Maoists!' 'National Rural Employment Guarantee Act to deliver 365 days of employment, not just 100.' Jostling with other village-level workers to get close to Madhusudanji whom they all admired, Birsa encouraged younger boys to do what he had once done for the Naxalites—run errands for the guerrillas, pass tightly folded handwritten messages, pick up rations and act as lookouts for police patrols.

These youths weren't paid for this work but, in times of need—for instance, a health problem in the family—they knew that the Naxalites would cover some, if not all, of their expenses, as they did for the poor. In time, they hoped that the Naxalites would reward their efforts by selecting them as contractors for some of the state-funded schemes or projects that were coming into the area—the building of a road, a useless community centre, or collecting *kendu* leaves—which would enable them to earn a decent amount of money.

Birsa's enthusiasm and hard work as a village-level worker was recognised and—like Rafiq—the Naxalites put him forward with another young man to get a contract for *kendu* leaves. Later, they also gave him the contract to build the primary health centre in Lalgaon, a building that was empty and disused when I arrived there.

Soon after gaining their first contracts, these young men changed their attire. Rafiq replaced his rubber sandals with bril-

liant white Nike trainers, his grey woollen shawl with an imitation black leather jacket. He spent ever more time in the all-
male drinking dens near Lalgaon. Birsa got a TVS motorbike
with a leopard-skin seat and his belly grew so large that the
white t-shirts he wore over the trousers that replaced his *lungis*
regularly rode up.

The Naxalites seemed to turn a blind eye to the changes in
their village-level workers and the fact that they seemed to look
more and more like the elites they had replaced. They needed the
infrastructure that these men could now offer. Yet, at the same
time, they knew that these men were also probably becoming
their weakest link within the villages—those most likely to
betray them as police informers—as their support was largely
utilitarian, predicated on the fact that they were prospering
through their involvement with the Naxalites.

* * *

Birsa's neighbour complained that Birsa and other men like him
were embezzling the *Jungle Sarkar* and getting rich. She said to
me, 'All these boys who became village workers, they earned a lot
of money from the Party and in the Party's name. Look at Birsa,
here he has a motorbike, but he also has a car and a four-wheel-
drive Land Rover in Ranchi city.' Birsa had changed, she said,
after he had been given responsibility for building the primary
health centre. He, who was supposed to ensure that not a cent
went astray, swindled away as much money as he could.

'Look at Rafiq,' she continued, 'he took 2.5 lakh rupees from
the income from *mahua* flowers in the cooperative set up by
Madhusudanji.' Rafiq had been given the responsibility of buying
the flowers from the villagers at market rates (9 rupees a kilo)
when they first fell from the trees in March/April, drying and
storing them, and then selling them back to the villagers in the
winter months at a fair price, undercutting the traders who

charged 15 or 16 rupees a kilo by then. The neighbour said the plan was a fiasco as the boys didn't know how to keep the *mahua* flowers dry during the monsoons. The flowers rotted and no one knew how many had been bought, because the books weren't properly maintained, and whether the young agents had in fact pocketed some of the Naxalites' money earmarked to purchase the flowers. Although Rafiq had been suspended by the Naxalites from village-level work for a while, he still got away with most of his shenanigans, she expostulated.

Meanwhile, a few years after Rafiq and Birsa began working for the Naxalites, the police climbed into the hills and found a register for a village-level workers' meeting of the Naxalites and filed cases against all the names on the list. Birsa's and Rafiq's names were there along with sixteen other men. The police cases against each of them began accumulating. After any explosion or incident in the area, it was their names that would immediately enter the police files. Birsa soon had three cases registered against him.

Birsa said he wanted to leave the area to work as manual labour in Gujarat. But Madhusudanji convinced him to go fully underground again for better protection. Birsa joined the platoons but was apprehended shortly afterwards when the deputy superintendent of police of the neighbouring district was blown up. They detained him in police custody for nine days and tortured him for information about the 'terrorists'. They tied his thumbs together behind his back and hung him from the ceiling for half an hour. The pain was so excruciating that eventually he promised to tell them all that they wanted to know. Nevertheless, the interrogator suddenly released the rope, making him crash onto the table, his nose and lips hitting the surface hard, spurting out blood. He was thankful that they had spared him worse torture techniques. Some of his peers had reported that the police would cut open the soles of the prisoner's feet with a blade and inject spirit into the wound. They did use the splits though; they forced his legs to spread, with one policeman sitting on each thigh and one holding down his feet, until the muscles tore in his groin. Finally, they threw him into a cell. Madhusudanji paid all his legal and family expenses while he was incarcerated, and they let him out on bail the year after.

By the time I arrived in Lalgaon, twenty-three such young men had police cases against them. Many were constantly on the move to avoid arrest. Others, like Rafiq, were considering 'surrendering', doing their time in prison and coming out on bail. Some had already done what they called 'their *darshan* (prayer) to the jail'.

Only those affluent enough to get lawyers to defend their cases, 'arrange' witnesses and pay off the judges, could come out of jail on bail quickly. I knew of an eleven-year-old girl, caught with a Naxalite woman commander, who was imprisoned for three years. No one knew where her parents were and the only person to have visited her in prison, presented her with a change of clothes and bars of soap, and met her lawyers was a man deputised by the Naxalite leader, Parasji. If Parasji had not kept an eye out for her, it was eminently possible that she would have spent all her teen years behind bars.

When he came out of prison, Birsa did not want to return to the Naxalites and his rancour towards them escalated. The closer he got to them, the more bitter he felt. He complained about the hierarchy in the movement despite the promise of equality. He said that the leaders of the mass organisations who worked openly in the cities and organised the rallies were never at the forefront of the public spaces, delivering speeches; it was only the young people who were put on stage and made the target of police repression. He complained that the leaders of many of these open mass organisations were old Brahmin men who could not even implement their ideals against casteism in their own homes; Birsa wasn't allowed beyond the front rooms of their family houses as they practiced untouchability and considered him polluted, even though he was not a Dalit but an Adivasi. When their daughters were married off, they had traditional Hindu weddings and even paid dowry, he complained. One such mass organisation leader had the gall to live off a Central Coalfields Pension fund, while organising marches against mining.

He also complained that too many rallies were being organised and people could not continuously take time out from earning their daily bread. 'The Naxalites are like teachers forcing the students to learn the entire alphabet in one day.' People who had once participated in the rallies with passion began losing their zeal. And finally, he said, while there might be a few Gyanjis, Parasjis and Madhusudanjis, there were also those Naxalites who did not even wash their own dinner plate unless they were told to do so.

Although the Naxalite leaders paid his bail, they stopped trusting Birsa, increasingly suspecting him of being a potential police informer. Even his family complained that he had ruined his life and he was at a loss about what he should do. Birsa said he was now 'killing flies and watching the dance of death' around him. He said he was 'neither of the hills, nor of the houses,' a phrase that I had heard from other young men in a similarly alienated position who felt that they belonged with neither the Naxalites nor the villages.

Most of the time Birsa was on the run. His wife had to hide every time the police climbed into the hills, so he moved her to Ranchi city. He sent his daughter to boarding school in yet another town. He said the 2,000 rupees he might get in five months from the Naxalites for household emergencies was insufficient; he needed at least 1,200 rupees a month to educate his two children. His younger brother had left for Ranchi to work as a labourer to escape police interrogations. If Birsa continued to stay with the Naxalites, all he would do, he said, was make bombs. But manual labour was no longer his cup of tea because he had become too educated, fought too hard for the cause of the Adivasis and seen too much of the world with the Naxalites. To earn a decent living or gain power, Birsa began considering pitching behind a Member of the Legislative Assembly for whom his older brother worked, in the hope that he could one day mobilise enough support to fight for a seat himself.

* * *

Entering the black economy to generate capital to fund the Naxalites meant intimate contact with the established elites of the contractor-politician-state official nexus—the rich, well-connected classes and castes. It meant that young men like Vikas or Birsa, whose ancestors had steered clear of these outsiders, had to learn how to negotiate with them in their cultural environment. For them to succeed in being accepted into this elite milieu, they had to participate in the activities that gained them access to that social world within which business transactions took place and political deals were struck.

In this process, without a strong counterculture, it was all too easy for them to internalise some of the capitalist and hierarchical caste values of these elites and seek to differentiate themselves from others, reproducing the inequalities that these values generated. This included the desire for the accumulation of private property, the increasing conflation of status with the acquisition of private wealth, the necessity to flaunt this wealth through conspicuous consumption and adopt increasingly patriarchal attitudes towards women. Riding around on motorbikes and four-wheel-drive Boleros rather than on bicycle or public transport or going on foot; wearing trousers, shirts and trainers rather than *lungis* and rubber slippers; aspiring to derive more wealth and power through engagement in party politics; drinking foreign-made liquor behind

183

closed doors away from their mothers, wives and daughters; and denigrating the women of their house as a second sex who should stay confined to their homes—the list could go on.

These values and the inequalities they nurtured were quite contrary to the ideal communists the Naxalites were seeking to make out of men like Kohli or Vikas or even Birsa. Used to a tough nomadic life, the Adivasis were from backgrounds where notions of private property, accumulation and social mobility were not well developed, and where egalitarian values were more prevalent than in the caste-divided plains. Joining a movement where all personal interests were to be sacrificed for the larger cause of the revolution, they simply needed to be 'politically educated'—that's how Gyanji put it—into a commitment to placing the revolutionary struggle above all else.

But contact with these upwardly mobile higher-caste elite networks—through the work they did for the Naxalites—had the potential to transform Adivasi youths like Vikas or Birsa, away from their humble family roots and the distance they had kept from the state and its related outsiders, into macho movers and shakers demanding respect for their authority while fattening their bellies. It seemed that although the Naxalites displaced the established elites with less privileged villagers as contractors and mediators, these progressive changes came at a huge cost because of the very processes of how they had to insert themselves into the markets of the black economy to fund themselves in a context of war. In giving more people the opportunity to accumulate a profit in this black economy, the Naxalites unwittingly spread the values of those elites more widely among the villagers and their own ranks.

Other ongoing political and economic processes might perhaps have had the same effect on Vikas, Birsa, or even Kohli— for instance, getting one of the 8 per cent of state jobs that are reserved for Adivasis across the country by the Indian Constitution, or becoming, also through these quotas, a politically elected leader. These situations would, similarly, have brought the state closer to Adivasi lives and with that would come the potential for upward mobility through accumulation, the penetration of the values of capitalism, the influence of the values of caste hierarchy and the resulting social stratification and inequalities within Adivasi communities.

Indeed, in other parts of the country like Kerala, Gujarat and even more developed parts of Jharkhand and in areas with high rates of Christian conversion, it appears that these processes of social stratification are well underway. Jharkhand has produced a series of notorious cases of corruption among Adivasi politicians. A notable one involved the Adivasi chief minister of the state, Madhu Koda, who was jailed for three years in 2007 for his involvement in a coal scam case.[7]

There were endless debates within Marxism about the extent to which a transition to capitalism was necessary to bring about a communist future. But the Naxalites saw themselves as a revolutionary group that prioritised learning from the masses: 'from the masses to the masses,' they called it, and they were working with relatively egalitarian societies into which capitalism had not penetrated with the longest of its tentacles. So, it was ironic that this movement for a communist future inadvertently brought the state closer to Adivasi lives, accelerated the spread of the values of capitalism and caste hierarchies amongst them, and thereby undermined its own visions for a communist society. The Naxalite aim was to create a casteless and classless society, but it was also accelerating class differentiation and at the same time nurturing some of the hierarchal values of caste amongst Adivasis.

* * *

It was challenging to produce a Prashant or a Gyanji who renounced the mainstream and committed to living out their communist ideals. Perhaps it did indeed take an ascetic—like Gyanji—to resist being drawn into the temptations of social mobility, accumulating wealth, status and power recognised by this locally powerful elite. And perhaps Kohli did have that potential.

Saintly figures, going against the current of political and economic change, who have often renounced certain aspects of Adivasi sociality (for instance drinking alcohol and eating meat) have long been a feature of Adivasi societies and have sometimes produced large followings in history. Many of the widely celebrated anti-colonial movements such as the 1914 Tana Bhagat movement, the Birsa movement of the 1900s, and the 1855–6 Santhal Hul were headed by such ascetic Adivasi figures. All their leaders—be it Birsa or Sidhu Kanhu—had divine revelations (in some cases described as millenarian), typically became vegetarians and teetotallers, and gained prophetic powers as healers and miracle workers. They were saintly.[8] But could the Maoists harness such potential amongst boys like Kohli?

The main problem, as Gyanji had once said, 'is that our capacity has been reduced to the military needs of the war.' In response to the intense state repression, they had increased their attention to military attacks and counter-attacks at the expense of the political education of their soldiers, the ethical foundation of their cadres, and the politicisation of their supporters. He said they spent far too much time on planning formations for attack, military drills and making weapons, and far too little time reading, debating and creating a community away from arms and the hierarchies of the society which surrounded them.

It is true that history has shown us that in situations of extreme violence and oppression, counter-violence may be the only way to achieve justice. And indeed, when one travels across the Indian countryside and witnesses the violence of systematic neglect and oppression that has been wrought on India's low castes and tribes, it is often hard not to feel that the only way to change things is for them to take up arms to make their demands. The danger, however, it seemed to me, is that this counter-violence becomes the purpose, a force that is an end in itself, and that the broader aims of achieving power through collective social change takes a backseat.

15

NIGHT FIVE

'We have to watch Vikas carefully,' Gyanji observed. I asked him what could be done. He said the first stage would be processes of criticism and self-criticism. Then there was demotion of rank. And finally, of course, there was always expulsion from the movement.

I remembered the last such case of expulsion and the minor, though unintentional, role I had played in bringing it to Gyanji's attention.

One evening I was returning home from a nearby village when I spotted Gyanji sitting under a mango tree full of mynah birds noisily chirping away. I asked if I could join him. I was burning to ask him about Madhusudanji, the state-level leader, who by then was in prison in a local town. Gyanji was very close to him and I wanted to know his opinion on the astonishing news I had just heard that Madhusudanji, from behind his prison bars, was apparently preparing to stand as an electoral candidate in the Jharkhand State Legislative Assembly elections.

Gyanji was silent for a moment and then asked me where I had heard such rubbish. When I told him, he reproached me for spreading rumours. I later realised that he had genuinely thought it was a hoax. I defended myself, saying I had watched at least twenty villagers board a local jeep in the *haat* to visit Madhusudanji in prison because he had asked for their assistance in electoral work.

Madhusudanji had grown up not far from where we were on the march. He was a Dalit who had been mobilised in the anti-feudal struggle, one of the few Dalits to make it to a Naxalite senior leadership position. I had not met him—he was arrested a year before my arrival—but many people in Lalgaon talked about him as a much-loved leader. A brilliant orator, he was thought to be fair and just.

Those who visited Madhusdudanji in prison said that they would do anything for him and they trusted that he would look after them in return. They came back from their visit to him with a list of canvassing tasks, all under the assumption that the Naxalites had decided to put him forward as their electoral candidate.

It took Gyanji and the other leaders several months to verify what was going on—whether Madhusudanji was indeed intending to betray the movement's policy of boycotting parliamentary elections.

Madhusudanji was finally expelled from the movement and notice of his expulsion was distributed by the guerrillas to the local newspaper, the *Prabhat Khabar*. Posters were pasted on the walls of houses across local villages telling people to boycott the elections. When the security forces came to occupy the health centre and schools at the time of the election, the Naxalites blew up these buildings as a reminder of their position on mainstream parliamentary elections.

Madhusudanji's defection was a shock to Gyanji. But it was not the first time that a Naxalite cadre, after a spell in the movement, had stood as a candidate in elections. After accumulating money as a contractor, it was in fact the next step for many ambitious young men from poor rural areas on the path of upward social mobility. Becoming a politician brought with it the possibility of accumulating more money and, especially, getting power and status of the kind that was recognised by those higher up the Indian social hierarchy. Dejected, Gyanji said that Madhusudanji, 'had lost all innocence, had lost the romance for the revolution.'

Later, with greater distance from the initial blow, Gyanji analysed further what had happened.

He said that Madhusudanji had given much to the Naxalites and was extremely committed and passionate. The police had killed his father-in-law, and two of his sisters' sons, who had joined the Naxalites, had been killed by the security forces. But, Gyanji reflected, Dalits and other low castes (he excluded Adivasis who have historically lived with more autonomy) who rose within the Naxalites' ranks often have an inferiority complex as they have suffered historic humiliation from those above them in the caste hierarchy, and this complex is dangerous. They want to undo the wrongs they have suffered and the injustices they have seen, but the result is that they can become extremely sectarian, Gyanji explained. Although they can fight for justice for their communities, when the fight becomes more abstract, for a different world for everyone—for a communist society—it is much harder for them to commit. Communism everywhere, Gyanji reflected, has usually failed to raise leaders from the working classes, the peasants; leadership remains the privilege of the educated bourgeoisie.

Gyanji said he used to tell Madhusudanji to read—to study communist literature—so that he could move beyond the struggle for the rights of Dalits and think more broadly about our global society. But he didn't read, Gyanji said sadly. It was his great weakness and one of the reasons why he could not see himself as part of human history, making history with others, not just an individual making history, Gyanji said. Gyanji reflected that Madhusudanji could have easily stepped away from the guerrillas silently but his ego got in the way and now he was ready to destroy the Naxalites.

Madhusudanji had been such a trusted and respected senior Naxalite leader that his actions cast a huge shadow over the movement. For several months, I recall Gyanji being extremely depressed. The increased penetration of the Indian security forces sent to wipe out the guerrillas was one thing, but this kind of betrayal from within was quite another. It was a stab in the back.

Vikas was now lying on a jute bed wearing dark sunglasses although the sun had set. Gyanji, staring at him, muttered under his breath, 'Frankenstein.'

I didn't quite understand.

'Frankenstein's monsters,' Gyanji repeated. 'That is what is happening, that's what we are creating here,' he said. From a beautiful dream and beautiful people, he said they were producing the very people who would destroy the movement and its vision for a different world.

With the haunting image of Frankenstein's monster in mind, I soon had to return to the survival strategies of the march. Eating as much food as possible given the uncertainty of the next meal; lacing trainers loose enough to slip them on and off in one quick movement, but tight enough for ankle support during the hours of relentless walking. Another night of walking; another 35 kilometres to cover?

We now needed the sweepers at the back of the platoon to erase the traces of our footsteps, for the area was one in which a mercenary gang, calling itself the Tritiya Prastuti Committee (TPC), also moved. The Naxalites had suffered recent casualties at the hands of the TPC—who were backed by the police, they said—and it was getting increasingly dangerous for the guerrillas to make the crossing from Bihar to Jharkhand.

The TPC wore uniforms like those of the Indian army, created military structures akin to the Naxalites' and funded themselves by demanding levies from coal mining and development projects in the area, competing with the Naxalites. Their sole declared aim was to eradicate the Maoists.

They had been formed eight years ago by Bharat, a man who had been demoted within the Naxalite ranks, on charges of embezzlement and sexually harassing women. The Naxalites claimed that, unable to face the humiliation of his demotion, he reacted by leaving with a range of the best weapons from his platoon and several young Naxalite recruits who were kinsmen from his village area. The man claimed that the Maoists were dominated by Yadavs who were middle-caste people from Bihar and that there was no space in the movement for Dalits.

In the areas where I had conducted my doctoral field research, a couple of hundred kilometres further south, another such gang who called themselves the People's Liberation Front of India (PLFI) had also gained ground. There were at least half a dozen such outfits in Jharkhand. MMMC, JPC, JLT—a spate of acronyms—whose roots could all be traced to Naxalites who had been expelled from the struggle and who had subsequently mobilised people of their own caste against the guerrillas. They also accumulated wealth using the threat of their guns in their areas of operation through levies on development, forest products and mining. Some, like the TPC and PLFI, lasted several years and managed to grow—at points—to a couple of hundred members. But many fizzled out within the space of a few months or their members were killed.

The Naxalites claimed that these gangs were state supported. It was rare, they said, for the police to kill or incarcerate gang members. Senior police officers themselves had admitted that these groups were different from the Naxalites—there was no ideological motivation to their struggle; they were purely extortion rackets, or 'money-minting' machines.[1] Whatever their exact connection with the state, in many ways gangs like the TPC were more dangerous to the Naxalites than the Indian security forces. They also had kinship connections in the villages they moved through and could traverse the forests and hills with the same agility as the guerrillas.

The day of bathing, relaxation and recuperation we had enjoyed seemed a long time ago. Reflecting on Gyanji's comments about 'Frankenstein's monsters' and on the potential of Vikas to defect from the guerrillas, I realised how easy it was for armed revolutionary movements like the Naxalites to give birth to such renegade gangs. I became ever warier of our platoon commander.

PART SIX

SOMWARI'S AUTONOMY FROM THE SHACKLES OF PATRIARCHY

16

NIGHT FIVE, CONTINUED

A special Maoist company composed of two platoons, known for its military skills, had been deputed from another part of the state to eradicate the TPC. Gyanji knew that the company was nearby and had been trying to make contact with it all day. Just before sunset, we got news that their commander had asked us to climb a hill with a school at the summit.

They were waiting for us, about fifty of them, standing in a straight line, with their bags on their backs and their rifles hanging off their shoulders in the dusty playground in front of the school, the sun setting behind them. The wind was whistling through the trees and a high-pitched orchestra of large bats flew above us in the sky as we approached. It was surreal to see them, a line of olive green, against the orange and pink sky, an elongated mirror image of us.

As we got closer, I saw that four of them were women. They had plaits braided down to their shoulders and the peculiarity of my own situation as a woman dressed like a man struck me. I asked Gyanji if I could have some time alone to speak with them.

The women were Santhals, an Adivasi community from the far east of Jharkhand, near the border with West Bengal. The youngest couldn't have been much older than sixteen. The oldest was in her early twenties. Gyanji said she was a gifted fighter and had been made deputy platoon commander.

I sat down on the ground with them and for a while we just stared at each other, laughing, holding hands. I admired their immaculately straight backs, a characteristic of all the Adivasi women I knew, a gift from having carried pot upon pot of water on their heads from the well to the house. They seemed just as delighted to see me as I was to see them. Gyanji had introduced me as a comrade making a radio programme, so they asked if I had learnt the latest song about resisting the mining companies—those who sucked the blood out of the country. They broke into song, their sweet voices producing a captivating melody, and ended on a high note of raising the red flag higher and higher before bursting out into soft shy laughter.

The deputy platoon commander soon grew more serious and asked if I had sanitary towels. She said that a decision had finally been taken that women were to be given a supply of pads rather than rely on scraps of old cloth, as most women did in those forests. However, they hadn't been able to find any in the markets they had passed and one of them needed the towels urgently.

I couldn't help but say that sanitary towels polluted the environment and that the old-fashioned ways, although not as convenient, were perhaps more environmentally friendly. There we were, immersed in the intimacies of our menstrual cycles, but I knew that it was futile to try to understand the depths of their personal histories—why they found themselves in these armies— the stories I most wanted to hear. Our time together would be brief, an hour at the most. It would take days for them to open up and they would in any case at first only be prepared to repeat their particular version of a well-rehearsed generic story involving experiences of feudalism, exploitation and police repression. I would have to live with them, in their villages, to understand the nuances of their complex stories.

Our platoon departed soon after. We shook hands with every member of the company in the customary Naxalite way followed by thrusting one's fist in the air. The girls led a song in chorus:

Goodbye friend,
Take care friend,
Be clever friend,
There are enemies ahead,
We will meet again,
Not just once but several times.

I was overwhelmed by the brief but intense encounter. What lay ahead for the women? Would I ever see any of them again?

By two in the morning, everyone was tired. We had been marching continuously for five hours. We were in a patch of forest which, though TPC territory, was deemed to be safe enough to stop, eat and sleep for a few hours. Here, we had to prepare our own food as it was not safe to enter the villages. Some young men from Section C dug a pit and laid a fire for cooking *khichdi*, a simple but nutritious one-pot mixture of boiled broken lentils and rice.

Kohli and Gyanji's bodyguard dug two holes, 2 metres apart, in a wet sandy patch in the riverbed. The water seeped in slowly from under the ground to create a pool and soon the moon was dancing off it. One waterhole was for drinking and cooking, the other for washing. From building the fire and finding water, to washing our dishes, it took less than an hour and a half for everyone to be fed.

Gyanji decided on a sleeping place away from the cooking site and sentry points were allocated. But there was a commotion in the platoon. Some of the young men were talking loudly between themselves. Gyanji went to settle the matter.

I asked Kohli what was going on. He said a woman had died in childbirth in the vicinity and her angry evil spirit was lurking above us in the foliage of the *neem* tree waiting to besiege passing prey. He said he had seen the madness that overcame men who were possessed by such spirits; it was not a good idea to sleep below her.

Gyanji came back exasperated. He said we had to move. Right now there was no point trying to convince the men that evil spirits don't exist. He had been in this situation before.

I was rather amused. There were so many dangers in the forests. Close to my house in Lalgaon I had heard stories of tigers and leopards stealing cattle. Elephants had mowed down houses. A neighbour had died of a venomous snakebite. And now, in the territory of a mercenary gang, these guerrilla soldiers were more afraid of otherworldly creatures, the evil spirits that might seize and possess them in the forest.

We crossed the riverbed and walked on for ten minutes. Sleeping arrangements were mapped, sentry positions decided, change of guard agreed. Finally, we could lay our heads to rest, although only for a couple of hours.

Gyanji was soon muttering away about the TPC, talking as he so often did in his sleep. But I kept seeing images of the women in the company we had just left. My head was abuzz with questions. How did they feel about the way they were treated by the men in the guerrilla columns? Did they want to have children? What was it like to be a woman in this male-dominated movement for a more egalitarian future?

I recalled with fondness Seema, the only senior woman Maoist leader I met, who had been with the movement for several decades, and the sleeping arrangements at the camp in Bihar, from where we had begun our journey. Gyanji had warned me that they would be rather 'conservative'. I would sleep in a separate tent with the new young female recruits, and not alongside the men of my generation who were the leadership. Seema had expressed to me her great frustration with those very same arrangements, which she had experienced many times. She had said, 'I spend all my time with the girls. It is not that I don't want to be with them. The problem is that in those important large conferences, the most significant decision-making takes place around the informal banter in the male tents, often at night. By sleeping apart, as women, we are invariably excluded.'

What would it be like to be Seema? There, in the territory of the mercenary gang, sleeping among men, knowing that this was the world I had to live in. Despite the years of feminist reading groups and discussions and activities mobilising women, and despite the Gyanjis of the movement, the Maoist leaders often reproduced the cultural norms of the structures they sought to attack. I began to feel terribly alone. Perhaps pre-empting my own thoughts, I recalled that Seema had said that the point was to stay within the movement and combat patriarchy within it, not to give up and leave.

17

GENDER, GENERATION, CLASS AND CASTE

In the same way that the Maoists gave importance to the political education of the cadres, the setting up of health camps, and the development of agricultural cooperatives, they argued that addressing inequalities in gender relations was crucial for the building of a more egalitarian future. 'Women hold up half the sky,' they said.

I knew from reading their documents that after years of internal critique, the Maoists had come to recognise the importance of gender. Just as 'caste' could not be ignored as simply 'superstructure' in favour of a more important focus on economic and material relations that were called the 'base-structure' or 'infrastructure', gender relations could not be left to culture, subjective relations and the private domain.

It was not enough to make the argument: 'Let's fight the war first; we will deal with gender later.' That would only pave the way for patriarchal authoritarian men to dominate the new future communities aspiring to be egalitarian. Gender equality had to be fought for during the struggle, addressed in the very ways through which social relations were nurtured amidst cadres and sympathisers to reflect—at least in the guerrilla strongholds—their ideal future communities.

The faces of women carrying arms had come to take pride of place in representations of the Maoists. A particularly captivating image—one that journalists liked to shoot—was a line of women with their feet placed a shoulder's width apart, their waists twisted at right angles to their feet, rifles perched between their right bicep and their shoulder, faces hidden by the butts of their guns, barrels aiming out at some imaginary target.

Over the last year in Lalgaon, on at least three different occasions, the young women who made up the *Nari Mukti Sangh*, the Women's Liberation Wing of the Maoists, wanted to pose in a similar line for my camera, just to see what they looked like carrying guns. They had borrowed the rifles from the men—only one of them knew how to use the weapons—lined up for the camera, and then ran back to see how the image looked on my digital screen.

'Wait, *Didi*! Sushila is not in line! Wait, *Didi*, I am smiling too much, you shouldn't have captured my teeth. *Didi*, can you take it from this angle?'

In some parts of the country, the Maoists said that 40 per cent of the cadres were women. The figure of 40 per cent appears to provide some kind of gender credibility stamp as it has cropped up in several struggles: in the 'People's War' of the Maoists in Nepal and the Kurdistan Workers' Party (the PKK) in Turkey, for instance.

International representation of these radical movements has been quick to focus on women with guns and the allegedly empowering changes the guerrilla war brought to women's lives. In Nepal this was shown by Li Onesto, who, writing for *Revolution*, the paper of the Revolutionary Communist Party USA, was perhaps the first foreign journalist to travel into the guerrilla zones in 1999. In India, it was Arundhati Roy, who toured the guerrilla zones of the Dandakaranya region in Chhattisgarh for ten days just after I met those Maoist women in TPC territory in Jharkhand. These voices told the world how the armed struggle was, in Onesto's words, 'like the opening of a prison gate ... with thousands of women rushing forward to claim an equal place in the war.'[1] The reality was more complex than that, as is so often the case.[2]

Women in the villages were vital for providing logistical support to the Naxalites—giving food, acting as couriers, caring for sick comrades in their homes and even hiding the guerrillas. They were also crucial in the protests organised by the Naxalites, often placed in the forefront of rallies in the hope that the protesters would be less likely to be attacked if there were women and children in the vanguard. In many parts of the country the Naxalites had set up women's organisations in the villages, demanding equal wages for agricultural work, seeking higher wages for *kendu* leaf collection, demonstrating against the rape of low-caste women by high-caste men.

After years of hard work among women, the Maoists had also trained up some women soldiers and were proud of those who had led platoons in battles. And in regions where the entire population had no other choice but to either be displaced from their homes or join the Maoist armies—such as the Dandakaranya region of Chhattisgarh—women had run overnight to join the guerrilla armies for the same reasons as men. The state-supported vigilante groups—Salwa Judum or 'purification hunt', as it was called, and the others which followed—were burning villages and raping and murdering those who were left behind. Like the Adivasi men in those regions, the women had nowhere else to run to and were left to choose between the brutality of life in the prison-like refugee camps that the Indian state had erected on the roadsides, escaping over the border to a different state, or roaming the forests with the guerrillas. Many already had children, siblings and other kinsmen who were with the guerrilla armies and life on the move was probably the most attractive option for some.

In other parts of the Adivasi Maoist strongholds, despite the existence of women's organisations of the Maoists, the number of women to take up guns was small and their participation was often fleeting. Most women who joined the armed squads were young—rarely older than twenty—and it was not often that they stayed with the guerrilla armies for more than a year. The handful of Adivasi or Dalit women who lasted underground for longer were usually there because they had married high-caste leaders, and they were eventually given leadership positions.

Seema, for instance, from the south of India, was perhaps even more a foreigner to Jharkhand than I, for she struggled with the local language. Although low-caste, she was clearly from a middle-class background, was well-educated and spoke excellent English.

For years Seema held down a job as a clerk in a post office in a large city in Andhra Pradesh, while at the same time mobilising slum-dwellers to fight for their rights as part of a human rights organisation. When state repression increased in Andhra Pradesh, the organisations that she was a part of were banned as a Maoist front. Although she tried to continue this 'overground' work in the city, under the cover of her clerical job, her friends were arrested and killed. Seema, at the age of forty, was sent by the Naxalite leadership to the relative safety of the forests of Jharkhand to, amongst other things, strengthen the women's wing of the movement there.

It was six months into my stay in Lalgaon when I finally met Seema for the first time. I was curious, as I knew that women like her were rare. Until then I had only met young women, like Kohli's sister Anju, who drifted in and out of the movement. Only two of the young women whom I met had been with the Maoists for more than a year and neither one for more than five years.

The first time that I met Seema it was in the forests near my home. I had missed her visits to the area on two previous occasions for she only ever stayed in the region for a day or two. As was the case with the other leaders, she had to keep moving to protect herself. The day we first met she was reading Ashraf Dehghani's *Torture and Resistance in Iran*.[3] She said that these memoirs of a woman guerrilla, tortured for her political beliefs under the dictatorial rule of the Shah of Iran, were like a bible; they would give her courage in the difficult times that lay ahead.

Seema later revealed that she had just received a letter from a female guerrilla who had been arrested and who said that during her torturous interrogation, the police had asked her about every scar on Seema's body, every mole on her face and every line on the palms of her hands. Alongside electrocutions, beatings and other torture techniques, a common tool used by the police was to reveal select information they already had about the guerrillas' comrades in order to extract further details from people who had been newly arrested.

As I approached her, Seema was standing in the shade of a guava tree full of fruit. Her greying hair was tied back in a pony-tail and she was dressed casually in black tracksuit bottoms and a long maroon cotton kurta. Surrounded by Anju and six other girls, she was saying goodbye to a thin spindly old man with a hunchback and a pretty nine-year-old girl whom I had seen in the village before.

Seema said the old man was the young girl's grandfather and also now her guardian; malaria had killed both her parents two years ago. He had come to take his granddaughter back home. His little girl, the old man had said, was too young to be with the *Jungle Sarkar* and he needed her at home to draw water from the well and for other household chores. Seema looked at me despondently. 'There was no way that I could keep her, so I told her she must go back home with her grandfather.'

We sat down under the guava tree. Seema told me that she had been trying to figure out all day which of the girls had joined the squad of the Women's Liberation Front since she had last come to the area three months ago, which of the girls had left, and what their different problems were.

I wasn't sure whether to tell her that the week before I had met two of the squad members at one of their parental homes. The girls had said that they were sick and had left the Women's Liberation Front for a few days. But I found them all dressed up in saris, with cheap costume jewellery and wearing bright red lipstick, getting ready for the weekly *haat*. They were delighted to see me and asked me to help drape their saris.

'I thought you were all sick!' I exclaimed. Savitri, whose home it was, said that four of them had fallen ill and had come to her house to recuperate. They had all recovered, two had left and only these two still remained here.

One of them, a Birjia Adivasi girl, who lived in a small village high up in the hills, had already returned to the Women's Front. She had joined the Naxalites because she had been lonely at home after her parents had gone off to Delhi as construction labour. When she fell ill she had come to Savitri's house to rest and then returned to the squads. Another, an Agharia Adivasi girl, who had been with the Women's Front for four months, also initially came to Savitri's house to recover but then left to go and work in a brick kiln in West Bengal with her cousins. Pratibha, the third girl, said she was torn. She wanted to go back to the Women's Front as she liked living with them but was worried about what it would do to her. She said her brother Ranjeet was in one of the platoons and he was so involved with the *Jungle Sarkar* that now he did not even acknowledge their parents. She said it really hurt her to see him turn his back on them and she did not want to become like him.

After a while, Savitri took me aside, sat me down and confided that in fact she had not been sick; she was 'love sick'. I asked her what she meant. She said she was in love with a boy who lived in a village about 40 kilometres away where the husbands of both her sisters hailed from. The boy had asked to marry her but her mother had refused even though he was from the right clan. The boy's village, her mother said, was bewitched as one of Savitri's sisters had died there after having been accused of being a witch, and the other sister was deeply unhappy. When Savitri told the boy what her parents had said he immediately married another girl. This hurt her so much that she had stopped eating. Her mother's brother, a Maoist platoon commander, found Savitri in her depression and suggested that she join the Women's Front for a 'change of scene'. It seemed a good idea.

She had come on the pretext of sick leave from the Women's Front but she told me that in fact she had used the occasion to go back to the boy's village to see him one more time. They had spent a beautiful night together and he claimed that he would leave his wife for her. She returned home and confided in her mother, who said she must not be 'kept' by him; she would always be treated as secondary to his first wife. She thought deeply about the situation and concluded that her mother was right, but was very upset because she still loved the boy.

I asked her what she would do now. She said she wanted to return to the Women's Front because at least she could sometimes forget about the boy there. But she was torn because she knew how much her parents needed her back at home. Her mother was nearly blind, her father did all the housework, and everyone in the village criticised her for abandoning her parents and joining the Naxalites to do nothing but grow 'fat'. She said it was true that she had put on weight. She had asked the local quack to provide her with some medicine to make her thin again, but he had told her that there was no such thing.

Seema did not know the histories of any of these girls and I wasn't sure what details to divulge, without breaking their confidence, so I asked her about Binita, whom I had seen a few days earlier in a house in a village nearby.

Glamorously dressed in a glittery bright red sari, Binita had been feeding her newborn son whom she had called 'Bispot Oraon', which literally meant 'Explosion Oraon'. Her delicate ears were stretched by dangly imitation gold earrings and a similarly patterned necklace adorned her chest. She looked out of place in the village. She belonged to a different province of Jharkhand and was one of the few girls who had been with the Maoist Women's Liberation Front for as long as a year and a half. It was long enough for the man she was in love with in the platoons to father her child.

I knew that the birth of her baby had been a problem for the Naxalites. While it was not uncommon for children to be born in the squads, the Naxalite leadership had taken the position that women fighters should not have children during the struggle. The movement could not look after them and they would be a threat to the safety of the squads. In most cases of pregnancy, the foetus was aborted, but Binita had managed to hide the bump that was her little Bispot until she was five months pregnant. If a child was born, the mother needed to give the baby to others to look after and eventually send the child to boarding school. It was difficult to find women who were willing to do that. I knew of only one.

As I suspected, Seema said that Binita was leaving the Naxalites and would soon return to her home village with her newborn. Trying to be optimistic, she said such women—those who had once experienced life in the squads—remain crucial Naxalite supporters in the villages. They become important providers of food, trusted messengers and couriers and much-needed guarantors of safe houses and security. In Bihar there were many stories of women who, during intense police repression, had protected Naxalite leaders, pretending they were in bed with their husbands, when there was nowhere or no time to hide.

Seema did not deny, though, that the question of children was an issue. Women leaving after childbirth is a major impediment to our female recruitment, she said. It was a common problem for such movements, I knew. Perhaps also involving fathers in childrearing might help resolve the issue of women leaving?

Seema and I talked late into the evening as though we were long-lost sisters. She told me how she admired leaders like Gyanji for their sensitivity to women's issues and their openness to rethinking gender relations. She said he encouraged the leadership, through his own actions, to alter their approaches and attitudes to women, and actively sought to address gender equality within the Naxalites. But men like Gyanji, she said, were few and far between.

Most men in the leadership found it difficult to deal with gender equality. There were always other, more important, needs of war. So, unless it was to celebrate a good woman fighter, gender issues were better left to women. That's how gender inequities perpetuated themselves—by acknowledging the significance of gender relations as 'the women's issue' and making a separate wing for women headed by women for women to deal with. In that process, women and gender relations were too easily ghettoised and became of secondary concern.

The Naxalites had given rise to impressive female leaders who produced sophisticated writings on gender within the movement. I had read the works of Anuradha Ghandy, who also went by the names Narmada, Janaki and Rama. It is possible to call her by her real name for she is now dead and is celebrated as a martyr by the Naxalites. She was killed, at the age of fifty-four, not by the police or the mercenary gangs, but by an Anopheles mosquito carrying the *Plasmodium falciparum* that gave her malaria. The disease rapidly took over her body, which was already weakened by systemic sclerosis, an auto-immune disease that had been attacking her lungs and heart. She died just a year before I met Seema in the forests of Jharkhand.

Born into a communist family, and a graduate of the prestigious Elphinstone College in Mumbai, Anuradha was involved in radical politics from a young age. Her parents had been part of the Communist Party of India; her father had taken up the legal cases of the communists arrested in Telangana and became a well-known progressive lawyer, her mother an active social worker. Her brother became one of Mumbai's noted progressive playwrights and theatre artists. Anuradha herself turned to a more revolutionary path. She had been moved by her visits to the Bangladesh refugee camps and the suffering of people from famine in Maharashtra in the early seventies and began participating actively in radical left-wing activities at college, where she joined the Progressive Youth Movement, which was affiliated with the Naxalites.

In Mumbai, she fell in love with a similarly well-heeled young radical, Kobad Ghandy (one of the most senior leaders of the Maoists when he was arrested a year after she died). Kobad, though without the same communist pedigree, was born into a wealthy Parsi family (his father was the managing director of a multinational company). He was educated at the country's most famous independent public school, the Doon School, often dubbed 'India's Eton' and went on to study chartered accountancy in London where he got involved in left-wing politics. He returned to Mumbai to work against the human rights abuses of Indira Gandhi's Emergency regime and met Anuradha whom he then married.

By 1982, Anuradha gave up her lecturing job in a Mumbai college and moved to Nagpur to teach sociology at Nagpur University. There, she organised 5,000 informal workers to strike at a thermal power plant, and mobilised house servants, railway workers, power loom workers and coal miners, all to better their terms and conditions of work. She also worked against the horrors of untouchability amongst the Dalits in the slums, eventually moving to live in the slum itself, and brought the Dalit issue in Maharashtra onto the revolutionary agenda. And she was instrumental in building a women's movement in Nagpur.

As police repression increased, she eventually gave up her position as a sociology lecturer and, in her forties, went underground. Three years before she died, she was sent by the Naxal leadership to live in Adivasi-dominated Dandakaranya, the other guerrilla stronghold—just as Seema had been deputed to Lalgaon—where the best protection could be provided to senior members by the guerrilla armies. In 2004, when the various Naxalite groups united to form the Communist Party of India (Maoist), she was the only woman to be elected to its Central Committee.

Anuradha was clearly a remarkable woman, both an impressive ground-level organiser and a critical thinker—putting into practice the precepts that the world was not only to be interpreted but changed, that thoughts had to be fought for. She was said to be fiercely critical of her own comrades and pushed the Naxalites to address issues that mattered, to 'rectify' the movement from within.

She wrote some of the most insightful reviews of 'the women's issue'. Drawing from thinkers ranging from Gerda Lerner, Simone de Beauvoir, Mary Wollstonecraft, Emma Goldman and Kate Millett to Gayle Rubin and Heidi Hartmann, she applied philosophical trends in the international feminist movement to the Indian context. She developed trenchant critiques of autonomous women's movements and cultural feminists who focused solely on patriarchy and who drew attention to reproduction but often ignored production. She argued that these versions of feminism failed to strengthen the broader movement against capitalism; they resulted only in small women's groups making lifestyle changes within an unchanged system. Her answer was that the shackles of patriarchy could be thrown off only if women participated in the revolutionary movement. 'Women need revolution and revolution needs women,' she said.[4]

213

At the time of her death, Anuradha was leading the women's wing of the Maoists and was said to have been educating Adivasis in Jharkhand against the oppression of women in their own societies, a role that Seema eventually took up.

I admired Seema for her fortitude. But would she have survived within the Maoists' ranks if she were not, as Anuradha had been, married to a high-caste, high-ranking leader, and if she had not upheld the monogamous family structure within the movement? Although single men in the leadership ranks were commonplace, single women in the movement—those who joined single and remained single, or who had husbands who were not involved in the movement—rarely lasted long. They would arouse too much suspicion in relation to their sexual propriety and were at risk of being accused of being 'loose' by others.

Seema's designated task was to fight the feudalism and patriarchy that the Maoists thought existed within Adivasi communities, to raise consciousness among Adivasi women, and to mobilise them for the revolutionary struggle. But was she constrained by the movement's middle-class, caste-based assumptions of what it meant to be a 'good woman'? Was she inhibited from experiencing the gender relations, kinship and family structures, as they existed amongst the Adivasi communities she now lived amidst?

* * *

The Naxalite gender problem seemed to be one that feminist activists and scholars have long called attention to. They have pointed to the necessity to understand the specificities of gender relations in particular contexts and not assume a universal notion of women's subordination and oppression. The idea of a 'universal Indian woman'—the 'patriarchally oppressed', 'disadvantaged woman' in need of 'empowerment'—was one too easily created by the middle classes and higher castes.

The Naxalites were not alone in this construction. I had seen numerous NGOs in Jharkhand holding meetings of so-called 'self-help groups' addressing 'women's empowerment'. They gathered women together in a pre-designed 'participatory' meeting to make them talk about husbands who stole money for drink, who didn't help with the housework and childrearing, assuming women everywhere faced the same issues. Rarely did NGO workers appear to understand what was really going on in these Adivasi households or had the opportunity to take the time to understand their specificities. The result was an assumption that Adivasi gender inequalities were similar to those found in other Indian communities.

I met Seema several times after our first meeting. Whenever she was in the vicinity, she would seek me out to visit her in whatever forest she was in. Just as I was intrigued by her life in the forests, she was intrigued by my life as an anthropologist living amidst the Adivasis in their villages. To my surprise, I discovered that she had not stayed in an Adivasi household for any significant period, although she had been tasked with building the women's movement in the region. I invited her to come home with me and told her that Somwari, whose house it was, would welcome her. I thought she might like to experience life as lived from the perspective of Somwari and the neighbouring Adivasi women.

I wanted her to see how it was common for Adivasi men to cook, wash their own clothes, and do all the household chores—to share the domestic tasks of reproductive labour with the women. I wanted her to know how Adivasi women worked in the forests and fields alongside men, also went to the local bazaars, brought home the bread, kept the home fires burning and maintained the accounts. To acknowledge how Adivasi women were on a far more equal footing with their husbands than was the case in most middle-class, middle- and upper-caste families, and how they were independent and autonomous from their partners, even those who came to be fathers of their children. They didn't wear a veil and were not afraid to flirt and flaunt their sexuality in public places outside the domestic confines of their houses. Most of all, I wanted to discuss with her the ways in which marriage and kinship relations constantly undermined the monogamous family structure that the Naxalites resurrected, and this did not seem to be to the detriment of Adivasi women.

Somwari's partner, Bimal, had in fact first been married off by his upwardly mobile parents to another woman, although he was in love with and already involved in a sexual relationship with Somwari at the age of sixteen. The marriage was a disaster and Bimal left his wife to be with Somwari. The couple started cohabiting and had two children. Amongst the Oraons—the Adivasi community that Bimal and Somwari belonged to—second marriages after children were so common that they even had a special wedding ceremony for such unions in which children were hidden under a wicker basket for the most important part of the marriage ceremony. Bimal and Somwari, however, never got around to having a wedding, although everybody in Lalgaon considered them husband and wife.

A few years after they started living together, the ex-wife decided to strike back. She made legal claims on their land and filed charges against Bimal and Somwari. She said that Bimal had left her for Somwari when she was pregnant with their son. They had to either give her compensation or face incarceration. To escape jail, Bimal spent most months of the year as a construction labourer in Chennai. It was Somwari who ran the household. She looked after their goats and chickens. She leased their land to a cousin to till in return for sharing half of the produce. It was also Somwari who began working as a part-time assistant health worker, when those jobs were introduced in Lalgaon in the year I stayed with her, earning a few hundred rupees each month, ensuring there was always rice and dal to eat. That was how she brought up their son and daughter.

The arrangement seemed to suit Somwari. She developed feelings for an attractive Adivasi teacher, who had come to teach in the local school, when the state had finally tried to fill those posts with Adivasis, and spent many evenings in the teacher's company. Bimal, worried that he was losing Somwari, returned to make his claims on her. The teacher had already left by then because he was afraid the Naxalites were going to accuse him of being a police informer.

During the time I lived with Somwari in Lalgaon, Bimal was present for only two periods of about a month in total. The last time I saw him leave the village, Somwari was expecting a third child, a girl she gave birth to by herself in her own house.

Somwari's case was not unusual. In all the Adivasi villages that I have lived in, it was common for girls and boys to choose their own cohabitating partners, to start living with them and even to have children, with weddings to follow only if they could afford them. It was also common—as common for women as it was for men—that if a relationship went wrong the couple would part and seek other partners.

I wanted Seema to come and live with me and see the relative autonomy of Somwari and my other Adivasi female neighbours, to understand what a large gap there was between the Naxalite assumptions of Adivasi women's subordination and patriarchal gender relations in households and what existed in practice. I also wanted Seema to come to the house and make *hadia* (rice beer) and *mahua* wine with Somwari, and to enjoy drinking it, as we so often did, in innocent merriment with other Adivasi women and men, building community after a hard day of shared work.

* * *

Overnight, writing appeared on the walls of houses and posters were pasted everywhere in Lalgaon, 'Women come forward to strengthen the fight against patriarchy: Ban the brewing of alcohol.' Shortly afterwards, a group of teenage girls of the Women's Liberation Front set about teaching a lesson to those who defied the Maoist decree.

Somwari described in detail the horror of watching Binita, dressed in her guerrilla fatigues, walk into our mud house with a torchlight and make her way to the kitchen. Binita had found all of Somwari's clay pots used for making *mahua*, carried them outside the house and, in full view of all the neighbours, smashed them against the mud wall and stomped on them with her boots. It was not surprising that the girls who willingly took up such tasks were, like Binita, from other areas. It was difficult to see how girls from Lalgaon could have inflicted such violence on their village aunts and uncles.

In non-Adivasi-dominated areas and amongst Hinduised non-Adivasi communities, the Naxalite anti-alcohol campaigns were perhaps warranted. During the 1990s in the caste-divided plains of Andhra Pradesh, the Naxalites had successfully mobilised thousands of rural women to demand the banning of arrack. For two years, the government had been forced to comply. In high-caste households and in Bihari feudal and patriarchal family structures, only men were permitted to drink, in exclusively male environments and behind closed doors. But here in the forests and hills of Adivasi India drinking practices were very different.

In several of the households that I knew, on the day of the *haat*, the one day of the week that was a day of festivity, it was the women who usually went to sell their household wares, who enjoyed rice beer at the *haat* with their male and female friends, and who came home rather merry to husbands who had stayed back and cooked. My neighbour Etwa would say to me that the day of the *haat* was always his turn to cook supper and his wife's to get drunk.

Making and drinking beer and wine, men and women together, signified Adivasi women's relatively egalitarian status in relation to their men. In destroying these cultural markers, were the Maoists harassing those women whose cause they wished to serve? Assumptions of feudalism and patriarchy within Adivasi households, in this respect, were not only out of place but potentially damaging.

* * *

Indian society is noted for a toxic mix of the effects of caste and class that is particularly lethal for the fate of women. Women who belong to elite families in the metropolitan cities and those who come from matriarchal societies are exceptions. In most of the rest of India, the further you move up the caste hierarchy, the less the autonomy for women, who are usually confined to domestic life in their homes. Moreover, when low castes become upwardly mobile and aspire to be middle-class, they often reproduce these upper-caste norms. Challenges to economic inequality through the upward mobility of low castes, therefore, can actually increase gender inequities within households as patriarchy emerges where it had barely touched before.

The problem, in the Maoist case, was the combination of status and upward mobility that being with the movement could bring to young Adivasi men like Vikas and girls like Binita. This sense of upward mobility was accompanied by a valorisation of a new set of middle-class upper-caste values around femininity and masculinity which had little space for respecting the independence, autonomy and lifestyles of Adivasi women like Somwari.

Over the time I lived with Somwari I watched her grow ever more anxious about the fate of her children. Her cousin's son had become one of the few Adivasi Naxalite couriers and small contractors and made bunkers in the forests to hide their arms. But one day the Naxalites accused him of becoming a police informer, tried him at a forest meeting, found him guilty, and shot him dead. Meanwhile, two of Somwari's sisters' children had joined the Maoist armies. One had a bad leg and the family was worried he would be caught in the crossfire and would not be able to run. The other had migrated to Maharashtra to work, had been beaten by the Hindu nationalist Shiv Sena men who wanted to send all the Biharis back to where they came from, and then joined the Maoists. Somwari did not like what she saw was happening to these children.

She said, 'They were the children of our homes and our villages, but when they join the *Jungle Sarkar* they can do anything, there is no guarantee that they won't turn against you. They can forget that we are their *chachis* and their *fufus* (aunts).' She said that they now had 'the power'. Binita coming around to smash her alcohol pots was a potent example. Somwari became more and more afraid that her own children might run away to the guerrilla armies too and turn against her. Would they become a Vikas or a Binita?

The irony of the situation—that perhaps it was the Maoists who were helping to promote and encourage the rise of patriarchal attitudes within Adivasi societies—was brought home to me in the celebration of International Women's Day on 8 March 2009 in Lalgaon.

Across the remote forests of central and eastern India, the Naxalites gathered villagers together for this celebration. They saw themselves as carrying on the legacy of the German Marxist theorist and activist, Clara Zetkin, who organised the first International Women's Day in 1911. I had received a two-page letter they had printed about Women's Day. It began with a women's oath to fight against American capitalist society and work for the welfare of the common people, moved on to the subject of the downturn in the Indian economy, causing women employees to be laid off and the extra burden that had fallen on women in the household, and ended with discussing the rape and killing of women accused of being Maoists. The letter arrived just before the Maoists asked for at least one person from each house to attend the International Women's Day celebrations.

I went with Somwari and my two neighbours. One of the neighbours came bearing a grudge. She was busy planting tomatoes in her garden and didn't want to leave the day's work incomplete. Somwari also only came reluctantly. She was upset because for at least a year she had been unsuccessfully asking the Naxalite leaders for help in fighting the charges that Bimal's ex-wife was pressing against them. No one had come to her assistance and instead Binita had broken her pots. If they won't help me, she said, why should I waste my day for them? But the third neighbour told them to stop being so moody. It would be a fun outing, she said, and raise everyone's spirits.

So off we walked, 4 kilometres into the forest of a neighbouring village where the Women's Day celebrations were being held. From a distance, it looked a pretty sight, with lots of women and a few men gathered in a clearing decorated with colourful bunting strung up between the trees. Journalists had been called in from the local city and an attractive picture of 'Red Guerrillas celebrating Women's Day' was presented in the local newspapers the following day.

As we got closer, however, I saw that the men and women had been segregated and were being pushed into disciplined lines. Binita's analogue—a new young Adivasi woman in her twenties from the Women's Liberation Front from another area—was wearing a black salwar dress with a scarf around her waist and a pistol secured to it. Together with Vikas, also with a pistol at his hip, she was strutting up and down the clearing, shouting at and even pushing women much older than herself into position. The ceremony proceeded on the orders of these young Adivasi cadres, as though the Adivasi women who had gathered there, many of whom were old enough to be the cadres' parents, were cattle.

In celebrating International Women's Day of all things, the Maoists had inadvertently given power to this new generation of young leaders to bully their elders. These young soldiers seemed to use their newfound authority to undermine the relations of respect and deference with which they would have behaved in their own households. After that incident, it was hard not to feel that Somwari and my neighbours didn't need the valorisation of Clara Zetkin to liberate them.

18

NIGHT SIX

The shadow of a soldier stirred. He bent down to awaken another. The hour was up and it was time to change sentry duty. There was some grumbling from under the blanket that he was shaking. 'Wake up! Wake up!' the soldier whispered. No response.

'Come on,' his voice grew louder and more agitated. The lump under the blanket finally moved and somebody staggered out, mumbling their annoyance at being awoken. Would he fall asleep again on sentry duty? Despite this noise, there was no movement at all from any of the other sleeping men.

I was becoming increasingly frustrated because I knew I desperately needed to rest to survive the next days of the march, for the end seemed nowhere in sight. Yet my mind just wouldn't shut down, and my thoughts kept racing back to Seema and Somwari.

The contours of Gyanji's face stood out dark against the moonlit night. Kohli was between us, under Gyanji's blanket, his head and entire body huddled under the covers where it was warm. I watched Kohli's silhouette turn over under the covers. If he stayed with the Maoists, what kind of a man would he become? Would he eventually develop a more patriarchal attitude

towards women than those that existed in the Adivasi households of Lalgaon where he had grown up?

It felt as though I was sleeping on a bed of rocks. I recalled that
Gyanji and I had once had a conversation about the Muria and
Gond Adivasi *ghotul* (a kind of dormitory—a spacious mud hut—
for youth to gather) in Chhattisgarh and the *dhumkuria,* its
equivalent in the Oraon and Munda Adivasi areas of Jharkhand. It
was a sacred tribal hut for youth—a 'children's republic', Verrier
Elwin had called it[1]—and existed in many villages, a place where
girls and boys came to sing and dance, tell stories, plan village
festivals, allot duties, and sometimes sleep together.

Gyanji had said, 'As communists we don't approve of the
ghotul; we are against premarital sexual relations because such
relations don't seem to be about much more than freedom of
choice.' I had tried to defend the *ghotul,* saying that it was not a
space of anarchy as he interpreted it; there were rules about what
you could and couldn't do. And besides, what was wrong with
premarital sexual relations?

I wanted to awaken Gyanji and talk to him about these
thoughts that were racing through my mind. To point out to
him the potential virtues of the romantic liaisons between
Adivasi youth who joined the Maoists, and to suggest that perhaps the guerrilla armies provided the space that the *ghotul* once
had in Adivasi society. I wanted to make the case for the possibility that premarital and extramarital sexual relations in fact
gave Adivasi women greater economic autonomy and respect in
relation to their men than their higher-caste counterparts could
enjoy. In a country which put so many constraints on women, I
wanted to ask him about the many women who came to live with
the guerrillas because of a man they had fallen in love with in the
squads. And of the virtues of being able to leave their partners if
they were unhappy with the relationship. So, I brought the subject up.

'Sexual anarchy,' muttered Gyanji as he drifted in and out of sleep. I had realised that this was how he slept. I could talk to him all night long in his state of semi-sleep and in the morning he would remember the entire conversation, but also say that he had slept well.

Annoyed, I asked him why he couldn't celebrate the Naxalites for inadvertently creating a space for voluntary sex-love relationships and why he had to be so moralistic about them. I can't understand, I continued, why as a Marxist you want to idolise family structures based on monogamous marriages. Weren't they often about the subordination of women for the protection of private property owned by men? I asked. Don't you think Engels, one of your heroes, was right?[2] That with the development of capitalism and the need to transmit wealth across generations, we have seen the increasing enslavement of women in monogamous family structures?

Gyanji was clearly getting upset with me for confronting him with these questions and brushed them aside, saying I didn't understand.

I knew that the Maoist leaders were concerned about the widespread media propaganda against them. Male leaders were accused of sexually exploiting low-caste female cadres. They wanted to maintain a 'pure image' of the movement, far from condoning casual sexual encounters. Any romantic liaisons were disrupted by the Maoists by assigning the couple to different platoons, by suspending one partner for a while, or, most commonly, by encouraging their marriage to make them 'legitimate'.

Although there were no Hindu rituals, a pledge of marriage was the only legitimate way in which a couple could be intimate amongst the Naxalites. Permission to marry had to be sought from the movement's leadership and would be determined by showing that the desire to be together was not just sexual but would help the revolutionary cause. Marriages were assumed to be lifelong partnerships, and the conjugal union was to be a democratic one, prohibiting inequalities of any kind between the husband and the wife. Couples had to be prepared to spend long periods apart due to the demands of war—many of the leaders like Gyanji often didn't see their wives for six months or more. Wanting divorce without good reason amounted to irresponsibility and anarchy, a product of individualistic thinking that did not prioritise collective interest. If disputes arose between a couple, other comrades had the responsibility of settling them, ensuring that divorce would not be granted unless there really was an insurmountable problem. Ultimately though, I said to Gyanji, what was or wasn't a problem would be decided by a male high-caste leadership and it seemed that the emphasis on marriage—as the only legitimate way in which two people could be close—was about controlling women.

Using Marxist terminology, Gyanji accused me of being 'mechanical' in my thinking. From his point of view, I knew this was a damning criticism. I wasn't sure exactly what he meant by 'mechanical' in this context, except that I wasn't applying the art of discussing and examining opposing arguments and ideas in order to find the truth.

'Then teach me to be "dialectical",' I retorted. But he only responded with a deep sigh, indicating that he had drifted back into unconsciousness. I didn't have the heart to raise the question about the Naxalite perspective on same-sex unions. I think I knew that there wasn't one.

I was surrounded by all the sleeping men, huddled together under blankets they had amassed, piled up on top of one another, seeking bodily warmth from each other. I felt bitterly cold. I wished Seema were with me and that we could talk about these matters. Seema hadn't been able to come and stay with me in Somwari's house in the end. There must have been concerns about her security, but I wondered if part of the reason was that we needed the permission of the male leadership for that.

PART SEVEN

WHAT CAME TO PASS

19

NIGHT SEVEN

I was told that the final night of walking lay ahead. How many nights had it been since we left the festive tents of the camp in the state of Bihar? I no longer knew. It felt as though we had been marching for years. A sense of timelessness and spacelessness had overcome me as we trekked endlessly through a huge distance across the centre of India. Time had done a peculiar stretching trick, as though it no longer existed. The different landscapes—rocky gorges, forested hills and rice fields—seemed to merge into each other.

War usually has beginnings, climaxes and ends, and the experience of it is sometimes described as long periods of boredom punctuated by short moments of excitement. But this kind of guerrilla war seemed above all else an eternal march of endurance to erase one's presence from a place and, at the same time, to survive in it. In some ways the seemingly endless quality, and the ups and downs, of the nightmarch seemed to be an encapsulation of the Naxalite struggle itself—its meanderings, let-downs, and puzzling persistence.

All I could remember was walking. Every muscle in my body was exhausted. My shoulders felt like a dead weight imposing themselves on the rest of my body. My legs tingled with numbness. My feet were tender. All conversation had stopped, as though it was a waste of the limited resources we had between us. It seemed crucial to conserve any remaining strength for essential tasks only. I tried to focus on copying Kohli's footsteps again. One foot in front of the other.

We were to cross a vast agricultural plain dissected first by a major highway and then by the ever-changing waters of a wide river. An impassable fast-flowing torrent of muddy brown water in the rainy season, it reduced to a mere trickle in the dry season and was now not likely to be more than knee deep.

Only six or seven more hours, I was told. Then we would be back in the forests of Jharkhand that marked my home territory, near to Lalgaon. I knew that 'six or seven hours' could easily mean ten or twenty. I was not sure whether this imprecision was an attempt to keep our spirits up or if the inability to judge the distance was the cause of the continually changing estimates for our arrival.

We stopped under two huge jackfruit trees in a forest. We were waiting for another platoon to join us for this, the last stretch. I imagined other platoons, like the spokes of a wheel, converging from many directions, from various corners of the country, sometimes branching together, as they all made their way to the central hub, the final camp for the Jharkhand State-level Conference.

They looked a motley crew as they walked towards us, very different from the disciplined company we had met in the territory of the mercenary gang. There was a shaggy dishevelled horse amidst them. Kohli's eyes lit up when he saw that with that platoon was Parasji, the man who had befriended his father all those years ago, and with whom Kohli had pleaded to take him into the *Jungle Sarkar*.

It was Parasji who had the idea of enlisting a horse to carry injured comrades, but Kohli and the other young men laughed at the sight of the animal. It was short and stout, more a pony than a horse. Kohli said it would never be able to climb the rocky trails we would encounter in the hilly forests of Lalgaon. Parasji had not yet dared to ride the animal himself, although he was limping. He had a huge raw gash across the back of his right foot, plastered with a dirty bandage that was beginning to unravel.

There was then another surprise. Seven women. Four were not much older than sixteen and one looked as if she were about twelve. Two wore saris and were clearly in their twenties. One of them had a baby on her back, harnessed in a shawl. None of them wore fatigues or carried weapons. I was told it was the Children's Cultural Wing and the Women's Liberation Front. A man from our platoon ran towards them and took the baby boy from his mother. The father of the child, Kohli said.

I recognised the woman leading them as Tara, Kohli's gentle and soft-spoken older cousin with a striking heart-shaped face and whom Kohli's sister and younger cousin had followed into the guerrilla armies. Even for an Adivasi she was petite. She had joined the guerrilla armies five years ago when she had fallen in love with a platoon commander who frequented her house. The couple now had a three-year-old son who was in an Adivasi Hostel. It made Tara deeply sad. We had talked about her situation before and she had said that she felt trapped. She couldn't leave the guerrilla armies now to look after her son as the security forces would pursue her; she had far too many police cases against her.

When Parasji came up to us, I could see Gyanji questioning him with his eyes, indicating towards the girls with a subtle glance. Parasji shrugged his shoulders and replied that he had not known what to do. The women had insisted on coming to the festivities of the camp in Jharkhand. How could he disappoint them? he asked. Tell them it was too dangerous to walk for a night when they knew this terrain like the backs of their hands?

There wasn't much time to chat. The sun had just set and we needed to start walking. Parasji and his bodyguard fell into line behind me and the rest of his platoon joined the back of our formation to make what the guerrillas called a 'company'. There were now eighty of us walking single file. I was impressed by the speed and discipline with which we all moved. Over two and a half hours we stopped only once, for a pee break.

A group of young men had been sent on ahead to prepare our evening meal. There were too many of us to burden one village so it was decided that we should cook for ourselves. The youths bought rice and dal from a village shop owner and acquired the keys to the kitchen in the local primary school. They cooked with the vats and on the hearths that in the daytime were used for the children's 'free midday meal'.

Gyanji said that in the fierce anti-feudal struggles of the 1980s, a courageous woman Naxalite leader had been killed by the security forces in this village. To commemorate her martyrdom, the Naxalites had built a memorial as well as the school. Although now it was not much more than a pile of crumbling rubble, traces of the concrete pyramidal monument still existed. The Naxalite-established school had, however, been taken over by the government, so it now looked like any other state primary school in the area.

By the time we arrived, the food was nearly ready. Parasji called me over and gave me a pot of water to wash my hands before eating; whether we were marching or not, basic hygiene was followed. To my surprise, it was warm. He said that he always tried to wash his hands in warm water as otherwise they developed cracks. Even in these tense moments of utter exhaustion, Parasji cared for his hands!

I walked over to the serving area to help. I wanted to talk to the commander of the new platoon who was dishing out the rice. 'You remind me of a lady I met many years ago,' he said. 'She spoke English just like you.' Intrigued, I asked him to tell me more. He said she was European but had been married to a Gujarati, and that he came to know her because he had kidnapped her to get her husband's guns.

I let out a gasp; I was serving rice and dal beside my Austrian friend's abductor. I reproached him for driving the poor woman away from her home in the countryside and into the city. Wasn't kidnapping precisely the kind of felony that tarred the Naxalites with the same brush as criminals and terrorists? I asked. He agreed but said that they had had little choice at the time as they needed those guns, and maintained that they had done their best to treat her with the distinction of a 'five-star guest' and ensure that she didn't face any kind of discomfort. He had a point, for although the incident had terrified my Austrian friend she had nonetheless developed a soft spot for the Naxalites because of the intimacy she had shared with them that one night.

It took more than an hour and a half for everyone to eat and put everything back as it had been found in the school. I devoured the dal and rice. The simplest of meals, it had become a banquet after the arduous trek on an empty stomach since that morning. I recalled Prashant teasing me the night before we left him back at the forest city-camp in Bihar. He had said that there was no way I would survive the long march ahead if I continued to eat like a mouse. He was right. I needed a big helping of rice now. Although my serving wasn't quite as large as the mountainous portions that the others consumed, it was at least twice as much as I had been accustomed to eating before embarking on the march.

I washed my hands and plate under the hand pump and went to talk to some of the other new arrivals. But, as I sat on the veranda of the school with Tara, tiredness overtook me and I fell asleep.

I was awoken for the roll call at 10:00 p.m. Gyanji assured me that this really was the last leg of the journey. We would not walk for much more than four hours across the plains before we would be in the safety of the forests not far from Lalgaon.

One foot in front of the other. Then there was a sudden jerk in my neck. The weight of my head had collapsed onto my chest. I realised I had dozed off while walking and awoke with a jolt. My eyelids were heavy and I struggled to keep my eyes open as we marched on. My neck jerked again, and then again.

'Sleep-walking', the guerrillas called it. They could all do it. I used to laugh in disbelief when they told me about it in the months before, not once imagining that I would share their lives to such an extent that I would find myself walking in my sleep as they did. I had never experienced it before. My head seemed to empty of all consciousness and awareness moved to my feet, which continued to place themselves one in front of the other with mechanical regularity. They intuitively appeared to sense the unevenness of the ground beneath them without recourse to the eyes or the brain.

Four hours later, it was obvious that something was wrong. We ought to have been surrounded by the forests by then. Gyanji had been uneasy for most of the previous hour. It became clear that we were not on the route they normally took through this area.

Moreover, there were two new Central Reserve Police Force camps with at least a thousand men of the security forces stationed in these plains now, all trained as commandos in counter-terrorism and jungle warfare tactics. They were there to conduct domination exercises to sanitise the area and get rid of the guerrillas by going out on regular patrols and setting up ambushes.

Vikas was leading us. He kept running back when Gyanji beckoned him, bringing assurances that everything was under control and that the pilots up ahead were on the right track. But clearly something was amiss.

I was annoyed with Gyanji. He seemed to be taking too lenient an attitude towards Vikas. Did Vikas know where he was going?

Was he deliberately leading us astray? Wasn't this exactly how ambushes were set up? We seemed to be sitting ducks.

Parasji, meanwhile, seemed oblivious to my concerns about Vikas. Noticing my struggle to keep up, he suggested that I should ride the horse. I tried to protest, afraid to lose control of my mobility to an animal. But he insisted. I was too tired to hold my ground. In any case, I wasn't sure I was the best judge of what was good for me at that stage and so I gave in.

The saddle was a pile of blankets and the stirrups were two loopholes knotted in a jute rope. It was far from comfortable but lolling up and down on the animal certainly kept me awake.

An ear-splitting bang resounded through the landscape. The horse bolted away from the line. With my heart in my mouth, I dug my calves into its side and tugged ineffectually at the reins for a few seconds and then wrapped my arms around the horse's neck, hanging on for dear life. Just as I was about to free my feet of the stirrups, there was another boom.

Kohli ran to my side, grabbed the reins and brought the spooked horse to a halt before helping me dismount.

'Run!' people were shouting.

'Let's go, *Didi*.' And so I ran, trying to keep up with Kohli. Earlier that night, when I had been constantly on the brink of falling asleep as I walked, I wouldn't have believed that I was capable of running at all. I hadn't known that when you think you have a gang of armed men after you, you find the strength to run. I was half sick with fright.

I passed others who had stopped in their tracks to fling themselves onto the ground and crouch down behind the rice bunds. Some of them appeared to be crawling on their bellies towards what look like the contours of reeds. I wondered whether I should follow suit. I couldn't keep up with Kohli and he disappeared from my sight.

Then I heard the voices of North Indian soldiers. And although I didn't know if they were imagined or real, and although I didn't know where I was going, the voices galvanised me into running faster.

'Everyone back in line!' I heard Gyanji, and then Parasji, shouting. 'Stop running! Calm down! Don't disperse!' Parasji's voice rang through the air.

They said it was only a shotgun. Probably a hunter in the jungle or someone just practising their shooting. The Indian security forces, they assured us, would not be out now.

I stopped running. Guerrillas emerged from all sides like ghosts. A company line was formed again.

But after the recent panic, the line kept breaking. It seemed that everyone's nerves were frayed. Soldiers were huddled together and the space between groups kept increasing. It was hard to keep eighty people together and we soon became a ragtag bunch of misfits roaming the landscape. Gyanji was in despair as he said we were losing discipline when we needed it the most. It was as though the gun had shot through the confidence of everyone in the guerrilla army.

I never discovered what the gunshot was but I grew increasingly frustrated with Gyanji for not taking Vikas to task and for not taking on the responsibility to lead the company himself. So many lives were at stake now. However, I was too shaken to speak, and focused my energies back on placing my feet one in front of the other.

It must have been five o'clock in the morning when we entered a patch of forest. We were to rest there for no more than ten minutes. Yet bags were thrown on the ground and people collapsed onto whatever clearing was closest to them. There was no attempt to keep any kind of military formation. Within minutes it looked like most of the eighty-odd crew was fast asleep. I wondered how people could sleep under such stressful conditions.

I sat beside Gyanji, fully aware that he was aghast that everyone had just dropped off to sleep. I knew that having stopped, everyone would now find it extremely hard to start walking again. With such exhaustion, it was more important than ever to keep the rhythm of the march going. I said to myself that under no circumstances must I allow my eyes to close, although my eyelids were like lead weights that wouldn't stop sinking.

I awoke to Gyanji's bellowing voice, a sound that I had never heard before. He could no longer contain his wrath with Vikas and was shouting at us from atop a small mound. 'Do you all want to die in this forest?' he thundered. He said that dawn would soon be upon us and then the two security camps would set out on their patrols. They would surround us within minutes and, in the state of exhaustion that we were in, any confrontation would be very dangerous.

I felt awful for having succumbed to sleep, but there was no time for regret. At the sound of Gyanji's angry shouts, everyone was up, slinging their bags and rifles across their shoulders. He split us into three platoons. He said that it was too close to sunrise to continue as one company and we would move faster separated.

Each platoon was to take a different path back into the hills. I was now being told that we would meet the next day at the final camp. With resigned disappointment, I wondered whether it would be just one more day.

A new leader who knew the route was allocated to each platoon. The women, girls and children were separated as one formation, led by Tara. Wearing saris and salwar dresses and not the olive-green fatigues, they were instructed to walk as ordinary villagers going to visit relatives. In case of danger, they could easily disperse and disappear amidst the villagers. Another group was headed by Parasji. Gyanji led the final formation which consisted of almost everyone from our original platoon. Kohli and I were to go with him, as was Vikas. These two platoons would walk about a kilometre apart so that they could support each other in case of an emergency.

There was no bidding farewell. There was no time for that. Nobody but Gyanji spoke and that was only to bark out instructions. Although the sun was rising, it felt as though an opaque dark cloud was hanging above us.

At dawn, a wide sandy riverbed with large craggy granite boulders jutting out at the shore edges lay before us. Some of the boulders towered above us. The water was so clear that you could see small fish darting around. We took off our shoes and rolled up our trousers to our thighs, adjusting our bags to make sure they hung above our waists. The water felt warm and refreshing against my legs. The sand, cool, soft and soothing between my toes. The river crossing seemed to calm everybody, reviving us for the last hurdle before the hills.

A railway line lay ahead of us. A train could be heard in the distance but there were rows of bushes between the line and us. We crouched amidst the thicket to hide. The train's horn, warning animals and people to get off the tracks, blared increasingly louder. The rumble on the tracks turned into a roar. The ground shook under me and the hairs on the back of my neck stood on end. My tiredness was overtaken by a surge of adrenaline. What would happen if we were spotted? What if there were security forces on the train? Which way would I run?

As the train rounded the corner, I could see that it was carrying goods. Its blue engine was hauling a long line of maroon wagons open to the skies and piled high with mounds of dark grey. Like the trucks we had passed earlier, it was carrying coal. Bogie after bogie thundered past, leaving me in a hypnotic trance. Perhaps fifty in all, they seemed never-ending. Where was it taking the coal? To the factories of which corporation? Tata? Jindal? Mittal?

I realised that these were the tracks that I had read about in the local newspapers. It was here that the guerrillas had, on several occasions, ambushed passing trains that were trying to cross on a day that the Naxalites had declared an economic blockade of the state. It was also here that they had blown up parts of the track for the same reason. It was surreal to think that the platoon I was with might, in another situation, be laying a landmine under those very tracks.

When the last of the bogies was well out of sight, we walked on. I began to see the shapes of individual *sal* trees and distinguish one bright-green mass from another. As the forest closed in on us, a small Adivasi hamlet emerged. There we took a short break as everyone wetted their parched throats, drawing water out of a well. Gyanji insisted that we would only rest when we had ascended some distance into the hills.

At long last, we stopped and I collapsed on a mossy grass bank by a bamboo grove. The tension began to leave my shoulders; my body relaxed despite my aching legs and feet. I slipped off my shoes and socks. The brand new green trainers that Prashant had given me at the start of the walk were now brown, ragged and looked like they had been worn for years. My feet, a startling white in comparison to my tanned hands, were damp and tender. I had not dried them carefully after wading across the river. I wriggled my toes to restore the circulation and sensation in them.

Gyanji sat down beside me. Do you think, I asked, that Vikas intentionally led us down that path so that we would end up exhausted, collapsing in that small patch of forest, at the mercy of the security forces?

Before Gyanji could respond, Kohli came to us with two cups of red tea. Like a magician doing a trick, from his pocket he produced a green custard apple as large as my fist, which he had just picked. His eyes were alight with boyish excitement and warmth. He wanted to surprise us with his find, hoping that we would be as delighted as he was. His spidery fingers adeptly pulled the fruit apart revealing the white flesh inside. He presented Gyanji and me with the biggest pieces and kept the smaller one for himself, laughing as his brilliant white teeth bit into the fruit and spat the pips onto the ground. In a moment of uncomplicated happiness, I inhaled its sweet fragrance deeply and sank my teeth into its creamy flesh.

In the years to come, this scene became one of my most enduring memories of Kohli. It was then that I felt we were finally in safe territory. We walked for one more day into the guerrilla stronghold, sleeping for a few hours in the dark on the outskirts of a village, under a haystack housed on a bamboo structure. Early the next morning, at 3:00 a.m., before the villagers stirred and it was still dark, we crossed by my home in Lalgaon.

We climbed high into the hills behind the house. There, another Naxalite forest city had been erected a week ago. At least 500 guerrillas, from various other parts of the country, were already gathered there. Halfway up the last hill, as we reached the clearing that had been made into a kitchen and dining area, we saw a line of guerrillas—soldier after soldier—waiting to welcome us.

The next few days were a blur. I remember eating, bathing and changing into the embroidered red salwar dress Prashant had given me, relieved to return the olive-green guerrilla uniform and no longer having to remember to be a man. I must have collapsed under one of the tents soon after and was overtaken by a deep sleep. When I finally awoke, I realised I had been asleep all night and all day.

I followed the sound of drum beats and singing. All the soldiers except those on sentry duty were gathered in one large circle in a clearing in the forest nearby. The atmosphere was jolly and the platoons from Bihar were leaping into the air, playing the *dhol*, a North Indian drum, and singing songs in Bhojpuri. But as one song medleyed into another, I could see some of the Adivasi soldiers standing on the side with their *nagda* and their *mandar*, Adivasi drums, looking on, getting increasingly agitated.

Gyanji was quick to notice their distress and intervene. He said that was enough Bhojpuri, we now needed the songs from the south, the Adivasi songs, in Nagpuri and Sadri. It pacified the soldiers. But the next day Kohli told me that all the Adivasis were talking about the Biharis taking over the Jharkhandis and the need to ensure democracy in the singing and dancing. The fault lines between the plains and the hills were difficult to erase.

I left the camp early one morning, escorted by Gyanji, Kohli, my Austrian friend's abductor and a few other soldiers who dropped me off in the woods by Somwari's house, where I had lived for the last year and a half and to which I returned for one last night. I couldn't look at them when we parted. I knew that it was probably the last time that I would see them.

Somwari had prepared my favourite dry potato curry and chilka roti made from rice flour for breakfast. I ate in silence. Then, with great attention to every fold, she carefully wrapped me in a green sari with white polka dots as though I were a delicate parcel that had to be safely sent off. I boarded the jeep and watched her trying to cheerfully wave me off but I could see the tears flowing down her cheeks.

I tried to stop the sobbing that was rising from my stomach, grateful to have to attend to the practical task of trying to squeeze into the jeep, squashed between eight women sitting on one small seat that was meant to hold four people. Like them, I was now an expert at adjusting to the space—one person leaning forward with half a buttock on the seat, another edging to the back of the seat with at least one person on her thigh, and so the pattern was repeated. The youths had climbed onto the roof and were hanging off the back, two sitting on the bonnet, leaving just half the windscreen for the driver to see through.

The owner of the vehicle clearly took pride in the jeep. Red velvet patterned with burgundy roses lined the inside of the roof and a fancy sound system was blasting Nagpuria music. The ground was so dry that, as we bounced across the rocky road, everyone's hair soon looked as though it had been dusted with Johnson's baby powder. We weaved through the forest and hurtled down the mountainside at great speed. My head was throbbing but I knew it was important for the driver to be hooting loudly and blaring out his music. This cacophony of sound had been agreed with the guerrillas so that they would know when a public jeep was descending—and not a police vehicle—and refrain from triggering the land mines laid under the tracks.

I could see from a distance that where the tarmac road began, the security forces had erected a new checkpoint. At least a dozen heavily-armed men were gathered there and had stopped a jeep that must have left some fifteen minutes before us. They had made everybody get out, were conducting body searches of the men and checking everyone's bags.

Sweat was dripping down my spine yet I felt a chill. My first thoughts were about my notebook, camera, mike and recorder. I could not afford to lose them at this final stage. But to my dismay, I soon realised that the stakes were higher. I desperately hoped I would pass off as a local and that they would not distinguish me from everyone else since we were all covered in dust. An outsider in these areas would immediately be taken to be a Maoist leader. I would be given no opportunity to bring out my British passport, my LSE university letters, or call a friend. It would be rough and tough with these men.

Flashing before me were images of the old disused oil factory that had recently been taken over as a Central Reserve Police Force camp in the nearby district town. Barbed wire fences ran along top of the high walls and sentry battlements, each with three soldiers, armed with machine guns poised to fire out. That was all one could see of the camp from the roadside. Inside, the compound was a black hole in my imagination. A place where people disappeared. That's where I would be taken. The villagers of Lalgaon called it 'the Torture Centre'.

Several young men from Lalgaon had already been taken there, severely beaten, legs split, limbs broken and given electric shocks, before they were presented in police custody. What would happen to a woman? The stories from women taken prisoners in other parts of the country were horrific. Being stripped naked. Sexual assault. Rape. Stones inserted into private parts. I shuddered.

The jeep came to a halt. I dared not look up. All I could see were big feet in tough black boots all around me. Their Hindi was rough. A stark contrast to the sweetly-spoken local language Sadri. These were Northerners.

They ordered us to get out. Before I could stop her, my neighbour, trying to be helpful, took my bag. I protested but she had already walked off with it towards the three soldiers who had formed a barricade for us to move past. In horror, I watched a tall, light-skinned, well-built man with a thick moustache shove the stock of his rifle into my neighbour's side and into my bag.

A feisty woman, she shouted at him to be careful. I held my breath and walked towards them wondering what to do. Should I approach him and claim the bag before he attacked her and threw her into the police jeep, or should I stay silent?

Then I recalled that I had buried my equipment in the bottom of the bag. Bras and pants were on top. Too embarrassed to delve deeper, the soldier removed the rifle from the bag.

His attention diverted by my neighbour and my bag, the soldier didn't notice me as I walked straight past him. I heaved a silent sigh of relief and walked rapidly towards our jeep that the passengers were clambering back onto.

This was the closest that a checkpoint had ever been to Lalgaon. They were slowly closing in on the guerrilla strongholds. How long would it be before they had tarmacked the road right up into Lalgaon and erected permanent barracks there? How long before a new influx of outsiders would set up business for a new infrastructure for the mining opportunities that surrounded Lalgaon? How long before the villagers were bought off, co-opted, shown as 'surrendered', or evicted? I felt like I was witnessing and leaving behind the juggernaut of perhaps one of the greatest people-clearing operations of our times.

20

INCARNATIONS

Trying to sink back into life in London was hard. Eating with a knife and fork, going to the cinema or the theatre, and sleeping on a soft mattress all felt like alien experiences that I somehow had to learn anew. Perhaps the most difficult was slipping through the barriers to march in line with the city workers going down into the stations of the London Underground. I found myself cycling along Essex Road, down Rosebery Avenue and onto High Holborn, talking to Kohli, turning to Gyanji, thinking of Prashant, joking with Somwari, as though they were all there. Everywhere I seemed to search for ways in which I could connect my life back to those I had left behind.

The road into the hills of Lalgaon has now been paved, electricity cables interrupt the skyline, and the spaces for the night-march that I embarked upon in 2010 have been closed. A security force camp has been established in Lalgaon. The military might of the Indian state has encircled the mineral-rich guerrilla zones and the voices of journalists, human rights activists and scholars trying to shed light on what is afoot in these remote parts of central and eastern India have been increasingly silenced.

In Lalgaon, the soldiers occupied the school where I used to teach for several months while a permanent barracks was constructed next door. Children now go to class against the backdrops of its high walls and barbed wire fences. At least 500 soldiers are based there. On many occasions, there are at least twice that number, I am told. It is one of eighteen such security camps constructed since 2014 in the remote forests of Jharkhand as part of the focused 'Action Plans' to erase the 'menace of Naxalism'. In 2018, thirty more security camps have been planned across the state.

Meanwhile, many people I know who had police cases against them—like Rafiq—have had no choice but to 'surrender'. In the six years after I left, the South Asia Terrorism Portal claims that over 6,000 people have surrendered across the country. The government offered handsome bounty—often between 1.5 and 2.5 lakh rupees (£1,700 to £,2800) and more for weapons—depending on the seniority of the Naxalite and the rifles with which he or she surrenders. But scholars, lawyers and human rights activists have said that many of these surrenders are 'fake' and that Adivasis are being coerced.[1] In Jharkhand, the National Human Rights Commission said that between 2012 and 2014 more than 500 Adivasi youths who had no links with the Naxalites were made to surrender.[2] Human rights activists also report that 4,000 Adivasis charged as 'Naxalite' are in the prisons of Jharkhand and kept incarcerated for years on end without trial.[3] The Jharkhand Director General of Police has promised to 'eradicate Naxalism' before the end of 2018.[4] It appears that this is to be at any cost.

Back in London, out of desperation, I threw myself into my academic writing and speaking, churning out one analysis after another. It was as though by abstracting Gyanji, Kohli, Vikas, Prashant or Somwari from the forests of Jharkhand I would achieve the distance I needed from them to know what to do with the significance of their stories.

INCARNATIONS

At the end of March 2013, three years after I had left the jungles of eastern India, I was sitting in my north London study with the sweet scent of jasmine diffusing through my open sash window when I received news of a military encounter. I saw it first as a news bulletin in the *Times of India*. Almost simultaneously it rang in my inbox as a press release from the Revolutionary Democratic Front, an Indian civil liberties and human rights organisation. I read about it in one Indian newspaper after another as I frantically searched the Internet, trying to piece together the puzzle of the story, even though I knew I would never establish the true course of events in this way.

On the same journey that I had embarked upon in February 2010, walking from Bihar to Jharkhand in a platoon of a similar size, ten Maoist guerrillas had been killed in the Lakarbandha forest by the Indian security forces. Alongside the empty cartridges, the police captured seven rifles including an AK-47, cane bombs and Maoist literature. The Indian security forces suffered no losses.

The tales of what exactly had happened varied. Some said that a mercenary gang engaged the guerrillas in a nightlong gun battle. By the time the Indian security forces arrived, the casualties had already been suffered. Washing their hands of the killings, the police said that the gang was a breakaway Maoist group. Meanwhile, sympathisers of the guerrillas claimed that the gang was a mercenary arm of the state. I knew that both these stories could be correct. The leading gang members could be renegade Maoists now working for the Indian government.

Other reports said the guerrillas were drugged while having their supper in the local village. The poison had been inserted in the sickly sweet Indian confection *barfi*, made of condensed milk and sugar, gifted by a road contractor to one of the guerrillas who had shared it with his comrades. A traitor within the guerrilla armies was likely to have been complicit in this act. Their sentries intoxicated, the guerrillas were easily surrounded, captured and killed.

As I read on, I saw flashes of Vikas bringing the *gulab jamun* to our platoon from the contractor three years ago.

Still other reports said that in the middle of the night, a 200-man-strong combined battalion of the Indian security forces and a mercenary gang had surrounded and overpowered the thirty guerrillas who were asleep under the trees. There had been an informer in the platoon. The battle began at 3:00 a.m. and two guerrillas died soon after. By noon the next day, the guerrillas had run out of bullets, and found themselves surrounded in a dry riverbed with no option but to surrender. The mercenary gang and the security forces accepted their surrender and their arms, but then they rounded up, tortured and shot dead eight of the most senior guerrillas.

It was only from the news stories of the encounter that I learned that the real name of the now-dead leader of that platoon was Lalesh Yadav. As the reports confirmed to me, Lalesh was the handsome young man with chiselled features and large brown eyes who was the first Naxalite guerrilla to welcome me when I transited from 'overground' to 'underground' in Bihar, and had greeted me with a rehydrating solution. He was known amongst the Naxalites by the *nom de guerre* Prashant.

Was there a Vikas on that journey; someone who had turned against the guerrilla armies from within?

And what about Vikas? One night several months after our march, when I managed to phone someone in Lalgaon, I heard that Vikas had mutinied from the platoon with eight young men and seven of the best rifles. It was rumoured that he was now working for the Indian security forces and for a mercenary gang, having formed his own branch of the TPC. He was said to be demanding levies from development projects, competing with the Maoists, and telling local people how he was going to kill Gyanji.

As had happened to others who had defected in the same manner before him, however, I heard later that the Maoist leaders had focused several platoons on the task of eliminating Vikas. It took four months before a Maoist sympathiser in Vikas's village informed the guerrillas of his arrival home. Two platoons surrounded his house and captured him. At a Maoist public hearing held in a nearby forest the next day, Vikas was accused of being a police informer and a leader of a mercenary gang. He was tried in a Naxalite 'people's court', found guilty and sentenced to death by firing squad.

As Gyanji had said, the Maoists are always in danger of giving birth to the Vikases of this world. When Prashant was killed in March 2013, it was likely to have been because another Vikas, an informer from within, had helped the police and a mercenary gang.

In a context of extreme state-repression the revolutionary guerrillas can easily be reduced to a movement of brute force, especially if they retract from being a broad-based organisation looking after the concerns of local people. The conditions were increasingly ripe to nurture the creation, destruction and recreation of what Gyanji had called 'Frankenstein's monsters'.

However, for every Vikas nurtured through the Maoists, there were bound to be others who took a different path. It was when I telephoned Somwari one day in 2013 that she told me that the sweet young Kohli, who had looked after me so tenderly as my bodyguard on the nightmarch, had returned to the village during the monsoon, but then had disappeared again one night. Perhaps he had returned to the Naxalite armies and been deputed to a different region. Perhaps he left with some friends to work in a factory in the neighbouring state of Chhattisgarh.

His parents had not heard from him since and worried about his fate. Would he be returned to them as a corpse killed in the counterinsurgency? Would he join the many instances of migrant construction labourers who disappear, never to be seen again? From my experiences, it seemed likely that Kohli would have continued in the guerrilla armies. He appeared to have the potential to emulate Gyanji. But the truth is that we may never know.

Somwari herself spent three months in prison because of the cases that her partner's ex-wife had filed against her and her husband. She took her youngest daughter, born when I lived with her, to jail as she was only three years old and there was no one else to look after her at home. Meanwhile the security force barracks inched from the plains and into the hills. One garrison settled near to Somwari's house.

Somwari became a convert to a Hindu spiritual sect that has been spreading in the area. She is now part of an older generation of Adivasis reacting against their world being rapidly torn apart by the guerrillas—against, for instance, the threat of their sons and nephews leaving home to become the Vikases of the world, against the security forces that the Maoists have inadvertently brought to their doorstep. Transforming herself by joining these spiritual sects was maybe a desperate attempt to put all aspects of her life back together. The irony, perhaps, is that that this sect, whose spread is umbilically tied to the extreme left (the Maoists), is likely to become co-opted by the forces of the extreme right, the Indian Hindutva.

And what of Gyanji? A few months after the nightmarch, I read in an Indian newspaper that police had surrounded a house in a city in Jharkhand. They had tapped Gyanji's phones and one of his aides had turned police informer. Gyanji had compromised his security and come out of the forests to meet his wife. He was arrested soon after she left him to return to her own home.

Gyanji had talked so often of the dangers of others risking their security and consequently the safety of the movement; therefore, it was surprising that in the end he succumbed to the same pressures. It had not been possible for him to entirely break away from his family and live out his ideals isolated in the Naxalite guerrilla community, as though their history were to be made on an island.

The owners of the house in which he was arrested must have alerted his wife as soon as the incident happened. With tactical skill and alacrity, she immediately spread the story widely, getting it broadcast on the TV and into the newspapers, in a deliberate attempt to save his life. Although it meant presenting him to the world as a 'Dreaded Terrorist Caught', and though it did not prevent the police from torturing him, it may well have saved him from being murdered by the security forces and then falsely described as having been killed in a violent 'encounter'.

The conditions at the prison he was incarcerated in are infamously appalling. From the villagers who have done time there, I know that it is common for several hundred prisoners to have to share two toilets. The water supply is unreliable and contaminated with iron. The food intended for prisoners is sold on the black market through collusion between prison authorities and the contractors who supply it. The rice and dal the prisoners are left with is more grit than grain. Bribes are required to access even the most basic of necessities, including the space to lay a sleeping mat. But it has always been in prison that such movements are rethought, reshaped and resurrected.

As I write, Gyanji is being moved around the prisons of Jharkhand, Bihar and Chhattisgarh, waiting to be tried for the forty or so charges that the Indian state has filed against him. These range from possessing a weapon on arrest and planning ambushes, to having participated in the killing of seventy-five men from the Central Reserve Police Force in the Dantewada district of Chhattisgarh in 2010. He had told me that he had never visited Chhattisgarh. Gyanji faces life imprisonment or the death penalty.

FIELDNOTES ON MAKING NEW FUTURES

Upon my return to London, my first 'knee-jerk' inclination was to write a book as fast as possible, one that countered the dominant representation of young people like Kohli, Vikas, or even Somwari, as 'terrorists'. This need for speed was perhaps inevitable given the wider political and economic context and the counterinsurgency operations it had nurtured. Since the 1990s, the Indian government paved the way for the increasing influence of the private sector in all aspects of life, encouraging national business and welcoming in multinational corporations, generating a surge in the economy and growth rates that economists all over the world marvelled at. But there was also an ever-greater polarisation of the country with the formation of a super-rich elite, whose accumulation of wealth was based on the oppression and exploitation of the poor, and whose power and reach seemed to be protected and supported by the state's military and police forces. Some of the world's most marginalised people were being displaced, dispossessed and discarded by the dramatic inequalities generated by economic growth, thrown into an Indian underbelly of extreme poverty, left to die young. It was against this backdrop of the uncaring advances of capitalism and entrenching inequality that India's Naxalite guerrillas had strengthened their half-century fight for a communist society. Yet it was also in this context that the Indian state had reinforced its resolve to eliminate them and evict the Adivasi people they live amidst, freeing up land for occupation by corporate mining interests and other resource extraction businesses. The escalated counterinsurgency efforts were often brutal and the rest of the world seemed to have little concern with the events unfolding in the remote hills and forests of central and eastern India. In this context, writing a book against the widespread representations of the Indian 'terrorist' seemed a noble cause. I had come a long way from seeing them as mere 'protection racketeers'.

However, my passion in writing such a book would have been driven by a counter-propaganda agenda that would have produced quick-fix representations of the Naxalites and the Adivasis they lived amidst. The emerging writings on the Naxalites were divided between the mass who were radically opposed to them and those who tried to counter that position, creating polarising views. I had gone to Jharkhand as a scholar—not as a representative of the state, a human rights activist or a Maoist, but as an independent researcher and reporter committed to understanding the complex lives of the Adivasi communities amidst whom this revolutionary struggle for social change had spread. A hastily written book would only have added to the binaries of condemnation or romanticisation and would have curtailed my ability to reach a deeper critical analysis of the experiences, visions and actions of the people whose lives I had shared. That needed much more time and reflection.

My journey to and from the jungles of Adivasi India and the Maoist guerrilla armies has made me think about revolutionary social transformation with insights and ideas that I could not have previously imagined, but it has also raised many more questions than it has resolved. There are a few issues, though, that keep coming back to haunt me.

To understand the persistence of revolutionary mobilisation is to explore the confluence of various groups of people. In India, there are those like Gyanji who have come from well-to-do, highly educated, upper- or middle-caste families, who, moved by the injustices around them, have sought to break from their pasts to be a part of a revolutionary community fighting inequality in the hope of a more equal future. These are the cadres who have been underground for twenty or thirty years and who lead the Naxalites today. There are also those from India's most marginalised populations, kept at the bottom of its caste and class hierarchies—in particular its Adivasi communities—who, like Kohli or Vikas, have drifted in and out of the revolutionary community as its foot soldiers, often treating the guerrilla armies as a home away from home. In a country deeply divided by caste and class, it is remarkable that these groups of people at polar ends of society have come together—with no promise of a wage or other material interest or any form of public status—to fight for a better world.

To grasp how movements like this evolve, one must seek to understand the drivers that allow various groups of people to coalesce in the revolutionary armies, their varied contexts, as well as relations between them. This in turn ought to shed light on not only what unites people to fight for change but also the potential internal contradictions between them and how such movements carry within their own ranks the seeds of self-destruction.

One of the striking things about the Naxalite leaders was their ability to renounce the world around them, break with their pasts, and sacrifice everything, including themselves, to fight for their ideals of human emancipation. Indeed, despite the differences between the renouncer and the revolutionary—the former seeks personal emancipation, the latter works for communal freedom—the continuities between communist revolutionaries and a long history of renunciation and sacrifice for liberation in India may be part of the reason why the ideal of communism thrives on in the subcontinent in this form. It is, perhaps, the very hierarchies of Indian society that have produced some of the world's most committed pursuers of a more equal society.

India has no end of battles to wage and the Naxalites have consistently fought for the rights of, and to mobilise, some of the country's most oppressed communities. In the caste-divided agricultural plains it was the untouchable communities, the Dalits, who came into its armies. In the last three decades, as the guerrillas retreated into the remote forests and hills of the centre and the east of the country, they joined hands with India's indigenous people, its Adivasis. How and why did these revolutionary leaders, from dominant-caste backgrounds, historically shunning and shunned by low castes, spread amongst India's low castes and tribes, particularly its Adivasis?

My journey has shown that the propositions of 'coerced between two armies' (that of the state and that of the rebels), 'greed', 'grievance', or a 'politics of identity', are partial at best for understanding the spread of the Maoists in India. They cannot explain why so many Adivasi youths gravitate towards the rebel armies. Crucially significant to the Naxalite spread were the relations of emotional intimacy they achieved with the people in their strongholds, which enabled them to become part of the family and kinship networks of the Adivasis. Although the Naxalites came as dominant-caste outsiders, their ideological commitment to an egalitarian society—a casteless and classless one—translated into their treatment of those they encountered with dignity, as equal human beings. Communism was not simply a utopian dream of a future society but influenced the remaking of revolutionary subjects and the restructuring of social relations in areas where the party held sway. So, despite a hierarchically governed organisation, an enormous effort went into superseding and negating the specificities of caste and class divisions between those who encountered the revolutionaries.

However, as we have seen over the course of the nightmarch, while the Naxalites were successful in generating the support of Adivasi communities in central and eastern India, it was also difficult for them to retain that support. Such radical struggles to create a more egalitarian future by trying to change the structures of the present are beset by some inter-locking contradictions that constantly undermine them and pull them apart. The Indian revolutionaries face several such contradictions.

One contradiction is that, while the making of emancipatory futures requires the creation of new communities that represent the values of the imagined ideal egalitarian future societies, there is also the need to rely on the support of pre-existing family relations which anchor one to the present and the past. For the Naxalites, their egalitarian values enabled them to form kinship networks into Adivasi communities, but it also led to a constant flux of youth like Kohli walking in and out of the guerrilla armies, as though they were simply the home of an uncle or an aunt. Immersion in local communities through kinship relations can be the strength of such movements, but it can also become an Achilles heel when the same battles and betrayals within families that bring people to the guerrilla armies begin to play a role in those very armies. Moreover, in the end perhaps even those leaders, such as Gyanji, who seemed to live like ascetics, apparently having subverted and left behind their pasts, found it difficult to totally break away from their families and thus submitted to domestic demands to the detriment of the revolutionary community.

FIELDNOTES ON MAKING NEW FUTURES

Another contradiction is that the creation of a more egalitarian future requires smashing the structures of capitalism that generate inequality, but immersion in the capitalist economy is necessary to fund and sustain movements against it. It is then, perhaps, inevitable that any such movement will create the Vikases of the world, cadres who get integrated into the imaginations and values of the very societies they are working against, conflicted by the desire to accumulate wealth and status for their personal gain, eventually turning them into betrayers of the revolutionaries. To fight these spreading cultural forces of capitalism a strong counterculture is necessary, something that the Maoists perhaps not only failed to nurture but whose destruction they even accelerated amongst the Adivasis communities.

The added problem for the Maoists, the basis of a third contradiction, is their adherence to an outdated analysis of the Indian economy as semi-feudal and semi-colonial. Elevating this economic analysis to what seems akin to a religious ideology that is hard to question may be one reason why a core group of leaders has stayed together in a kind of transcendental purity of collective commitment to the idea of the execution of the struggle. But, it has also meant that challenges to the economic analysis from within are portrayed as a betrayal of the revolutionary cause, losing potential supporters and establishing a dogma.

Although, on the ground, the Maoists interpreted actions based on local conditions, the untouchable status of the economic analysis also disabled them from fully addressing major issues stemming from the wide and deep reach of capitalism across the country and, therefore, the concerns of a majority of the Indian poor. For instance, in their own guerrilla strongholds they did not address the circumstances faced by the many who were migrating seasonally from their small parcels of land to work as informal sector casual labour in faraway construction sites, brick factories or agricultural fields of large capitalist farmers. It also meant that they were not able to give due recognition—except through violent measures such as suspension, expulsion or killing—to how capitalist values were permeating their movement, affecting their cadres and destroying the movement from within.

Crucially, in the Adivasi areas that were neither feudal nor dominated by capitalist values, the Maoist adherence to the ideology of semi-feudalism and a particular vision of a linear development to capitalism led to a fourth contradiction. Just as they had once been criticised for not taking the 'caste question' seriously in the plains, ignoring it as 'superstructure' in relation to a more significant focus on 'infrastructure' or economy, they had not given the 'indigenous question' sufficient thought. This not only disabled them from taking full cognisance of the relatively egalitarian systems and values that already existed amongst the people they were living with, which had a great deal in common with the egalitarian utopia they were fighting for, but it also led to the destruction of those values within the Adivasis communities.

A fifth contradiction is that mobilising people to fight against inequality and injustice may require the use of arms, but violent resistance will attract the violence of state repression. The danger is that mastering the art and discipline of guns becomes the focus of the struggle, overriding and thus destroying the move to mobilise people towards new ideals and new communities. This problem became acute for the Naxalites when one of the world's most powerful states began to send their military apparatus to destroy them and the communities they lived amidst. When the Naxalites retreated into the Adivasi heartlands of India and started to wage their protracted people's war from there, they became trapped—in the face of the Indian security force battalions—focusing only on their military strategy at the expense of working with the people for a new imagined future.

A final contradiction is that such movements seek to create new casteless, classless communities where women will be equal to men, but are most often led by men from elite backgrounds. In their challenge to the structural inequalities of society, they too often neglect the incipient inequalities within. In the Maoist case, although many Adivasis and, in some areas women, joined the revolutionaries, the higher-caste leaders not only failed to give space for the nurturing of lower-caste, Adivasi and women leaders, but also seemed to neglect the fact that the societies they worked amidst had more egalitarian gender-relations than the ones from which they had come.

The most sophisticated explanations of the appeal of the Naxalites have suggested that they are the combined outcome of the steady democratisation of the political process in India and the failures of its developmental reach. As the state has become more and more available to people who were kept on its margins and more of India's marginalised peoples have participated in its democratic processes, democratic aspirations have flourished. At the same time, though, the failure of Indian democracy to give adequate space in which a sense of public purpose can be articulated has left vast sections of society disenchanted, and their resulting grievances have made them turn to the Naxalites.

Living in the hills and forests of eastern India, however, I was struck by the reality that the opposite is true. The irony, it seems, is that a movement fighting against the character of Indian democracy has expanded its reach amongst people who had previously been left on the margins of the state, alienated from it. By fighting for their human rights on an equal footing with dominant and higher castes and classes, the Naxalites have nurtured Dalits and Adivasis who would ultimately seek not the withering away of the state that is the revolutionary ideal, but would want a greater share of the state, as a part of it. Indeed, in many countries of Latin America, class-based guerrilla wars eventually gave rise to indigenous movements that sought not to challenge the state but to have greater control over it (as in the case of the rise of Morales in Bolivia) or of territories within it (as in the case of the Zapatistas).

With the ongoing state repression and the contradictions and conflicts that beset the Naxalites, one wonders about the future of such armed struggles towards a communist society in India. Historically, even in times of extreme repression, India has produced educated, well-to-do leaders from its universities and its prisons, people who were repelled by the inequalities that surrounded them, sought to fight them, organised amongst the masses, and espoused the communist ideals of a society where caste and class will disappear, laying down their lives for the cause. Despite all their problems, the Naxalites have provided a rare alternative vision of a commitment and sincerity to a way of life and a future, rejecting and fighting against the spirit of individualism, accumulation and competition based on exploitation and oppression that prevails in our globalised world. Whether India continues to produce such revolutionary spirited youth remains to be seen. Whether the revolutionary ideology and practice can be reformed in the prisons and the jungles to take full account of the changes and challenges that are affecting the country today also remains to be seen.

NIGHTMARCH

This Indian Maoist-inspired Naxalite struggle for a communist society will, however, have given rise to and emboldened Dalit, Adivasi and women's movements, demanding their rights to be treated on equal terms as the dominant classes and castes, seeking a greater share of space within Indian democracy, keeping alive a dream for a better more equal world. Perhaps then one of the furthest-reaching consequences of the Naxalites might have been as a democratising force in India, catalysing those who want to fight for a more equal world, who are mobilised by the spirit of revolutionary struggle, even if they have been, at the same time, disappointed and disillusioned by its practice.

A BIBLIOGRAPHIC ESSAY ON THE NAXALITES

Nightmarch is a creative nonfiction elaboration of some of the articles I have written for academic journals. For those interested in the more detailed intellectual and political contexts of specific arguments, as well as the relationship between method and theory that forms the backdrop for this book, the following articles may be of interest. The relationship between ideology and political economy that frames *Nightmarch* was the subject of the 2012 Malinowski Memorial Lecture published in the *Journal of the Royal Anthropological Institute*.[1] The journal *Economy and Society* published the analysis of the significance of relations of intimacy, in particular kinship, in explaining the reach of such movements, moving the established debates beyond greed or grievance.[2] In a special issue of the *Journal of Agrarian Change*, the Maoists' overall analysis of the agrarian political economy is challenged in their own terms.[3] *Critique of Anthropology* published some reflections on citizenship, the state and revolutionary struggle.[4] In *Economic and Political Weekly*, Feyzi Ismail and I examined the relationship between class relations and indigenous politics in class struggle, exploring both the Indian and the Nepali Maoist cases.[5] An earlier volume, *Windows into a Revolution*, edited with Judith Pettigrew sought to think about the Indian and Nepali Maoists in one frame and to bring together empirically based ethnographic studies on both movements.[6] For reflections on the relationship between religion and the secular left, through a comparison of the Maoists with the Birsa Munda movement a hundred years before, see a piece in *Anthropology of this Century*.[7] An article in *Modern Asian Studies* analyses the debates of the early subaltern school through the spread of the Maoists, focusing on their anti-alcohol campaigns.[8] My thoughts on the 'markets of protection' through which the Naxalites get funding and competed with the state in their initial spread were published in *Critique of Anthropology*.[9] In *Dialectical Anthropology*, I also explored the relationship between certainty and uncertainty, through the case of one man who got stuck between these 'markets of protection'.[10] For the relationship between the theory and methods that have guided the research that went into this book, and why participant observation is a potentially revolutionary praxis, a few thoughts published in *Hau: Journal of Ethnographic Theory* might be helpful.[11]

Since I began preparing for the research that led to *Nightmarch*, there have been few issues in South Asia that have attracted as much scholarly and activist attention as India's Naxalite movement. At least fifty scholarly or political books, several novels, and numerous essays have been published since 2007. The literature that has poured out on the Naxalites is fascinating for the array of writing it represents, the different kinds of interest it has generated, and the questions that it has raised. There remains a dearth of first-hand, sustained research on the Naxalites and the people they live among, but the literature is as interesting for what it says about the authors and their perspectives as it is for its analyses.

For the interested reader, I present a bibliographic essay on this literature.[12] We see several trends. The first genre—emanating mainly from sociologists, political scientists, security studies specialists and administrators—sees the Naxalites from within the perspective of the Indian state and, as such, as a problem to be addressed, but is critical of India's military response to the insurgents. The second genre—produced mainly by scholars of political science as well as activists—takes seriously the Naxalite project of revolutionary social change, reflects on the nature of the Indian state and its democracy, and thus seeks to explain the spread of revolutionary violence in India. The positions taken are varied—from an avid defence of the Indian state and a view of the Naxalites as extremists, to those who are more reflective about the challenges posed to the state and democracy that lie at the heart of the spread of the revolutionary violence. The third genre, emerging mainly from journalists and activists, partly aided by the

A BIBLIOGRAPHIC ESSAY ON THE NAXALITES

Naxalites, attracted to some degree by the romance of the revolution—seeks to document (through travelogues and short trips to Naxalite regions) what life might be like in the guerrilla territories and armies. The fourth genre is the analysis of sociologists and anthropologists, based on sustained empirical research, concerned with the experience of the oppressed communities who have become part of the Maoist fold. There are also novels inspired by the Naxalites, some of which are notable for highlighting the challenge posed by revolutionary politics and mobilisation to ideals of the conventional family structure. The final genre is literature written by participants in the Naxalite movement itself, or by those who have been close to the movement.

Seeing Like a State

With the Naxalites once again taking centre-stage in Indian politics came a realisation that there was a major gap in our knowledge of contemporary India. We did not know much about either the clandestine movement that had existed underground for more than half a century or about the Adivasi populations it lived amidst. What mainly emerges, whether from political scientists or government administrators, is a strong critique of the military focus of the Indian state's response to the Maoists and a call to develop Adivasi areas.[13] The premise is that the Naxalites have gained strength because they address the genuine grievances of India's tribal communities.

A range of edited collections and books provide this message.[14] Perhaps the strongest one is from a 2008 Government of India report submitted by a sixteen-member expert group appointed by the Planning Commission, which sought to recognise the Maoist movement as a political force, arguing that in its day-to-day manifestation it had to be seen as a fight for social justice, equality, protection, security, and local development.[15] The call is for a response to the Naxalites that addresses the various developmental problems and—crucially—that moves away from a military-centred focus, which, it is argued, can cause considerable collateral damage and lead to the greater alienation of the affected communities. There is also a strong repudiation of state-sponsored vigilante groups, such as the Salwa Judum in Chhattisgarh, which the Government of India expert group report says 'delegitimizes politics, dehumanizes people, degenerates those engaged in their "security", and above all represents abdication of the State itself.'[16] The report recommends the effective implementation of existing protective legislations for India's Dalits and Adivasis; measures to resolve problems of land alienation, bonded labour and indebtedness, and land reform; rehabilitation and resettlement; livelihood, security and rural development; universalisation of basic social services like education and healthcare; the empowerment of local democratic structures such as *gram sabhas* and *panchayats*; and the proper extension of good governance to affected areas.

In *Maoists and Other Armed Conflicts*, Anuradha Chenoy and Kamal Chenoy further argue that looking at conflict through the lens of national security or even simply underdevelopment is insufficient, and an approach founded on dignity, justice, equity, rights and human development that addresses structural inequalities is crucial.[17] They suggest that the Indian government has rejected such an approach and is relying on 'fear mechanisms', including torture, encounters, crackdowns, enforced disappearances, strategic hamlets and the formation of local militias, in the wider context of a network of over-reaching undemocratic laws and Acts that legitimise these practices, and create the conditions for impunity.[18] These human rights abuses of counterinsurgency in Chhattisgarh are also the central focus of Nandini Sundar's *The Burning Forest*, discussed later.[19]

Overall, these are powerful arguments in the face of what has indeed been an overwhelming military attack by the Indian state on the Naxalites and the people with whom they live. But the Planning Commission expert group report was never presented in Parliament for debate. Instead it was an Intelligence Bureau report describing Maoist violence as the 'biggest internal security threat' to India that grabbed the attention of home ministers and precipitated the security-centred response to the Naxalites and the deployment of huge numbers of central armed police forces in the tribal belts of eastern and central India.[20]

The Legitimacy of Revolutionary Violence

Another genre of political science literature takes more seriously the ideological project of revolutionary social change itself, although the authors concerned do not necessarily agree with the Naxalite methods or analysis. Here, the questions addressed are much more about the relationship between democracy, the Indian state and Naxalite revolutionary violence. The premise of this work is that under certain conditions, revolutionary violence is legitimate.[21] The question, then, is whether revolutionary violence is justifiable in the contemporary Indian context (a question which requires an analysis of the Indian state) and, if so, whether the Naxal violence, in particular, is legitimate.

Indian democracy, Neera Chandhoke says, whilst robust, is characterised by violence, and thus revolutionary violence cannot be treated as an aberration, in just the same way that democracy cannot simply be regarded as a farce forced onto unsuspecting innocent people.[22] Chandhoke reminds us that revolutionaries seek to make people's lives less unequal and more just by transforming, through armed struggle aimed at taking over the state, the institutional context in which they live. She stresses that proponents of this form of politics believe 'that the state is not only unwilling, but incapable of institutionalizing the basic preconditions of justice for the most vulnerable.'[23] Revolutionary violence, then, is based on the political mobilisation of peasants on whose behalf the guerrillas have picked up arms.[24] Chandhoke's overall message is that when democracies fail in their responsibilities to democratic justice—as the Indian state so often has— then revolutionary violence can occupy the same space as democracy. She writes: 'Even if revolutionary violence is riddled with contradictions between theory and practice, it mounts a powerful challenge to violations of democratic justice and to an unfulfilled democratic agenda.'

Although she makes theoretical space for the legitimacy of the Naxalite cause through her critique of the Indian state, in her final analysis of the revolutionary violence of the Maoists, Chandhoke points to its ambiguities. She ends by noting that the Maoists are in danger of spearheading political violence without political mobilisation, leading only to more violence.

While Chandhoke's book is pitched at the level of theoretical debate on the relationship between democracy and revolutionary politics, Nirmalangshu Mukherji purports to provide an empirically grounded overall analysis in his book *The Maoists in India*.[25] The book, however, is based entirely on secondary sources. Mukherji admits that armed resistance is sometimes necessary—he applauds the Nepali Maoist revolutionary struggle for having overthrown a brutal monarchy—but the overall thrust of his book is to show, chapter by chapter, that the Indian Maoist upheaval does not signify 'genuine resistance'.[26] Mukherji argues that the prioritisation of the annihilation of class enemies, which was promoted by Charu Majumdar, persists in the twenty-first century through the brutal killing of informers. Considerable effort is spent discrediting the public intellectuals and activists—such as Arundhati Roy, Gautam Navlakha, and forums such as Sanhati—who have portrayed the Maoists and their work among the Adivasis in a favourable light. Even more effort goes into saying that the Adivasis are stuck between two armies—that of the Maoists and that of the state. Mukherji further argues that the the Communist Party of India (Maoist) is detrimental to the activity of other left-wing parties that are working within the democratic framework of the Indian state, though he characterises India as a 'fragile democracy' and argues that widespread mass movements on basic issues of life and livelihood are necessary to enable vast sections of the people to access the state.[27] Ultimately the overall aims of Mukherji's book are to show that the Maoists are an anti-democratic force; to propose saving the Adivasis by creating conditions for their safe and secure surrender from the People's Liberation Guerrilla Army; and to expand the scope and space for parliamentary democracy.

Contra Mukherji, Bidyut Chakrabarty and Rajat Kumar Kujur, based on an analysis of the spread of the Maoists in Odisha, regard Maoism to be the outcome, ironically, of the steady democratisation of the political process in India (beyond mere voting).[28] As the state has become more and more available to people who had been left out or firmly kept at its margins, and more of India's marginal peoples have participated in its democratic processes, democratic aspirations have flourished. At the same time, though, the failure of Indian democracy to give adequate space in which a sense of public purpose can be articulated has left vast sections of society disenchanted. In particular, they argue that representative democracy has not only failed but has also become oppressive, as it serves the interest of the market and acts as a collaborator of global market-capitalists. For Chakrabarty and Kujur, it is this paradox of Indian democracy that explains the appeal and spread of the Indian Maoists.

Manoranjan Mohanty, in his *Red and Green*, a republication of his 1977 book *Revolutionary Violence* alongside a series of published essays that he has written since, argues similarly that the Maoist movement has shifted focus, from armed squad actions around a revolutionary programme that targeted landlords, to an emphasis on a mass movement of Adivasis and peasants around issues like land, forest rights, basic civil liberties, and an alternative path to development.[29] Unlike Mukherji, Mohanty maintains that these latter phases of the Maoist movement are predicated not only on an 'Adivasi awakening', asserting 'the right to livelihood', but also the right to dignity and to selfhood. He claims that many Adivasi struggles—for instance, land struggles—started as peaceful campaigns within the framework of the law but that when they were suppressed by the security operations of the state, the activists joined hands with the Maoists.

In *War and Politics*, Gautam Navlakha presents a philosophical complement to Chakrabarty and Kujur's, as well as Mohanty's, overall analysis.[30] A prominent civil rights activist who has visited the Maoist areas (his *Days and Nights in the Heart of the Rebellion* will be discussed in the next section), like Chandhoke he explores the place of revolutionary violence in the Indian context and points to what he sees as the incapacity of the state to address the issues of democratic justice. 'There are many who believe that this system is incapable of delivering without an overhaul because it is loaded in favour of the rich, privileged and powerful who do not hesitate to take recourse to tyranny to maintain this system.'[31] Though acknowledging that there are cases of individuals being given justice, welfare policies being enacted, and corrupt political parties being democratically replaced, Navlakha maintains that there is no end in sight to the cycle of oppression and exploitation. He points out that the dominant economic discourse is circumscribed by the imperative of foreign direct investment which entails structural reforms that cut social services and increasing legal and military security for investments, reminding us that the Indian state's escalation of war has been to free up the Maoist areas for economic interest, especially mining.[32] When the very survival of the population is at stake because of the structural violence being wrought against them, and since it is hard to see how a peaceful civil society engaged in electoral democracy could make the Indian state more responsive to their needs, Navlakha argues that force may be necessary. Following Clausewitz and Marxist conceptions of war, Navlakha proposes that the guerrilla war is thus a political war, given that war is a continuation of politics. Peace, Navlakha reminds us, if it rests on tyrannical rule, is not in itself a 'positive value' and there can be a virtue to war if it helps in the removal of tyranny.[33]

Navlakha nevertheless criticises the Maoists for unnecessary, or what he calls 'criminal', acts of violence, like attacks on public vehicles.[34] The closing chapters of the book are dedicated to critically analysing the role of the Maoists in Junglemahal and to arguing that the Maoists need to shift away from what could be regarded as a militarist strategy towards a struggle combining possible electoral openings and mass and legal struggles, all of which require a multi-party pluralistic vision of struggle.[35] He warns the Maoists that, given that guerrilla revolutionary war is predicated on its popularity amongst the people, cruel and reckless conduct must be avoided.[36] He urges them to adopt the Geneva Conventions, and to wage their battle not through a concept of reciprocity—doing what the state does—but with respect for political ethics. In his closing notes, Navlakha reminds the Maoists that, while it is idealistic to believe that change in India will come through peaceful means alone, it is equally idealistic to believe that it will come through military means alone. These more critical comments on Maoist violence are nevertheless laced with a revolutionary optimism: given that the CPI (Maoist) itself always critically analyses its role and has on several occasions apologised for its mistakes, its members do indeed show that they learn from their blunders.[37]

If Navlakha sees the Indian state as 'predatory' and 'coercive', Ajay Gudavarthy, in *Maoism, Democracy and Globalisation*, sees it as simply 'violent'.[38] He argues that although Indian politics has seen a 'deepening' and an 'expansion' of democracy through 'robust bottom-up mobilization', democracy has also been 'arrested' through 'top-down counter-mobilisation, actively aided by insular public institutional structures, promoting globalisation and neoliberal reforms and worsening socio-economic conditions for large sections of society.'[39] Violence, Gudavarthy says, is now endemic to the state system and is no longer used just against the Maoists but has extended to all forms of protest politics, even non-violent forms, through a combination of extraordinary laws—such as the TADA, POTA, AFSPA, and Sedition Laws, among many others—and extra-judicial killings, torture and cases of disappearance, custodial deaths and even sexual violence by the armed forces.[40] Gudavarthy thus characterises India as a 'violent democracy.' Gudavarthy argues that the Maoist movement had 'waged a relentless battle in favour of some of the most dispossessed "basic classes", including the landless, Dalits, rural poor, workers and Adivasis, and questioned the very nature of the economic model of development and political model of governance.'[41] Walking a difficult line between scholarly analysis and what is a message, perhaps even a seminar, to the Maoists, Gudavarthy's overall critique is that the Maoist movement has fought this battle through a relatively singular focus on armed violence, and he is much less hopeful than Navlakha about the possibilities offered by them.[42]

Though critical of the Maoist movement to varying degrees, what emerges clearly from this genre of literature from political science and activist intellectuals is the necessity for revolutionary violence—armed struggle—in the context of highly oppressive state regimes. There is a strong critique of the Indian state, pointing to how its violence, predation and coercion have threatened the very nature of Indian democracy, creating the legitimacy, necessity and space for the Naxalite revolutionary violence.

Eyewitnessing Days and Nights in the Heartland of Rebellion[43]

If the aim of the literature covered thus far has been to impart an understanding of the problems of the Indian state and a philosophical basis for the legitimacy of revolutionary violence, what is largely absent from it is first-hand research by the authors into the spread of the Maoist movement in central and eastern India (Navlakha is an exception, as we shall see). Those who bring us closest to what life may be like in the rebel heartlands are in fact journalists and activists, and, as the next section will show, a handful of sociologists and anthropologists.

A BIBLIOGRAPHIC ESSAY ON THE NAXALITES

In 2009–10, the CPI (Maoist) welcomed a number of activists and journalists into the guerrilla stronghold in the Dandakaranya region of Bastar, Chhattisgarh. Given that much of India's ideological space was full of voices opposed to the movement, the Naxalites actively tried to fill the information void around them. The 'exposure visits' made by journalists and activists were intended to show to the Indian and international mass audiences the inequalities into which the Maoist movement had grounded itself, the movement's goals, and its history.

The visits to the Naxalite strongholds were generally short (ranging from ten days to several visits of a few days over the course of a few months) and the books were written fast—almost as if they were all racing to be the first eyewitness account of the hidden heart of India. The journalists Rahul Pandita and Shubhranshu Choudhary and activists Arundhati Roy, Gautam Navlakha and Jan Myrdal all wrote books. Satnam's travels much earlier (before the unification of the parties into the CPI (Maoist)) into these same areas of Dandakaranya to live with the rebel armies of the People's War Group were translated and published as *Jangalnama*.[44] There was also another earlier attempt, in 2007, by the journalist Sudeep Chakravarti although he did not make it to the guerrilla heartlands to meet the rebel armies or their leadership.[45]

These books come from very different perspectives on the Maoists, although at some level the authors are all attracted by the romance of revolution. Their virtue is that they make the guerrilla landscape come alive and humanise a movement that is otherwise talked about in abstractions or using the language of terrorism. However, the visits were highly monitored and organised by the Maoist leadership and there was inevitably little possibility for deep, sustained engagement with the Adivasis outside of the context of the rebel armies. So although we get a strong flavour of the landscape and daily life in the guerrilla armies, as well as a clearer idea of what the Naxal leadership wishes to tell the outside world, it is difficult for these books to show what everyday life is like for Adivasis in these areas, the multiple reasons why the Adivasis might join the rebel armies, and the intimacy, frictions, and contradictions that have developed between the Adivasis and the Naxalites.

A BIBLIOGRAPHIC ESSAY ON THE NAXALITES

The journalists Pandita and Choudhary present travelogues into Naxalite strongholds that are pitched at urban, English-speaking, upper-middle-class Indians for whom the forests of the centre and the east of the country are a black void, a world imagined as *jungli* (wild and savage). They seek to answer some basic questions for this audience. Who make up the Maoist leaders and cadres? What is their alternative vision of development? How do they continue to exert a powerful influence on Adivasis, Dalits and the disenfranchised? Although sympathetic to the plight of the Adivasis and offering critical praise to the Maoists for filling the development gaps left by the Indian state, both authors firmly distance themselves from the aims and objectives of the Maoist movement itself. Both journalists present a disjuncture between a high-caste leadership and their Adivasi foot soldiers, and believe that the armed movement could be ended if the miserable conditions of Adivasi life were ameliorated. Both argue that, apart from the high-caste leadership, the majority of the cadres are not concerned with revolutionary goals such as the overthrow of the national government. As such both Pandita and Choudhary broadly adhere to what political science literature refers to as the 'grievance' theory of conflict—that it is inequality, weak institutions, poverty, and lack of social services that are the root causes of conflicts.

The accounts of the activists—Gautam Navlakha, Jan Myrdal and Arundhati Roy—invited in by the movement to the forests of Bastar, all in the space of a few months in early 2010, are in contrast more sympathetic to the Maoists than their journalist counterparts. The emphasis here is different—rather than suggesting that Adivasis are caught in a war between the Maoists and the Indian state, they stress that the Indian state is waging a war against the people of India, under the guise of a Maoist threat. They argue that the lower classes, lower castes, and Adivasis have been economically, politically and socially deprived, and that the Indian state has no interest in giving them redress. And they broadly ascribe to the Maoist movement a challenge to the nature of the Indian state and, in particular, the revolutionary demand for alternative people-oriented forms of governance and economic development. Navlakha and Myrdal undertook their tour in Dandakaranya together in January 2010, laying the ground for

271

Roy to follow in their steps a few weeks later. The books are fascinating as much for what they say about their authors and the nature of their tours as they are for their content.

Myrdal ended his 1980s book, *India Waits*, with a vision of a Maoist-inspired revolution, signalling the existence of today's movement. The Maoists invited him in 2010 to serve as a kind of Edgar Snow figure of the contemporary movement.[46] Myrdal's nod to Snow is clear in the title of his book, *Red Star Over India*, channelling Snow's classic text about the Chinese revolution, *Red Star Over China*.[47] Then aged eighty-three, Myrdal had the kind of international track record that, perhaps, the Maoists hoped would make their struggle known to the wider world. He had some stature in the international communist movement, was a key European figure in speaking out against the Vietnam War, and had written several books about the continued support for Mao and the Cultural Revolution in China. Myrdal tries to replicate Snow's narrative structure and style through his interview with the general secretary of the CPI (Maoist), Muppala Lakshmana Rao, alias 'Ganapathy', and the party documents he reads. Much of the book, though, becomes a meandering journey through international communist history, Myrdal's reminiscences, the current situation in India, and the trip that he made with Navlakha. In itself the trip was clearly far too short to give Myrdal the kind of depth of understanding that Snow had of the Chinese situation. The book was published by a small Indian publisher and was available to a limited Indian audience; ultimately it did not succeed in its mission to introduce the Maoist movement to an international audience.

Where Myrdal failed in attracting international attention for the movement, Arundhati Roy, a Booker Prize-winning author who had earlier turned her attention to Adivasi activism in the Save the Narmada Movement, succeeded. Roy's book was initially published as three essays in the Indian magazine *Outlook*, and soon after as a book entitled *Broken Republic*, before it was remarketed as *Walking with the Comrades*.[48] One of its three essays is based on Roy's ten-day tour of the guerrilla areas of Bastar, following on from the visits of Navlakha and Myrdal. Roy's prose is characteristically sharp, the narrative powerful, the text full of irony, and the overall book is damning of the connections between the interests of large corporations, the Indian government, and police brutality. She does, though, re-inscribe the Maoist movement and its goals within a discourse of indigeneity. She suggests that the Maoist movement is in fact an Adivasi movement, effectively evacuating the Maoist movement of its history of class struggle, its goals, its structures, its leadership, and so on, in favour of a vision of a spontaneous uprising of Adivasis in a struggle against the collapse of their societies.[49] Thus, while Myrdal grounds the Maoist movement's history too neatly within the history of the international communist movement, Roy erases it.

Of all the 'eyewitness' accounts, it is perhaps from Navlakha's *Days and Nights in the Heartland of Rebellion* that we learn most about the war in the Adivasi areas of Bastar.[50] The book is in three parts. In the first Navlakha asks the question: why did the Maoists become such a threat to the Indian state? He establishes the connection with the state's need to cleanse the mineral-rich areas of central India for land grabs by the corporate sector, suggesting that the actual threat of Maoists taking state power was negligible. The middle sections of the book seek to show what Navlakha learned while he was in Dandakaranya. This includes the large number of women involved, life in the movement, their rules around killing, and their reflections on mistakes. The final section discusses wider issues regarding violence and the challenges and prospects faced by the movement. Written and published against the backdrop of 'Operation Green Hunt', his over-arching agenda was to humanise the movement, to provide a 'true' account of what was going on in central India. For, as Navlakha reminds us, 'truth is the first casualty of war'. But what differentiates Navlakha's book from the other eyewitness accounts is his critique of the Maoists from the perspective of a critically sympathetic person situated within the democratic rights movement. Amongst several criticisms, he points to the dangers of a sole focus on revolutionary violence, laying the seeds of the arguments that he later develops in *War and Politics*, discussed earlier.

These 'eyewitness' accounts give us a flavour of life in the rebel armies and have gone a long way into humanising a movement that is otherwise presented in the dominant media accounts only by pointing fingers at its acts of terror. However, what none of them does is give us an understanding of the complexity of the Adivasi communities of central and eastern India and how and why they have become involved with the Naxalites. The books are based on just 'days and nights in the heartland of rebellion'. No time was invested in being with the Adivasi communities, trying to understand them and their histories, outside the official tours of the Naxalites and the authors' own imaginations. That would have required much deeper sustained first-hand field research and analysis.

Empirically Researched Analysis

Of the more empirically researched scholarly texts on the Naxalites that have come out in recent years, there are four monographs which stand out. Two focus exclusively on gender, the third on Dalits, and the fourth on the impact of counterinsurgency operations on Adivasis.

Srila Roy's *Remembering Revolution* and Mallarika Sinha Roy's *Gender and Radical Politics in India* both focus on women who joined the Naxalites in the late sixties and early seventies, and what the women's experience may reveal about revolutionary violence and politics.[51] Both books focus on research done in West Bengal, and rely on multiple sources, including the personal narratives of women who had once been a part of the movement, based on interviews, women's published autobiographies, and cinematic and literary sources. Although both books highlight what M.S. Roy calls the 'magic moments of Naxalbari', i.e., the liberation that the women experienced in participating in the movement and their idealisation of it, ultimately both are also an important critique of the gender and sexual politics of the movement.

What emerges is a gender critique of the movement that is as intimately tied to the 'declassing' of urban middle-class male activists, bound up with refashioning masculinity through self-control and suppressing sexual desire, as it is with the neglect of the specific needs of women in the movement. S. Roy shows particularly sharply that, 'the party became the social consciousness of the collective, substituting for parental authority and mimicking middle-class morality in the underground.'[52] The result is that although the Naxalites are fighting for exceptional political causes including against

Dalit and Adivasi women's oppression, and many middle-class women joined them because of the potential of liberation from bourgeois family life, in the everyday life of the movement it was the patriarchal morality of upper-caste, middle-class India that was being reproduced. The hierarchies of caste, class and gender that thus resurfaced within the movement meant not only that women were more often than not confined to positions of care and support through the stereotyping of their roles as mothers, wives, and widows, but also that sexual violence and other forms of women's oppression within the movement were often ignored. For some women, over time, the violence of the state receded into the background because of the violence of the patriarchy they faced within the movement.

Together these books contribute to an important gap through their focus on women and in revealing the central role that patriarchy plays within such revolutionary movements. As ambitious as they are, in neither book do we get a broader analysis of whether or not the women who joined and participated in the movement accepted gender oppression for the sake of the 'bigger cause'; what the relative differences may have been between gender oppression within and outside the movement; what these women's present perspectives are on the need for revolutionary movements to place gender centre-stage; and whether and how these women's collective experiences have led to a gender critique and changes within the movement. (We know from the essays of Anuradha Ghandy—discussed in the last section of this chapter—that there were activists, like her, who tried to fight patriarchy from within.)[53] Above all, what is missing is an in-depth analysis of the gender, class, and caste dimensions of the different kinds of women who are members of the movement, in particular the experiences of the many Dalit and Adivasi women who joined and how their stories relate to those of middle-class women, and, indeed, how participation may have enabled social mobility for some women and, accompanying this, an increase in patriarchy. But for this, interviews and oral histories are not sufficient and need to be supplemented by more ethnographic research that will enable one to analyse the differences between what people say and what they do.

If S. Roy and M.S. Roy present nuanced accounts of gender relations in the early Naxalite movement, George Kunnath's *Rebels from the Mud Houses* is an analysis of the relationship between the Dalits and the Naxalites in the plains of Bihar in the 1980s and '90s.[54] Based on ethnographic research living in a Dalit colony in a village in Jehanabad district that was once the heart of the activities of CPI (Marxist-Leninist) Party Unity, Kunnath explores how the Dalits recount their experience of the spread of the Naxalites in the decade before his field research. In a highly feudal context, Kunnath argues that Dalits supported the Maoists not because of an absence of education or health facilities but because of the dignity they afforded in the face of extreme caste violence. As a result of Maoist activities, the lower castes were now able to hold their heads high in front of higher-caste landlords. This was also the argument presented in Bela Bhatia's remarkable unpublished PhD thesis, and in Prakash Louis's book.[55]

Over time, things changed and Kunnath shows that in the 1990s, the Naxalites in Bihar shifted their emphasis from mobilising landless Dalits to uniting the middle peasants by addressing the latter's demands for government subsidies and remission of rents, as well as protecting them from the demands of the classes below them. Unsurprisingly, the Dalits in Jehanabad district of Bihar were suspicious of the Maoist alliance with the middle peasantry, and the basic contradiction between the landed Kurmis (the middle peasantry) and the landless Dalits was never resolved. The Dalits were alienated from the movement in the 1990s and Kunnath thus shows us the difficulties of forming the wider class alliances that several authors have urged the Maoists to engage in. Like others, Kunnath also shows an 'uneasy marriage' between Maoist mass mobilisation and armed action. The 1980s mobilisation of Dalits in Bihar was accomplished through Maoist mass fronts, in particular the Mazdoor Kisan Sangram Samiti, whereas the 1990s saw a shrinking of the space for mass mobilisation and an increasing reliance on armed action, which had a negative impact at the local level. But Kunnath does not suggest that the armed struggle should be dropped: armed action continued to be crucial to Dalit needs as they were necessary for their protection from middle- and upper-caste peasants. The key problem with the Naxalites for the Dalits was not the new focus on armed action, but that this focus resulted in the decline of a mass politics and the replacement of Dalits' needs with those of the middle peasantry.

A BIBLIOGRAPHIC ESSAY ON THE NAXALITES

What we have in these empirical accounts are refreshing and unique insights through first-hand field research that enable us to understand much better the impact and spread of the Naxalite movement as well as its nuances and contradictions, an understanding which takes us beyond armchair condemnations, reflections and speculations. Although not focusing on the Naxalites but on the impact of the civil war on Adivasis in Bastar, central India, equally insightful is Nandini Sundar's *The Burning Forest*.

Sundar has known the area through earlier ethno-historical research but this book is based on her field visits as an activist, which led to a public interest litigation in the Supreme Court to ban the government-backed, state-armed private vigilante force Salwa Judum, as well as to disbanding the appointment of young (mainly Adivasi) men as Special Police Officers. The book's focus is on Adivasis caught in the midst of the armed conflict and it powerfully documents the severe human rights abuses taking place at the behest of the state security forces and their private armies: the forced displacement of Adivasis into desolate camps, the rape of women by the security forces, the government's use of starvation and denial of basic services (such as transportation of rice) as a weapon of control over the people, the burning of villages, and the forced surrender of villagers who were then conscripted as police informers and armed as Special Police Officers. Despite the detailed documentation of gross human rights abuses and the failure of electoral democracy to stem these abuses in these remote parts of India, Sundar keeps open the possibility of hope for accountability and the rule of law.

Novels

The initial Naxalbari struggles of the 1970s that once inspired filmmakers and novelists[56] have in recent years once again captured the imagination of award-winning international authors. The Booker Prize-shortlisted novels for 2013 and 2014 included two whose central characters are urban, middle-class Naxalites in the 1970s. The first was Jhumpa Lahiri's *Lowland* and the second, Neel Mukherjee's *Lives of Others*.[57] Interestingly, in both novels the central Naxalite characters are more or less absent from the novels' present timelines. Both books are more focused on the characters' families than on their participation in the movement itself. Both are set within Kolkata-based Bengali middle-class families—one in Tollygunge (Lahiri), the other in Bhowanipore (Mukherjee).

Lahiri's novel centres on two brothers and the one woman they both marry. One brother, Udayan, joins the Naxalites and marries Gauri, a girl he meets through the movement. The other, Subhash, leaves India for Rhode Island in the United States to study for a PhD, but returns to Kolkata when he hears about his brother's murder by the police for allegedly having killed a policeman. Subhash then marries Udayan's widowed pregnant wife. The bulk of the novel is set in the United States and focuses on the relationship between Subhash, Gauri, and her daughter, Bela. Their relationship is haunted by the dead Naxalite brother/husband and the effects of Gauri's early activism. The events of the book serve as a metaphor for the idea that Naxalites only kill. The Naxalites were not only responsible for the death of her first husband but also of Gauri herself, for she is unable to feel any emotional attachments and in the end leaves both her husband and her daughter.

Mukherjee's novel is about a Bengali middle-class family whose protagonist, Supratik, joins the Naxalites. It is a masterpiece of description and analysis of a particular kind of Bengali family life: the head of the household is a businessman who owns several paper mills; there is a daughter who cannot find a husband because she is dark-skinned; several sons, one of whom delights in perverse sexual activities; servants, and so on. Supratik, the grandson of the eldest child, leaves to join the Naxalites. Each chapter concerning the family is punctuated by letters he writes to a widowed aunt (with whom he is in love) about his experience as a Naxalite activist and life in the rural areas where he is mobilising peasants.

In both novels, the Naxalites form a foil for what are ultimately stories about the crises experienced by Bengali middle-class families, although they are perhaps represented with greater sensitivity in Mukherjee's novel. Lahiri gives us no insight into the political motivations of the Naxalite movement, and we have no understanding of the wider social context that compels Udayan to join the movement. How and why did so many 'Udayans' break away from general middle-class indifference to fight for the cause of the poor? Mukherjee reflects more on the political appeal of the movement for urban, middle-class youth. He focuses on the contradictions and contrasts that Supratik faces between the wealth of his household and the poverty of those he lives among as a Naxalite. Ultimately, though, Supratik's lasting gift to the movement is the making of landmines. The book ends with present-day Maoists setting up a landmine under a train in Jharkhand in what is represented as a terrorist attack.

As with Dilip Simeon's *Revolution Highway*, focusing on idealistic Delhi University students in the 1960s who join the Naxalites—a novel based on personal experience—what is highlighted is the futility of this means of resistance, presenting the Naxalites as ritualistic killers, as terrorists.[58] What is significantly missing in all of these novels is any deep analysis or understanding of how the Naxalites have attracted so many peasants and Adivasis into their movement and the complexities, nuances, and contradictions that have played out in their lives as a result of this movement. Mukherjee, however, offers a rich description of the plight of the disenfranchised and, in a series of essays published later, *A State of Freedom*,[59] while the terror theme continues through the unexplained amputation of a hand, he ventures further from Bengali middle-class family life to explore his empathy for the poor. The story of one of the five central characters—an Adivasi servant in a Bengali middle-class household—is intimately weaved in with that of an Adivasi woman back in Jharkhand who joins the Naxalites.

The Stories from Within

Perhaps the books that to some extent will determine the shape of future research and writing are those that are emerging from the Naxalite movement itself or those working on its fringes. These are fascinating for the issues they address, the analysis they wish to provide, and the evidence they use to this end. But perhaps, above all, their importance will lie in the fact that they are also, in the long run, historical artefacts that document the continuities and changes and the experiences and thoughts of the people within the movement.

First there are the analyses of intellectuals in the movement whose primary audience was often the movement itself. Perhaps the best example is the essays of Anuradha Ghandy. Published posthumously by Anand Teltumbde and Shoma Sen as *Scripting the Change*, the first two parts of the book are an insight into, amongst other issues, the challenges of the theory and praxis on caste and gender within a Marxist-Leninist class struggle in India with sweeping reviews of the literature (across both time and space).[60] The third part is an eclectic collection of the various public political interventions by Maoist activists on some of the important issues facing the Indian poor, ranging from changes in labour laws and the difficulties of mobilising contract labourers to deaths in police custody, published most often in the pages of *Economic and Political Weekly*. In her foreword to Ghandy's essays, Arundhati Roy writes that it is difficult to know how to read these writings and concludes that they must be seen as notes to Ghandy herself. Undoubtedly they are, but perhaps above all they are notes for her comrades, especially her argument that caste and gender ought to be central to the class struggle and not, as has happened all too often, left out. They leave a footprint of an intellectual engaged in a political struggle every step of the way, documenting not only the revolutionary struggle but also the movement's internal battles.

Whether we will see the publication of more such analysis from within remains to be seen. Security concerns and the emphasis within the Naxalites on decentring the ego mean that it is unlikely that these would be published from the contemporary forests or prisons. It is usually only when someone dies that the concern for de-emphasising the self, not being egocentric, falls away. For after death, focusing on the individual also enables resurrection of the martyr for the revolution.

Indeed, a collection of the Central Committee leader Azad's writings, similar to those of Ghandy, was published as a book by his friends after his death in 2010.[61] As with an earlier book on the martyred Central Committee leader Naveen Babu, the tributes by Azad's friends provide a revealing insight into the sociology and character of the revolutionary leader.[62] Born in 1954 in Krishna district, Andhra Pradesh, Cherukuri Rajkumar (Azad) moved with his family to Hyderabad where he went to primary school. Like so many of the leaders of the CPI (Maoist) who came from the People's War Group, Rajkumar was born into a higher-caste, middle-class family (his father had once been in the Indian Armed Forces) and was radicalised when he went to the Regional Engineering College in Warangal to study chemical engineering. He went on to pursue postgraduate studies in ore-dressing at Andhra University in Visakhapatnam. At the Regional Engineering College, he was a member of the Radical Students Union and spent a few months in jail when he was twenty-one during Indira Gandhi's Emergency in 1975. Five years later, he went fully underground and for the next thirty years worked in various parts of the country, from Gujarat to Karnataka, becoming a key leader in guiding the peace talks of 2004. Within the movement, he was widely known as an important intellectual figure.

Unlike the first two parts of Ghandy's book, the essays edited by Azad's friends are primarily texts that had already appeared in the public domain because Azad was the Maoists' spokesperson. They therefore address an external audience, and range from correcting various misinformed positions on the Maoists in the public realm (for instance, a response to a special issue of *Economic and Political Weekly* on Maoists, which takes up central issues such as the criticisms of violence, the treatment of tribe and caste, the misconceptions of being 'caught between two armies') to commentary on the various stages of the Nepal movement, the Maoist position on peace talks, and a substantive interview he gave to *The Hindu*. Chillingly, they also contain two accounts of the killing of comrades who were brutally tortured and murdered by the police and then placed in a forest as if killed in an encounter—as though Azad were foretelling the story of his own death.

There are also a few books from those who have worked on the fringes of the Naxalite movement that also provide internal insights into the movement.[63] N. Venugopal's, *Notes from a Participant Observer*, for instance, is a compilation of essays from someone who for years was associated mainly through the Revolutionary Writers Association (Virasam) in Andhra Pradesh, once banned along with the Naxalites.[64] As well as a chapter on this banning, the book also includes published and unpublished essays (many for *Economic and Political Weekly*). Some of the most valuable parts document the various people's struggles in Telangana and the Naxalites' involvement with them: Sikasa-Singareni coalminers, the Rythu Coolie Sangham, Tendu Leaf Labourers, the Radical Youth League, the feminist movement, the Dalit movement, the formation of the Andhra Pradesh Civil Liberties Committee in 1973, and so on. These struggles of the 1970s laid the foundation for the formation of the People's War in 1980 and contribute lessons of the significance of mass struggle for the Naxalites today. Equally valuable is the documentation of fake encounters; attempts on various people's lives, including the revolutionary balladeer, Gaddar; and the cultural literature being produced underground. The obituaries are moving, and the two on Azad and Kishenji are insightful for the information they provide, probably for the first time, on two of the influential leaders of the last two decades. As is characteristic of much of this genre of literature, they don't make up a coherent whole nor are they comprehensive, but for anyone interested in learning more about the history of the Andhra Pradesh-based Naxalites, they are crucial reading.

Contributing to this genre are the historical accounts of the Naxalites from intellectuals who are close to the movement or were once part of it. The work that claims to present the most comprehensive critical history of the movement (from 1972 to 2014) is Amit Bhattacharya's *Storming the Gates of Heaven*.[65] Although it covers many different topics such as 'Women and the revolution', as well as containing a chapter on guerrilla activities in Dandakaranya and Gadchiroli, it is perhaps most useful for bringing to wider public attention some of the inner party history and sources. For instance, it outlines the many different splits and mergers within the various factions of the Indian communist movement that lay claim to the heritage of Naxalbari and which led to the formation of the CPI (Maoist). It has some details on the Naxalites' various mass organisations, and an explanation of its transition from Mao Zedong's thought to Maoism.

A different angle on the Indian Naxalites is presented in exploring the intellectual history of Maoism. This is the focus of Bernard D'Mello's work, *What Is Maoism and Other Essays*, which identifies Maoism at its broadest to be a commitment to radical democracy.[66] Incorporating essays by Marxist scholars such as Paul Sweezy and William Hinton, D'Mello charts how the idea of Maoism evolved from Marxism, Leninism and Stalinism, thus providing the ideological backdrop for its adoption in India. For any serious scholar of radical politics, understanding this intellectual history is as important as tracing the history of the Naxalites themselves, and D'Mello takes us some way towards this.

Just as useful are the books that focus on one moment in the movement, written by civil society members and activists practically involved in the region or the issues. One example is the case of Lalgarh in the western hinterlands of West Bengal, where an Adivasi-led movement against state police excesses and land dispossession resulted in a direct confrontation between the CPI (Maoist) and the Indian state, and failed peace talks between the CPI (Maoist) and the West Bengal government in 2011. Two useful and complementary collections were published on this case. The first, edited by Biswajit Roy, is *War and Peace in Junglemahal*. It reflects the broad-based discussion within civil society about the incidents in Lalgarh, the resulting 'Operation Green Hunt' consisting of joint operations by the central and West Bengal governments, and the rise of Mamata Banerjee's Trinamool Congress Party (TMC) in the state effectively ending nearly forty years of Left Front rule.[67] The voices of the leadership of the People's Committee Against Police Atrocities (PCAPA)—in six letters written between 27 March and 6 August 2010—are the focus of *Letters from Lalgarh*.[68] The six letters were written in the midst of state-authorised violence in the region, and were sent (with great difficulty) to civil society members and organisations. They are an interesting source for those seeking to map out the relationships between the state and the indigenous populations of Junglemahal; the Maoists and the PCAPA; the TMC and the PCAPA; and urban civil society, the PCAPA, the Maoists and the indigenous populations. They also provide data about numerous individual arrests and acts of violence against indigenous people and PCAPA activists by the state, which would be near impossible to gather from official government sources.

In recent years, we have also seen the publication of accounts from people who joined the early Naxalite movement and helped in founding the struggle. Part (auto)biography, part diary, part chronicle, these memoirs, although often written decades after their authors' involvement, contain fascinating insights into the Naxalite movement. They are, though, overwhelmingly from the literate, well-to-do classes and must be read as just one type of account of mobilisation. (The experiences of the poor villagers, for instance, the Dalits and Adivasis, who joined the Naxalites are likely to be very different and would shed an important light on our understanding of the movement, but it is much harder for these voices to be published.) Two recent examples are *The First Naxal: An Authorised Biography of Kanu Sanyal* by Bappaditya Paul and Abhijit Das's *Footprints of Foot Soldiers*.[69] Written from the perspectives of two men born into middle-class, upper-caste Bengali families, one generation apart, they are interesting to consider together. Sanyal was born in Kurseong in Darjeeling in 1929 and Das, less than twenty years later (in 1948), in English Bazaar, Malda district. Both books begin with observations of the injustices that surrounded the authors, which led to their political mobilisation. Both describe the ways in which they came into contact with radical comrades from similar backgrounds who inspired them; how they in turn inspired youth from middle-class, upper-caste families to become politicised; the ways in which they went to work in the villages to organise and mobilise peasants and workers behind the revolutionary cause, and through that process 'declassed' themselves; and their experiences in prison (which for Sanyal was a time of greater political mobilisation). Both ended up parting ways with Charu Majumdar's legacy. While Sanyal, who had originally worked very closely with Majumdar in founding the movement—so much so that he was seen as Majumdar's lieutenant—split from the Majumdar line in his revolutionary work, Das eventually gave up altogether and went to work in Mumbai. The details reveal the sociology, psychology, and experiences of middle-class, upper-caste youth who were central to the initial Naxalbari struggle.

Interestingly, both accounts were written right at the end of the authors' lives. Das died a few months after his book was published, while Sanyal did not live to see the publication of his biography. What comes across overwhelmingly in both accounts is their desire, right at the end of their lives, to set the record straight in relation to any doubt about their commitment to the revolutionary struggle. There are of course differences in the way they do this. Sanyal is more bitter than Das, and his narrative focuses on the organisational work that he did in the villages and tea plantations in the years before and after Naxalbari that were crucial to the spread of the uprising. Das, in some ways, gives a more straightforward account—almost a diary—of his involvement in the movement. His book is a testimony to the sincerity with which he worked, his increasing concern about the party line, and his disappointment at meeting with Politburo members who either disregarded his concerns or told him that now was not the time to raise questions. Both books critique Majumdar's focus on the annihilation of class enemies for the way this alienated ordinary villagers, arguing that it was the struggle among, and with, the masses that was crucial. What comes across is the authors' commitment to the revolutionary cause and the overwhelming passion they continued to have for the Naxalbari movement.

It is worth mentioning here the re-publication of Suniti Kumar Ghosh's *Naxalbari, Before and After: Reminiscences and Appraisal* for its similar contribution, although it is perhaps much more clearly a political appraisal of the revolutionary organising after Naxalbari and until the death of Charu Majumdar.[70] In the aftermath of the Naxalbari upsurge, Ghosh, who had been closely associated with the 1946–7 Tebhaga struggle, became a member of the All India Coordination Committee of the Communist Revolutionaries and, later, a member of the Central Committee of the CPI (ML). From the perspective of someone deeply committed to the legacy of Naxalbari, the book charts the rise of the CPI (ML), beginning with the ideological differences that arose within the communist movement in India, and explores the initial spread of the Naxalites. Perhaps the most interesting parts are his critical accounts of the revolutionaries based on his personal experience of being a member of the Central Committee. He explores how it was formed, the tensions around the questions of whether Majumdar should have been a revolutionary leader or a revolutionary authority, the roles allocated to each member, and then the growing differences between them. Ghosh accused some of the other members of political careerism, which eventually led to him being accused by Majumdar of bringing 'bourgeois influences' into the party. Ghosh himself criticises Majumdar for having been theoretically weak, for pursuing the annihilation of class enemies, which led to terrorist acts, and giving up on mass mobilisation, and for having had a blind faith in Mao Zedong and the Chinese path, despite instructions from China that India needed to create its own political line. (There is a fascinating appendix on the comments of Zhou Enlai and Kang Sheng on the CPI (ML)'s political line as told to one of the Central Committee members when he visited China.) For Ghosh, the overwhelming motivation in writing the book, as it is for some of the other authors reviewed here, may also have been to set the record straight about what had actually happened from his point of view. What comes across is a sincere account that tells us as much about the emotional life of the leadership, the kinds of issues that caused inner party divisions leading to accusations of betrayal and of Ghosh's own commitment to the legacy of Naxalbari and the revolutionary cause in India, as it does about the history of the initial movement.

Most of these biographical accounts/memoirs of middle-class activists have been written by men, but we may also see the emergence of those coming from women. A precedent has been established by K. Ajitha, from Kerala, whose memoirs were serialised in the Malayalam magazine *Kalakaumudi* in 1979 and have recently been translated into English as *Kerala's Naxalbari: Ajitha, Memoirs of a Young Revolutionary.*[71] Born at around the same time as Das, in the early 1950s, she was from a middle-class communist family. Unlike many of the other comrades from her background who broke with their pasts, it was her parents who encouraged her participation in the movement. She was influenced by the books she read—many on Mao's China—and began by joining in demonstrations and distributing pamphlets and books disseminating Mao's ideas. Ajitha's parents also loom large in her politicisation. She describes how she went to mobilise peasants in the countryside with her mother and when she fell in love with another comrade, her father discouraged her from getting married, as it would have harmed both the movement and the couple.

In 1968, together with her lover and 300 armed guerrillas, and barely nineteen years old, she was involved in a series of attacks on police stations in Wayanad, Kerala (with the aim of stealing arms) and on two local landlords whose food reserves they distributed to the Adivasis. The details of the attacks reveal not only the spirit of adventure and revolutionary zeal of the mobilised youth but also their tragic inexperience and the mistakes they made; one comrade was seriously injured when he fell with a hand grenade he had himself made and another was similarly blown up by his own handmade bomb. Their stories provide a rare insight into what it must have been like on the frontline. In the raids that followed, Ajitha's lover was killed and she herself was captured, tortured, and sentenced to nine years of solitary confinement. The latter part of the book focuses on the humiliation and torture by the police and her grim life in jail. When she came out of prison, at the age of twenty-seven, she married a Muslim comrade eight years her junior and turned away from the armed class struggle to set up a women's rights NGO.

As the Indian prisons fill up with Naxalite prisoners, we see an emerging genre of books in the form of diaries and reflections of inmates who have been arrested under charges of being Maoists. A recent contribution is Arun Ferreira's *Colours of the Cage*.[72] Vividly illustrated with the author's pictures, the book documents his experiences of custodial torture, fighting the battle against false charges, the grim conditions of Indian prisons where corruption is endemic, and the everyday life that prisoners create in these dismal conditions.

Ferreira, a middle-class Roman Catholic from Bandra, a well-to-do neighbourhood of Mumbai, was arrested by the Nagpur police on charges of being a Naxalite under the Unlawful Activities (Prevention) Act 2004. He was accused of being the chief of communications and propaganda for the Maoist party and charged with murder, criminal conspiracy, rioting, and possession of arms. Fighting these charges from prison with the help of his family and lawyers, while undertaking postgraduate study with the Indian Institute of Human Rights in Delhi by distance learning, he was acquitted of all charges in 2011. But—as seems to be common for detainees alleged to be 'Maoist'—he was abducted at the prison gates and re-arrested.

The book begins with an unsentimental description of the torture that Ferreira faced while under arrest, including medieval techniques of stretching the body (which the complicit hospital doctors did not record), as well as narcoanalysis, lie detectors, and brain mapping tests. It is interspersed with Ferreira's brilliant ink drawings of the prison. These illustrations, which other prisoners referred to as 'the colours of the cage', are meant to give the outside world an idea of what life is like in Indian prisons. The letters he sent back to his family (it is not always clear whether they were to his parents or his wife) also paint a picture of the anxieties his family suffered and the work they did to get him out of prison. The book is a lucid account more generally of jail life—the awful food, the rapid spread of disease, coping with the shortage of water, and the physical beatings received by prisoners, which were a daily affair. One wonders what—if anything—has changed since the days when Mary Tyler wrote her 1973 book, *My Years in an Indian Prison*, about the five years she spent in a jail in Jharkhand awaiting trial, accused of being a Naxalite.[73] The torture of prisoners, the dismal prison conditions, and the indifference of the authorities to the legal and civil rights of prisoners all seem to still be in place. Tyler described in great detail the poverty of life in prison, but also the poverty and oppression of the women wardens at the hands of the male chief wardens and jail superintendents.

Ferreira's account is also important because it provides us with an insight into the everyday life that prisoners jailed in the name of fighting Naxalism have tried to create in prison—whether in Madhya Pradesh (as in this case) or Jharkhand. This involves the struggles they have undertaken to improve the conditions of prison life, backed by hunger strikes; the ways in which more educated, better-off prisoners tried to help illiterate, lower-caste inmates by teaching classes and sharing out their food.

If Ferreira's imagination and political messages escape the iron bars of the prison through his drawings, others do the same through poetry. His account joins the moving *Captive Imagination: Letters from Prison*, written by the revolutionary poet Varavara Rao.[74] This is a collection of Rao's meditations written between 1985 and 1989 from Secunderabad jail in what is now the state of Telangana. They were originally published as regular columns for the Telugu daily newspaper, *Andhra Prabha* (now part of the *New Indian Express*), and recently have been translated from Telugu into English and published with a foreword by Ngũgĩ wa Thiong'o. (The Naxalites have long admired the Kenyan writer for his writings and especially the novel, *Devil on the Cross*, which was written on toilet paper when he was in prison.)[75] Rao, who has been in and out of prison several times, has spent more than ten years of his life behind prison bars for his bold criticisms of the violence of the Indian state and his open sympathies for the Naxalite movement. Ferreira's book was written after his release, but Rao's letters were written and published while he was in prison. Despite the censorship Rao faced (he was unable to write directly about the social history of his time in prison and those around him in the way Ferreira could), his letters are remarkable for the emotional and political sentiment and sensibility they convey about being a political prisoner. Rao shows how those who imprison him cannot hold captive his imagination, which slips through prison bars as poetry.

Part poetry, part prose, Rao's writing takes the reader into his solitude and his profound inner thoughts, which are metaphors for the inner strength and defiance against life in prison faced and embraced, according to him, by all political prisoners. Through his poetry—which he sees as synonymous both with suffering and the struggle to end suffering—we learn about the emotional fight to endure the endless waiting for news of encounters and of friends who have been killed or are dead; the cultivation of patience and equanimity in the face of grief as well as joy; and the keeping at bay of despair and frustration in even the most trying of times. Though Rao suggests that grief is meant to be hidden (pondering on his daughter who comes to visit him in prison), those who spend time reflecting on his poetry and his prose are very likely to be moved.

> How long
> Can prison walls
> And iron bars
> Cage the free spirit?[76]

Rao tells us that the late human rights lawyer, K. Balagopal, sent him a copy of D.D. Kosambi's historiography in jail, with a note, 'While not in a position to participate in events that shape history, you may make use of this temporary rest period in studying history.' What both Ferreira's and Rao's books show us is that, contra Balagopal, through the social life of the prison and the power of imagination, prison bars cannot indeed cage the political prisoner who is making history from within.

A BIBLIOGRAPHIC ESSAY ON THE NAXALITES

The Literature Making History

The attention given to the Indian state's counterinsurgency against the Naxalites since 2006 has resulted in an astonishingly large number of books on this movement being published in recent years. What is truly remarkable is the vast and diverse literature that the Naxalite struggle has inspired, the reflections on the Indian state and parliamentary democracy that it has nurtured, the open debate it has provoked on the necessity for revolutionary violence in the contemporary world—a debate which is dead in most other parts of the world—and the imagination of a different and more equal world that it has kept alive. Whether wittingly, or unwittingly, those who have taken the interest, time and dedication to publish on the Naxalites have been participant in the making of history, against the grain of history.

Although there are exceptions, many of the books are hastily written, perhaps understandably so, and only a few are based on serious empirical research. The strength of this literature rests in its cumulative effects, in the combined intellectual and political contributions when the books are read alongside each other. Sorely lacking are empirically grounded studies of the contemporary guerrilla strongholds that focus both on the Maoist armies and the people they mobilise and move among. This is, of course, one of the main gaps that I hope *Nightmarch* will fill.

NOTES

PREFACE

1. https://www.state.gov/j/ct/rls/crt/2016/272241.htm. Last accessed 25 April 2018, 12:38.
2. http://www.financialexpress.com/india-news/rajnath-singh-outlines-new-aggressive-operational-strategy-to-take-on-maoists/659673/. Last accessed 25 April 2018, 12:38.

1. FOLLOWING THE CALL

1. K.P. Kannan (2012) 'How inclusive is inclusive growth in India?' *The Indian Journal of Labour Economics* 55 (1): 33–60, 36; Sabina Alkire and M.E. Santos (2010) 'Acute Multidimensional Poverty: A New Index for Developing Countries.' *Oxford Poverty and Human Development Initiative, Working Paper* 38.
2. https://kafila.online/2009/04/22/the-art-of-not-writing-shubhranshu-choudhary/. Last accessed 25 April 2018, 12:38.

2. HALF A CENTURY OF ARMED RESISTANCE

1. The best account of the early Naxalite movement, up to the death of Charu Majumdar in 1972, is probably still Sumanta Banerjee's (1980) *In the Wake of Naxalbari: A History of the Naxalite Movement in India.* Kolkata: Subarnrekha.
2. Sreemati Chakrabarti (1990) *China and the Naxalites.* London: Sangam.
3. Paul Bappaditya (2014) *The First Naxal: An Authorised Biography of Kanu*

Sanyal. New Delhi: Sage. See p. 130; Suniti Kumar Ghosh (2009) *Naxalbari: Before and After*. Kolkata: New Age Publishers. See especially Appendix B.

4. The 1948 Sunder Lal report on the aftermath of the military invasion by the Indian Army of the Hyderabad State was only released in 2013.

5. See Richard Wolin (2010) *The Wind from the East: French Intellectuals, the Cultural Revolution, and the Legacy of the 1960s*. Princeton: Princeton University Press.

6. See August Nimitz (2014) *Lenin's Electoral Strategy from Marx and Engels through the Revolution of 1905: The Ballot, the Street or Both*. New York: Palgrave Macmillan.

7. See Alpa Shah, Jens Lerche, Richard Axelby, Dalel Benbabaali, Brendan Donegan, Jayaseelan Raj and Vikramaditya Thakur (2018) *Ground Down by Growth: Tribe, Caste, Class and Inequality across India*. London: Pluto Press.

8. The best account of this period is Bela Bhatia's unpublished PhD thesis. Bela Bhatia (2000) 'The Naxalite Movement in Central Bihar' (PhD), University of Cambridge, Cambridge.

9. Although there are of course differences between all these groups, and names and classifications are often contested, in this book I generally refer to them by the popular term Adivasi, which emerged in the 1930s from their cross-group mobilisation in Jharkhand and which spread to many parts of the country.

10. There are clear parallels here with what has been described by Pierre Clastres (1974) as the 'societies against the state' of the Amazonian Indians or more recently by James Scott (2009) as the 'anarchist histories' of the ethnic groups who fled from the expanding nation-states of the plains to the hills of South East Asia to form 'stateless societies'. Pierre Clastres (1987 [1974]) *Society Against the State: Essays in Political Anthropology*. New York: Zone Books; James Scott (2009) *The Art of Not Being Governed: An Anarchist History of Upland Southeast Asia*. New Haven: Yale University Press. See also my earlier arguments on Adivasis: Alpa Shah (2007) 'Keeping the State Away: Democracy, politics and the state in India's Jharkhand.' *Journal of the Royal Anthropological Institute* 13 (1): 129–45; Alpa Shah (2010) *In the*

Shadows of the State: Indigenous Politics, Environmentalism and Insurgency in Jharkhand, India. Durham, N.C. and London: Duke University Press.

11. See also Frederick Bailey (1961) '"Tribe" and "Caste" in India.' *Contributions to Indian Sociology* 5: 7–19.

12. The people who had some success in infiltrating some pockets of the forest were Christian missionaries from the 1850s onwards. Some of them tried to learn the local languages and ways of life and help the Adivasis they came in touch with to fight off the oppression of the high-caste outsiders.

13. One of the best accounts of the Santhal Hul is in Vasudha Dhagamwar's (2006) *Role and Image of Law in India.* New Delhi: Sage.

14. Kumar Suresh Singh's (2002) *Birsa Munda and His Movement, 1872–1901: A Study of a Millenarian Movement in Chotanagpur.* Kolkata: Seagull Press, is a classic. See also Alpa Shah (2014) 'Religion and the Secular Left: Subaltern Studies, Birsa Munda and the Maoist,' *Anthropology of this Century* 9.

15. Neighbouring areas benefitted to some extent from Christian missionaries through the schools they set up and their attempts to call the state to account to serve local people. It was from these areas that saw Christian missionary and conversion activitiy that, from the 1930s, the first Adivasi social movements demanding land rights, forest rights, education and jobs for the Adivasis arose. But in the hills and forests where the Naxalites made their home, despite sixty years of independence, there was little attempt to incorporate Adivasis as citizens of the Indian state.

16. See Brian Morriss (2013) 'Anarchism, Individualism and South Indian Foragers: Memories and Reflections.' *Radical Anthropology*, November: 22–37.

17. See Shah (2010) *In the Shadows of the State.*

18. For a brilliant analysis among the Muria, see Alfred Gell (1986) 'Newcomers to the World of Goods: Consumption among the Muria Gonds' in A. Appadurai (ed.) *The Social Life of Things: Commodities in Cultural Perspective.* Cambridge: Cambridge University Press, 110–38.

19. See Nurit Bird David (1983) 'Wage-Gatherings: Socio-economic Change and the Case of the Naiken of South India' in P. Robb (ed.) *Rural South Asia*. Salem: Merrimack Publishing Circle, 57–86.

20. In this book I use 'Naxalite' and 'Maoist' interchangeably.

21. Most notably a Government of India (2008) report argued that the Maoist movement was a political movement and had to be seen as a fight for social justice, equality, protection, security, and local development. Government of India (2008) *Development Challenges in Extremist Affected Areas: Report of an Expert Group to the Planning Commission*. New Delhi: Government of India. However, an Intelligence Bureau report, which argued for a more robust security-centred approach, was favoured over this report for presentation in parliament. See K.S. Subramanian (2010) 'State Response to Maoist Violence in India: A Critical Assessment,' *Economic and Political Weekly*, 7 August: 23–6.

22. The best account of these peace talks is in Committee of Concerned Citizens (2006) *Negotiating Peace: Peace Talks between Government of Andhra Pradesh and Naxalite Parties*. Hyderabad: Committee of Concerned Citizens.

23. http://www.thehindu.com/todays-paper/555-fake-encounter-cases-registered-across-india-in-last-four-years/article4916004.ece. Last accessed 25 April 2018, 12:38.

24. See http://www.hrln.org/hrln/defend-the-defenders/pils-a-cases/1511-a-landmark-judgment-in-salwa-judum-case.html. Last accessed 25 April 2018, 12:38. See also Nandini Sundar (2015) *Burning Forests*. New Delhi: Juggernaut.

3. LIVING IN A MUD HUT

1. For how participant observation amongst the Naxalites have shaped my own understandings of this praxis of anthropology, see Alpa Shah (2017) 'Ethnography? Participant Observation, a Potentially Revolutionary Praxis,' *Hau: Journal of Ethnographic Theory* 7 (1): 45–59.

8. SACRIFICE, RENUNCIATION, LIBERATION AND VIOLENCE

1. See Maurice Dobb's (1946) *Studies in the Development of Capitalism.* London: Routledge. See also Paul Sweezy's 'Critique of Dobb' in R.H. Hilton (ed.) (1976) *The Transition from Feudalism to Capitalism.* London: New Left Books. Dobb's 'A Reply' and 'A Further Comment' and Sweezy's 'A Rejoinder' are also in *The Transition from Feudalism to Capitalism.*

2. Karl Marx (1845) *Theses on Feuerbach,* accessible at https://www.marxists.org/archive/marx/works/1845/theses/theses.htm. Last accessed 21 March 2018, 15:22.

3. Alpa Shah (2013) 'The Agrarian Question in a Maoist Guerrilla Zone: Land, Labour and Capital in the Forests and Hills of Jharkhand, India,' *Journal of Agrarian Change* 13 (3): 424–50.

4. Henri Hubert and Marcel Mauss (1981 [1899]) *Sacrifice: Its Nature and Function.* Chicago: University of Chicago Press.

5. Maurice Bloch (1992) *Prey into Hunter: The Politics of Religious Experience.* Cambridge: Cambridge University Press.

6. Emile Durkheim (2002 [1897]) *Suicide: A Study in Sociology.* London: Routledge.

7. Louis Dumont (1970) *Homo Hierarchicus: The Caste System and Its Implications.* London: Wiedenfeld and Nicolson, 184–6.

8. See Khare, for instance on untouchable renouncers. R.S. Khare (1984) *The Untouchable As Himself: Ideology, Identity and Pragmatism among the Lucknow Chamars.* Cambridge: Cambridge University Press.

9. As described by Chris Fuller (1992) *The Camphor Flame: Popular Hinduism and Society in India.* Princeton: Princeton University Press, 17.

10. See Jonathan Parry (1994) *Death in Benares.* Cambridge: Cambridge University Press.

11. Alongside individual ascetics, there has also been an Indian tradition of organised groups of renouncers, although Romila Thapar has argued that these groups were attempting neither to negate society nor to alter it radically, but just to create a parallel separate society. See Romilla Thapar (1978) *Ancient Indian Social History: Some Interpretations.* New Delhi: Orient Longman. See also William Pinch (1996) *Peasants and*

Monks in British India. Berkeley: University of California Press; Dirk Kolff (1971) 'Sanyasi Trader-Soldiers,' *Indian Economic and Social History Review* 8 (2): 213–20; Bernard Cohn (1964) 'The Role of the Gosains in the Economy of Eighteenth and Nineteenth Century Upper India,' *The Indian Economic and Social History Review* 1 (4): 175–82.

12. Richard Burghart (1983) 'Renunciation in the Religious Traditions of South Asia,' *Man* 18 (4): 635–53; Dumont (1970) *Homo Hierarchicus*; Fuller (1992) *The Camphor Flame*; Parry (1994) *Death in Benares*.

13. Maurice Bloch and Jonathan Parry (eds) (1982) *Death and the Regeneration of Life*. Cambridge: Cambridge University Press. See also Alpa Shah (2014) 'The Muck of the Past: Revolution, Social Transformation and the Maoists in India (The Malinowski Memorial Lecture, 2012),' *Journal of Royal Anthropological Institute* (n.s.) 20: 337–56.

14. Arundhati Roy (2011) *Broken Republic*. New Delhi: Hamish Hamilton.

15. See Jean-Paul Sartre's preface to Frantz Fanon's (2001 [1963]) *The Wretched of the Earth*. London: Penguin.

9. MORNING ONE

1. As Max Weber would classically have it: Max Weber (1921) 'Politics as a Vocation' in Weber, *Rationalism and Modern Society*, translated and edited by Tony Waters and Dagmar Waters. New York: Palgrave Books 2015, 129–98.

10. NIGHT TWO

1. See Karl Marx (1976 [1867]) *Capital: A Critique of Political Economy, Volume 1*. London: Penguin, 284.

11. EGALITARIAN IDEALS, HUMANENESS AND INTIMACY

1. http://www.ilo.org/global/about-the-ilo/newsroom/news/WCMS_005176/lang—en/index.htm. Last accessed 25 April 2018, 12:38.

2. David Stoll (1993) *Between Two Armies in the Ixil Towns of Guatemala*. New York: Columbia University Press.

3. As also pointed out by Radha D'Souza (2009) 'Sandwich Theory and Operation Green Hunt,' *Sanhati Journal*.

4. Samuel Popkin (1979) *The Rational Peasant: The Political Economy of Rural Society in Vietnam*. Berkeley: University of California Press.

5. Paul Collier and Anke Hoeffler (2004) 'Greed and Grievance in Civil War,' *Oxford Economic Papers* 56 (4): 563–95. Collier and Hoeffler later modified their 'greed' thesis to account for broader factors like 'feasibility'. See Collier and Hoeffler (2009) 'Beyond Greed and Grievance: Feasibility and Civil War,' Oxford Economic Papers 61 (1): 1–27. For an overall critique, see David Keen (2000) 'Incentives and Disincentives for Violence' in M. Berdal and D. Malone (eds) *Greed and Grievance: Economic Agendas in Civil Wars*. Boulder, CO: Lynne Rienner, 19–43.

6. See, for instance, Jason Miklian and Scott Carney (2010) 'Fire in the Hole,' *Foreign Policy*, http://www.foreignpolicy.com/articles/2010/08/16/fire_in_the_hole. Last accessed 25 April 2018, 12:38.

7. James Scott (1976) *Moral Economy of the Peasant: Rebellion and Subsistence in Southeast Asia*. New Haven: Yale University Press; E.P. Thompson (1971) 'Moral Economy of the English Crowd in the Eighteenth Century,' *Past & Present* 50 (1): 76–136.

8. The most powerful proponent of the grievance argument was Government of India (2008) *Development Challenges in Extremist Affected Areas: Report of an Expert Group to Planning Commission*. New Delhi: Government of India.

9. Arundhati Roy is perhaps the best example of those who hold this position and once claimed that since the movement is 99.9 per cent Adivasi, it is open to debate whether this movement is Maoist or Adivasi. Arundhati Roy (2011) *Broken Republic*. New Delhi: Hamish Hamilton.

10. See also Alpa Shah (2013) 'The Intimacy of Insurgency: Beyond Coercion, Greed or Grievance in Maoist India,' *Economy and Society* 42 (3): 480–506.

12. NIGHT THREE

1. McKinsey and Company (2014) 'Putting India on the Growth Path: Unlocking the Mining Potential,' http://www.mckinsey.com/global-themes/india/putting-india-on-the-growth-path-unlocking-the-mining-potential. Last accessed 25 April 2018, 12:39.

2. A good recent summary of these debates is provided by Kevin Anderson (2010) *Marx at the Margins: On Nationalism, Ethnicity, and Non-Western Societies*. Chicago: University of Chicago Press.

14. ACCELERATING THE REACH OF THE STATE AND CAPITAL

1. Details of how this operates are in Alpa Shah (2006) 'Markets of Protection: The "Terrorist" Maoist Movement and the State in Jharkhand, India,' *Critique of Anthropology* 26 (3): 297–314.

2. https://wikileaks.org/cable/2010/01/10MUMBAI12.html. Last accessed 25 April 2018, 12:39.

3. The most insightful study of these mechanisms of corruption is Robert Wade (1982) 'The System of Administrative and Political Corruption: Canal Irrigation in South India,' *Journal of Development Studies* 18: 287–328.

4. For further details on these processes and the moral justifications, see Alpa Shah (2009) 'Morality, Corruption and the State: Insights from Jharkhand, India,' *The Journal of Development Studies* 45 (3): 295–313. See also Jonathan Parry (2000) 'The "Crisis of Corruption" and "The Idea of India": A Worm's Eye View' in I. Pardo (ed.) *Morals of Legitimacy: Between Agency and System*. Oxford: Berghan Books, 27–55.

5. Each bundle of fifty leaves fetched 70 paise (£0.007). After the Naxalites doubled the rates, it became possible for a husband-wife team to earn 1,500 rupees (£15) a day picking leaves—a decent wage considering the daily wage for manual labour set by the government (but rarely met) was 100 rupees (£1).

6. Harijans is the word Gandhi used for Dalits.

7. https://timesofindia.indiatimes.com/india/coal-scam-madhu-koda-sentenced-to-3-year-jail-term/articleshow/62093513.cms. Last accessed 17 May 2018, 17:00.

8. See Alpa Shah (2014) 'Religion and the Secular Left: Subaltern Studies, Birsa Munda and the Maoist,' *Anthropology of this Century* 9.

15. NIGHT FIVE

1. http://www.indiandefencereview.com/news/splintering-naxalism-in-india-maoism-or-money/2/. Last accessed 25 April 2018, 12:39.

17. GENDER, GENERATION, CLASS AND CASTE

1. Li Onesto (1999) 'Report from the People's War in Nepal.' http://web. archive.org/web/20050104155223/http://rwor.org/s/dispatch-e.htm. Last accessed 25 April 2018, 12:40.

2. For an astute analysis on Nepal, see Judith Pettigrew and Sara Shneiderman (2004) 'Women and the Maobaadi: Ideology and Agency in Nepal's Maoist Movement,' *Himal South Asia*, 17 (1): 19–29.

3. Ashraf Deghani (1978) *Torture and Resistance in Iran: Memoirs of the Woman Guerrilla.* https://web.archive.org/web/20051022120534/http:// www.ashrafdehghani.com:80/books-english/memoirs/part1.htm. Last accessed 25 April 2018, 12:40.

4. Anuradha Ghandy (2011) *Scripting the Change: Selected Writings of Anuradha Ghandy.* New Delhi: Daanish Books.

18. NIGHT SIX

1. Verrier Elwin (1947) *The Muria and their Ghotul.* Bombay: Oxford University Press.

2. Friedrich Engels (1884 [1972]) *The Origin of the Family, Private Property and the State.* London: Lawrence and Wishart. Engels did, however, at the end of the book, romanticise a new form of monogamous love.

20. INCARNATIONS

1. https://thewire.in/142377/srp-kalluri-iimc-bastar/. Last accessed 25 April 2018, 12:40.

2. http://www.sundayguardianlive.com/investigation/6434-over-500-in-nocent-youths-were-made-surrender-naxalites. Last accessed 25 April 2018, 12:41.

3. http://peoplesvoice.in/2017/09/16/adivasis-in-jail-and-no-one-to-lis-ten-their-cries/. Last accessed 25 April 2018, 12:41.

4. http://indianexpress.com/article/india/naxalism-shall-be-eradicated-from-jharkhand-by-2018-dgp-5019506/. Last accessed 25 April 2018, 12:41.

A BIBLIOGRAPHIC ESSAY ON THE NAXALITES

1. Alpa Shah (2014) 'The Muck of the Past: Revolution, Social Transformation and the Maoists in India (The Malinowski Memorial

Lecture, 2012),' *Journal of the Royal Anthropological Institute* (n.s.) 20: 337–56.

2. Alpa Shah (2013) 'The Intimacy of Insurgency: Beyond Coercion, Greed or Grievance in Maoist India,' *Economy and Society* 42 (3): 480–506.

3. Alpa Shah (2013) 'The Agrarian Question in a Maoist Guerrilla Zone: Land, Labour and Capital in the Forests and Hills of Jharkhand, India,' *Journal of Agrarian Change* 13 (3): 424–50.

4. Alpa Shah (2013) 'The Tensions Over Liberal Citizenship in a Marxist Revolutionary Situation: The Maoists in India,' *Critique of Anthropology* 33 (1): 91–109.

5. Feyzi Ismail and Alpa Shah (2015) 'Class Struggle, the Maoists and the Indigenous Question in Nepal and India,' *Economic and Political Weekly* 50 (35): 112–23.

6. Alpa Shah and Judith Pettigrew (eds) (2011) *Windows into a Revolution: Ethnographies of Maoism in India and Nepal*. New Delhi: Social Science Press. Based on Alpa Shah and Judith Pettigrew (2009) 'Windows into a Revolution: Ethnographies of Maoism in South Asia,' *Dialectical Anthropology* 33: 225–51.

7. Alpa Shah (2014) 'Religion and the Secular Left: Subaltern Studies, Birsa Munda and the Maoist,' *Anthropology of this Century* 9.

8. Alpa Shah (2011) 'Alcoholics Anonymous: The Maoist Movement in Jharkhand, India,' *Modern Asian Studies* 45 (5): 1095–117.

9. Alpa Shah (2006) 'Markets of Protection: The "Terrorist" Maoist Movement and the State in Jharkhand, India,' *Critique of Anthropology* 26 (3): 297–314.

10. Alpa Shah (2009) 'In Search of Certainty in Revolutionary India,' *Dialectical Anthropology* 33: 271–86.

11. Alpa Shah (2017) 'Ethnography? Participant Observation, A Potentially Revolutionary Praxis,' *Hau: Journal of Ethnographic Theory* 7 (1): 45–59.

12. This is an abbreviated and updated essay originally co-authored with Dhruv Jain. Alpa Shah and Dhruv Jain (2017) 'Naxalbari at Its Golden Jubilee: Fifty Recent Books on the Maoist Movement in India,' *Modern Asian Studies* 51 (4): 1165–219.

13. Exceptions are the security-focused state response captured in the two

books brought out by P.C. Joshi on the Naxal movement, addressed in particular to the police and security services, which mainly provide as much information as possible on the Naxalites in order to 'counter' them. P.C. Joshi (2013) *Naxalism: At A Glance.*

14. For instance, Robin Jeffrey, Ronojoy Sen, and Pratima Singh (eds) (2012) *More than Maoism: Politics, Policies and Insurgencies in South Asia.* New Delhi: Manohar; Santosh Paul (ed.) (2013) *The Maoist Movement in India: Perspectives and Counterperspectives.* New Delhi: Routledge; C. Sinha (2014) *Kindling of an Insurrection: Notes from Junglemahals.* New Delhi: Routledge.

15. Government of India (2008) *Development Challenges in Extremist Affected Areas: Report of an Expert Group to Planning Commission.* New Delhi: Government of India.

16. Ibid., 77.

17. A. Chenoy and K. Chenoy (2010) *Maoists and Other Armed Conflicts.* New Delhi: Penguin. Their canvas includes movements from the Northeast to Punjab and their work on the Maoists is only through secondary literature.

18. Ibid., 80–1.

19. Nandini Sundar (2016) *The Burning Forest: India's War in Bastar.* New Delhi: Juggernaut.

20. See K.S. Subramanian (2010) 'State Response to Maoist Violence in India: A Critical Assessment,' *Economic and Political Weekly*, 7 August: 23–6.

21. Neera Chandhoke (2015) *Democracy and Revolutionary Politics.* London: Bloomsbury Academic.

22. Ibid., 30.

23. Ibid., 34.

24. Ibid., 35.

25. Nirmalangshu Mukherji (2012) *The Maoists in India: Tribals under Siege.* London: Pluto Press.

26. Ibid., 146.

27. Ibid., 138.

28. Bidyut Chakrabarty and R.K. Kujur (2010) *Maoism in India: Reincarnation of Ultra-Left Wing Extremism in the Twenty-First Century.* Abingdon: Routledge.

29. Manoranjan Mohanty (2015) *Red and Green: Five Decades of the Indian Maoist Movement*. Kolkata: Setu Prakashani.

30. Gautam Navlakha (2014) *War and Politics*. Kolkata: Setu Prakashani.

31. Ibid., 2.

32. Ibid., 87, 94.

33. Yet Navlakha himself notes that one must be careful about this latter claim as it has often been used as a 'facade' to justify the imposition of a 'foreign yoke', as evidenced in Libya and more recently in Syria. Ibid., 11–12.

34. Ibid., 72.

35. Ibid., 113–48.

36. Ibid., 84.

37. Ibid., 102–12.

38. Ajay Gudavarthy (2014) *Maoism, Democracy and Globalisation: Cross-Currents in Indian Politics*. New Delhi: Sage Publications India.

39. Ibid., 1–2.

40. Ibid., 8–9.

41. Ibid., 10.

42. Ibid.

43. 'Days and Nights in the Heartland of Rebellion' is taken from the title of Gautam Navlakha's (2012) book of the same name.

44. Satnam (2010) *Jangalnama: Travels in a Maoist Guerilla Zone*, translated by V. Bharti. New Delhi: Penguin.

45. Sudeep Chakravarti (2007) *Red Sun: Travels in Naxalite Country*. New Delhi: Penguin.

46. Jan Myrdal (1986) *India Waits*. Chicago: Lake View Press.

47. Jan Myrdal (2012) *Red Star Over India: As the Wretched of the Earth are Rising. Impressions, Reflections and Preliminary Inferences*. Kolkata: Setu Prakashani.

48. Arundhati Roy (2011) *Broken Republic*. New Delhi: Hamish Hamilton.

49. See Alpa Shah (2012) 'Eco-incarceration: Walking with the Comrades,' *Economic and Political Weekly* 47 (21): 32–4.

50. Gautam Navlakha (2012) *Days and Nights in the Heartland of Rebellion*. New Delhi: Penguin.

51. Srila Roy (2012) *Remembering Revolution: Gender, Violence, and*

Subjectivity in India's Naxalbari Movement. Oxford: Oxford University Press; Mallarika Sinha Roy (2011) *Gender and Radical Politics in India: Magic Moments of Naxalbari (1967–1975)*. Abingdon: Routledge.

52. Roy (2012) *Remembering Revolution*, 109.

53. Anuradha Ghandy (2011) *Scripting the Change: Selected Writings of Anuradha Ghandy*, edited by A. Teltumbde and S. Sen. New Delhi: Daanish Books.

54. George Kunnath (2012) *Rebels from the Mud Houses: Dalits and the Making of the Maoist Revolution in Bihar*. New Delhi: Social Science Press.

55. Bela Bhatia (2000) 'The Naxalite Movement in Central Bihar' (PhD), University of Cambridge, Cambridge; Prakash Louis (2002) *People's Power: the Naxalite Movement in Central Bihar*. New Delhi: Wordsmiths.

56. Paul Basu (ed.) (2011) *Red on Silver: Naxalites in Cinema*. Kolkata: Setu Prakashani.

57. Jhumpa Lahiri (2013) *The Lowland*. London: Bloomsbury; Neel Mukherjee (2014) *The Lives of Others*. London: Chatto and Windus.

58. Dilip Simeon (2010) *Revolution Highway*. New Delhi: Penguin.

59. Neel Mukherjee (2017) *A State of Freedom*. London: Chatto and Windus.

60. Ghandy (2011) *Scripting the Change*.

61. Azad (2010) *Maoists in India: Writings and Interviews*. Hyderabad: Friends of Azad.

62. Y. N. Babu (2008) *From Varna to Jati: Political Economy of Caste in Indian Social Formation*. New Delhi: Daanish Books.

63. Included here are only the books that directly address the movement. But for those interested in a wider literature that has been produced because of the impact of the Naxalites on the writers' lives—though they do not say much about the Naxalites per se—the writings of one of India's most important civil rights activists and lawyers, K. Balagopal, in *Ear to the Ground*, will be of interest. Also see Ilina Sen's *Inside Chhattisgarh*, which begins as an account of the police harassment the family faced on charges that her husband Binayak Sen, a doctor, was a Naxalite. K. Balagopal (2011) *Ear to the Ground: Selected Writings on Class and Caste*, New Delhi: Navayana Publishers; I. Sen (2011) *Inside Chhattisgarh: A Political Memoir*. New Delhi: Penguin.

64. N. Venugopal (2013) *Understanding Maoists: Notes of a Participant Observer from Andhra Pradesh.* Kolkata: Setu Prakashani.

65. Amit Bhattacharyya (2016) *Storming the Gates of Heaven: the Maoist Movement in India: a Critical Study 1972–2014.* Kolkata: Setu Prakashani.

66. Bernard D'Mello (2010) *What Is Maoism and Other Essays.* Kolkata: Cornerstone Publications.

67. B. Roy (2014) *War and Peace in Junglemahal: People, State and Maoists.* Kolkata: Setu Prakashani.

68. People's Committee Against Police Atrocities (2013) *Letters from Lalgarh: The Complete Collection of Letters From The Peoples Committee Against Police Atrocities.* Kolkata: Setu Prakashani.

69. Paul Bappaditya (2014) *The First Naxal: An Authorised Biography of Kanu Sanyal.* New Delhi: Sage; Abhijit Das (2015) *Footprints of Foot Soldiers: Experiences and Recollections of the Naxalite Movement in Eastern India 1960's and 70's.* Kolkata: Setu Prakashani.

70. Suniti Kumar Ghosh (2009) *Naxalbari: Before and After.* Kolkata: New Age Publishers.

71. K. Ajitha (2008) *Kerala's Naxalbari: Ajitha: Memoirs of a Young Revolutionary,* translated by S. Ramachandran, New Delhi: Srishti.

72. Arun Ferreira (2014) *Colours of the Cage.* New Delhi: Aleph Book Company.

73. Mary Tyler (1977) *My Years in an Indian Prison.* London: Gollancz.

74. Varavara Rao (2010) *Captive Imagination: Letters from Prison.* New Delhi: Penguin.

75. Ngũgĩ wa Thiong'o (1982) *Devil on the Cross.* London: Heinemann.

76. Rao (2010) *Captive Imagination,* 102.

ACKNOWLEDGEMENTS

A book is based on imagination, ideas and experience shaped by our encounters and interactions with others. This book would not have been possible without the journeys of thought, emotion and action I have shared with many people over the last decade. There are more people to thank than I can possibly do justice to here.

Those in the fields and forests of India whose names I cannot reveal, who led me into their lives and stories as though I were family; the Somwaris, Seemas, Vikases, Kohlis, Prashants and Gyanjis of this world. Some have since been killed; some are now caged behind bars; and others try to carve out a life despite the forces of history that seem set against them. These are the people who, wittingly or unwittingly, have become part of the making of history but whose lives no history book is likely to record.

George Kunnath, who caringly shared many of my experiences in Jharkhand and Bihar.

The UK Economic and Social Research Council and the EU European Research Council who awarded me the research grants that gave the generous time and resources to undertake fieldwork and writing. My colleagues in the Department of Anthropology at Goldsmiths and at the London School of Economics and Political Science who believed in and supported the making of

ACKNOWLEDGEMENTS

this book. My colleagues who work on Nepal who helped me understand the multiple facets of their 'People's War' to think comparatively about the Naxalites—in particular, David Gellner, Judith Pettigrew, Sara Shneiderman, Anne De Sales and Feyzi Ismail. The many colleagues who helped analyse the arguments that shape *Nightmarch* by inviting me to their seminars: University of Oxford Department of Anthropology and South Asia Studies; University of Cambridge Department of Geography, Department of Anthropology and South Asia Studies; British Academy; University of Edinburgh Department of Anthropology and South Asia Studies; University of Kent Department of Anthropology; SOAS Department of Anthropology and Department of Development Studies; University of Stockholm Department of Anthropology and South Asia Studies; University of Copenhagen Department of Anthropology; University of Oslo Department of Anthropology; Ghent University Department of Political Science; Bielefeld University; Central Eastern European University Budapest Department of Anthropology; University of Zurich Department of Anthropology; Max Planck Institute Hale and University Department of Anthropology Hale; Nice Department of Anthropology; George Washington University International Relations; University of Massachusetts Amherst Department of Economics; Yale University Department of Anthropology and Agrarian Studies Colloquium; University of California, St Davis Department of Anthropology; Stanford University Department of Anthropology; Princeton University Department of Anthropology and South Asia Studies.

Simon Chambers for encouraging me and helping me to step out of the cloak of academic writing. Hugh Levinson for seeing the significance of people's stories from the forests of India and making them accessible to a wider public through BBC Radio 4's *Crossing Continents*, even though I had no training as a presenter

ACKNOWLEDGEMENTS

or recorder. The friends who provided essential advice at crucial junctures or read all or parts of the script: Jonathan Parry, Maurice Bloch, David Graeber, Yasmin Khan, Jens Lerche, Orlanda Ruthven, Margaret Dickinson, Stuart Corbridge, Stephan Feuchtwang, Ashutosh Varshney, Barbara Harriss-White, Chris Nineham, James Palmer, Orin Starn, Laurie Taylor, Ian Jack, Ken Wissoker, Rita Astuti, Sumanta Banerjee, Bernard D'Mello, Gautam Navlakha, the late Sashi Bhushan Pathak, Kathinka Sinha-Kerkhoff and Vinod Sinha. My students Thomas Herzmark, Megnaa Mehtta, Itay Noy and Maka Suarez, who shared their insights on an early draft over an unforgettable Hyderabadi biryani. Dhruv Jain who wrote an extended version of the bibliographic essay with me.

Helen Garnons-Williams and Victoria Hobbs for believing in *Nightmarch*. Michael Dwyer and Farhaana Arefin, Priya Nelson and Siddhesh Inamdar—and the teams at Hurst, Chicago and HarperCollins India—for bringing the book to fruition.

My incredible family—who never expect or ask for thanks—for standing by me, even as I tried to break with the past. Rob—whom no words could ever thank—for the patience and endurance that mark the depth of his love, kindness and generosity, and for Amarirosa, who gave new hope and helped me see a path beyond the endless march.

INDEX

Adivasis: xiv–xxi, 10, 21, 24–32, 40, 43, 60, 67, 81, 99–101, 106, 112, 122–229, 246, 253–260, 264, 266, 269, 274–5, 284; Agharia, 208; autonomy of, xv, 25, 32, 147, 191, 217, 224; Bhumij, 26; Birhor, 125; Birjia, 208; Chero, 26; culture of, 30–1, 126–7, 131, 140, 150, 160, 162, 185, 215–16, 218–19, 224, 240–1, 271; displacement of, 28, 41, 142–3, 146; Gonds, 24, 26, 224; Hos, 24, 26; Kherwar, 125, 140; Kols, 26; Konds, 24, 26; Koyas, 24, 26; legal protection of, 22; Lohras, 162; Mundas, 24, 26, 30, 40, 126; Murias, 24, 26, 224; Oraon, 24, 30, 67, 73, 125–6, 131, 162, 177, 216; rebellions of, 27, 147, 186, 261, 273; Santhals, 24, 26, 197; Sarhul (festival), 122, 124; Sarna (sacred grove), 122

affirmative action: 21, 29; and upward mobility of Adivasis, 184–5

agrarian transition: 86; Maoist analysis of, 13, 18, 257

agriculture: agricultural servitude, 20–21, 25, 27, 264; labour, 22, 205, 257; Maoist agricultural activities/cooperatives, 165, 203; plains, 20, 24, 30, 74, 116, 133, 230, 255

Ahluwalia, Montek Singh: Deputy Chairman of Planning Commission, 142

alcohol: Adivasi culture of drinking, 149–150, 186, 218; *hadia* (rice beer), 131, 149, 217–8; *mahua* (wine), 28, 76, 100, 131, 134, 140, 141, 149, 162, 179–180, 217; Maoist policy on, 149–150, 218, 220, 262

Ambedkar, Bhimrao: 21, *see also Dalits*

anarchy: Adivasi social systems

INDEX

INDEX

INDEX

Mombasa, 37; Nairobi, 37, 92, 105

Khan, Shahrukh: 158

Khmer Rouge: 16, 59

Khrushchev, Nikita: 12

kinship: 138–9, 194, 206, 216, 256, 261, 278

Koda, Madhu: Chief Minister of Jharkhand State, 185

Kolkata: 13, 82, 278

Kollontai, Alexandra: 61

Kristeva, Julia: 16

Kurdistan Workers' Party (Partiya Kakerên Kurdistanê/PKK): 16, 204

labour: Adivasi sharing of labour (*madaiti*), 31, 130–1; bonded 22, 25, 27, 81, 86, 264; industrial fatalities, 129; manual labour, xv, 11, 13, 15, 20–2, 25, 27, 31, 37–8, 63, 83, 86, 89, 122–3, 125, 128–130, 132, 138, 162, 166, 169, 170, 172–4, 176, 180, 182–3, 208, 216, 250, 257, 264, 280–1; Maoist division of labour, 11, 59, 114; reproductive labour, 213, 215, *see also migrant workers*

land alienation/land grabs: xvii, 25–7, 136, 146, 149, 253, 264, 283; *see also displacement/dispossesion*

land, protection of: xvii, 27, 147, 293, *see also Chotanagpur Tenancy Act*

land mines: *see weapons*

landlords: 13–5, 22, 27, 45, 54, 63, 72, 83, 86, 89,97, 267, 276, 286

land redistribution by Maoists: 35, 149

Lal Chingari (Red Spark): 63

Lenin, Vladimir: 54, 57, 59, 82; theories of, 86; *see also Marxism-Leninism*

Lerner, Gerda: 213

Liberation: 18

literacy: *see education*

London School of Economics (LSE): 242

Madhya Pradesh: 23, 112, 212–213, 288

Maharashtra: 23, 33, 112, 212–13

mahua (mahua wine): see alcohol

Majumdar, Charu: 14, 63–4, 266, 284; death of, 285; 'Historic Eight Documents', 14; imprisonment and death of, 18; role in Naxalbari Uprising (1967), 13, 57

Makerere University: 38

malaria: 118, 134, 155–7, 207, 211

Malayan Communist Party: National Liberation Army, 36

Malinowski, Bronislaw: 39–40

Mao Zedong: 12, 14, 54, 57, 82, 285–6; influence of, 22, 129–30, 282; strategy of protracted people's war, 19

INDEX

INDEX

317

INDEX

INDEX

Shining Path: xix, 16; influence of, 19, 22

Sierra Leone, conflict: 120

Singh, Manmohan: xvi, 34, 142

Singh, Rajnath (Indian Home Minister): xviii, 34

Sino-Indian War (1962): 64; political impact of, 12–13

Sino-Soviet split: 12–13

sortition: 30

South Asia Terrorist Portal: xvii, 246

Soviet Union (USSR): 11, 82

Stalin, Josef: 57

Stalinism: 282

suicide: 90

Supreme Court: 277

Sur Empire: Delhi, 6

Suri, Sher Shah: 175; infrastructure developed by, 6

'surrender': 181, 246

Sweezy, Maurice: 82

Tagore, Rabindranath: poetry of, 61

Taliban: xvi

Tana Bhagat Movement (1914): see *adivasi* rebellion

Tata Group: 146–7, 238

Telangana: xvii, 12, 23, 288; *see also Andhra Pradesh*

Telangana Uprising (1946–51): 15, 285

terrorist: xv–xvii, 9, 144, 155, 165, 180, 233, 251, 253–4, 279, 285

torture: 35, 47, 79, 90, 180–181,

203, 207, 242, 248, 264, 269, 281, 287–8

Trinamool Congress Party (TMC): 283

Tritiya Prastuti Committee (TPC): 66, 192, 194, 200; branches of, 248; members of, 192–3; territory occupied by, 199, 205, *see also gangs*

United Nations (UN): Children's Fund (UNICEF), 123; International Labour Organisation, 129; personnel of, 120

Unlawful Activities (Prevention) Act: 287; Section 39, 9

untouchable/untouchability: *see Dalits and discrimination*

Urdu (language): poetry, 76

Uttar Pradesh: 58

utopia: 59, 88, 91, 150, 256, 258

Vedanta: xvii, 34

Vietnam: xiv; Vietnam War (1955–75): xvii, 82–3, 135, 272

violence and Maoists: xviii, 20, 77, 90, 94, 96–102, 106–7, 133, 151, 166, 186–7, 218, 262, 264–5, 268–70, 273, 281, 290

violence of state: *see counterinsurgency and police*

weapons of Maoists: 20, 41, 52–3, 71, 76, 94, 96, 98, 101–2, 105–7, 151, 170, 193, 186, 204,

319